TREES

Broadleaf and conifer models (all variations covered)

First published in March 2019

British Library Cataloguing in Publication Data
A catalogue record for this book is available from the British Library.

ISBN 978 1 78521 201 7

Library of Congress control no: 2018938909

Published by Haynes Publishing,
Sparkford, Yeovil, Somerset BA22 7JJ, UK
Tel: 01963 440635
Int. tel: +44 1963 440635
Website: www.haynes.com

Haynes North America Inc.
859 Lawrence Drive, Newbury Park,
California 91320, USA

Printed in Malaysia

Author acknowledgements

In no particular order the authors would like to express their thanks to the following people who were consulted for their expertise on various sections of this book, or who provided their time, support and advice:

Dr Bob Watson, Dr Neil Strong, Dean Bowie, Simon Richmond, Dr David Nowak, Andy Hirons, Sue James, Kevin Frediani, Nick Betts, William Crumby, Ellen Carvey, Dave Partridge, Karen Stretch, David Rogers, Neil Coish, Dr Kathleen Wolf, Annabel Buckland, Tim Harry, Alexia Smith and Dan Lambe.

The Arboricultural Association, the International Society of Arboriculture and The Tree Council for providing input into the Trees and the law section and Hiring a tree care professional sections. Barcham Trees for assisting with the *Tree Species* profiles and photos.

A special thankyou to Dave Hansford and Kieth Sacre who also contributed to this book.

And finally to our respective families without whose support this manual would simply not have been possible.

Credits

Authors:	Kenton Rogers Tony Kirkham
Project manager:	Louise McIntyre
Copy editor:	Jane Simmonds
Page design:	James Robertson

TREES

Broadleaf and conifer models (all variations covered)

Owners' Workshop Manual

A comprehensive guide to selecting, planting and maintaining trees

Kenton Rogers and Tony Kirkham

Contents

WHY A MANUAL FOR TREES?

This is a book for people who already own trees or who are thinking of planting one. It is also a manual for enthusiasts, those people who appreciate trees in the wider environment and who want to understand more about what trees do.

For professionals engaged in managing and maintaining trees there already exists a vast array of technical books and manuals. However, there is nothing practical written for the homeowner, despite around 60–70% of all trees in our towns and cities being in private ownership.

We felt that this needed addressing. Your tree may be important to you, but it is also part of a greater whole, what some call the 'urban forest': the collection of trees, shrubs, grass and plants in and around human settlements. Whether your tree is already established or yet to be planted, it could be providing pleasure (or pain) to many different people, for the next 100, 200, 300 years or more.

So, that given, it's probably important to understand a bit more about what owning a tree really means. Which species of tree is best for your home and garden? How should you look after it to get the most out of it? How and where do you get impartial advice?

These are just some of the questions we will be answering in this book. The manual guides the reader through selecting the right tree for the right place, planting, and how to establish, care for, prune and maintain your tree. The manual also serves as an introduction to the care and growing of trees (the science of arboriculture). Arboriculture is a vast technical subject and so references for further in-depth reading and professional advice are also provided.

We hope you find this manual useful and that your grandchildren and future communities will benefit for years to come from the trees you may be planting and nurturing now.

Kenton Rogers and Tony Kirkham

INTRODUCTION

As some of the largest and longest-living organisms on our planet, trees are often seen as particularly strong, resilient life forms. Unfortunately, this perception can lead to them being inadvertently ignored and neglected, left to get on with it, so to speak.

Despite generally being fairly robust, trees can also be rather vulnerable. They are, in the main, gregarious forest organisms growing in forest conditions. When they are taken out of this context, for example when they are grown as individual specimens in our gardens, streets, cemeteries and parks, they are often subject to stresses that affect their health and performance. This stress can be as a direct result of growing in an altered environment, but it is mainly due to inappropriate species choice, poor planting, lack of good soil for rooting and inadequate care and maintenance.

As a consequence of stress, trees will be much more prone to the effects of other pests and diseases, which will in turn lead to even further decline and poor performance.

In the majority of cases all this can easily be avoided. Appropriate species selection, preparation, planting, care and maintenance are all covered in this manual. Following the advice given here will contribute to a healthier tree that will require less maintenance (and therefore cost less) and provide a greater benefit for a longer period of time.

Trees contribute directly and indirectly to creating liveable places and healthy communities. These benefits are greatly enhanced in our towns, cities and villages, because that's where most people live.

We inhabit an increasingly urbanised society and this rapid shift from rural living is unprecedented in human history. In 2014, around 54% of the world's population were living in towns and cities, and this number is projected to increase to nearly 70% by 2050. Already, in the UK, over 90% of the population lives in urban areas.

It's also in our urban areas where (like trees) people are generally under greater stress. In evolutionary terms the urban realm is a relatively new environment. Urban living is often found to be a major contributory factor for a whole range of modern health and well-being problems. In addition, the urban setting presents a range of environmental challenges from localised storm water flooding to increased urban temperatures and poor air quality.

Finally, nearly two-thirds of the urban area that is predicted to exist by the year 2050 is yet to be built, so it is vital that we take the opportunity to locate and maintain healthy trees that will significantly contribute to making better places to live, work and play.

How do trees do this? Read on…

1 WHAT IS A TREE?

Archaeological evidence shows that the earliest types of tree were simple, fern-like plants, which first came to prominence during the Carboniferous period (approximately 380 million years ago).

The tree forms that we are familiar with today started to emerge during the Cretaceous period and went on to dominate the planet's ecosystem by the Tertiary period (around 66 million years ago). Despite being periodically driven back by ice ages as the planet cooled, trees have maintained their ecological niches and are adapted to virtually every terrestrial habitat. They are found on every continent except Antarctica.

Most of us should be able to identify a tree, but it's important to know what differentiates them from other types of plants. The distinction between shrubs and trees is often less clear, even among professionals. Often, a tree can also be classed as a shrub (and might in time become a tree) but not all shrubs will necessarily become trees.

Essentially, in botanical terms, a tree is a type of long-lived, perennial plant. Typically (but not always) it is characterised by a long woody stem or stems, rough bark and branches. Botanists tend to define trees more narrowly, as woody plants with secondary growth. All plants are capable of primary growth, which is the process by which the root tips and branch tips elongate. Trees, however, also increase in girth, thickening their trunk and branches outwards and producing wood; this process is termed secondary growth.

The *Oxford English Dictionary* defines a tree as: 'A woody perennial plant, typically having a single stem or trunk growing to a considerable height and bearing lateral branches at some distance from the ground.'

In 2009 a High Court judge took 12,000 words to define a tree for the purposes of an exact legal definition of what a 'tree' was and was not in the eyes of the law. In 2015 the UK Court of Appeal issued a decision that confirms that the word 'tree', for the purposes of a Tree Preservation Order or Tree Replacement Order, includes seedlings and potential trees, although it does not include seeds.

Cross section of a palm.

Cross section of a pine.

Types of tree

In this manual we mainly consider the broadleaf and conifer types of tree. Palms and tree ferns are also occasionally referred to, although in botanical terms these are not trees but large, woody herbs. This is because palms and ferns do not perform the 'secondary growth' necessary to create the actual woody tissues that we associate with a tree's structure.

Broadleaves and conifers are also often referred to as deciduous (trees that lose all of their leaves for part of the year) and evergreen (where leaves are shed over a longer period, therefore appearing to remain green all year round). However, some conifers are deciduous, like the larches (*Larix*) and some broadleaves are also evergreen such as holly (*Ilex*) and holm oak (*Quercus ilex*).

In warmer climes some trees can also be intermediate, and may be termed semi-deciduous (losing old foliage as new growth begins) or semi-evergreen (retaining their leaves over the cold winter months before shedding them in the late winter or early spring and replacing those leaves with new leaves almost immediately). Examples of these include the semi-deciduous custard apple (*Annona squamosa*) from the West Indies and the Australian jacaranda tree (*Jacaranda mimosifolia*).

In the tropics, some broadleaf trees like the kapok or cottonwood (*Ceiba pentandra*) will shed their leaves during the hottest, driest parts of the year (after the wet growing season) rather than in the winter as in the northern and southern hemispheres.

Broadleaved trees are also sometimes known as hardwoods, and conifers as softwoods, but again this can be misleading, as some conifers like the yew (*Taxus*) have a very hard wood capable of dulling the teeth of a chainsaw, while some broadleaves have a very soft wood such as the balsa (*Ochroma pyramidale*) or poplar (*Populus*).

A clearer distinction can be made by describing trees botanically as either those with 'naked seeds' (the Gymnosperms, which includes conifers, cycads, and the ginkgo) and those which have their seeds encased within a fruit (the Angiosperms, which includes all of the broadleaved trees).

Throughout this manual, however, the terms conifer and broadleaf will generally be used.

Parts of a tree

Conifer model

Broadleaf model

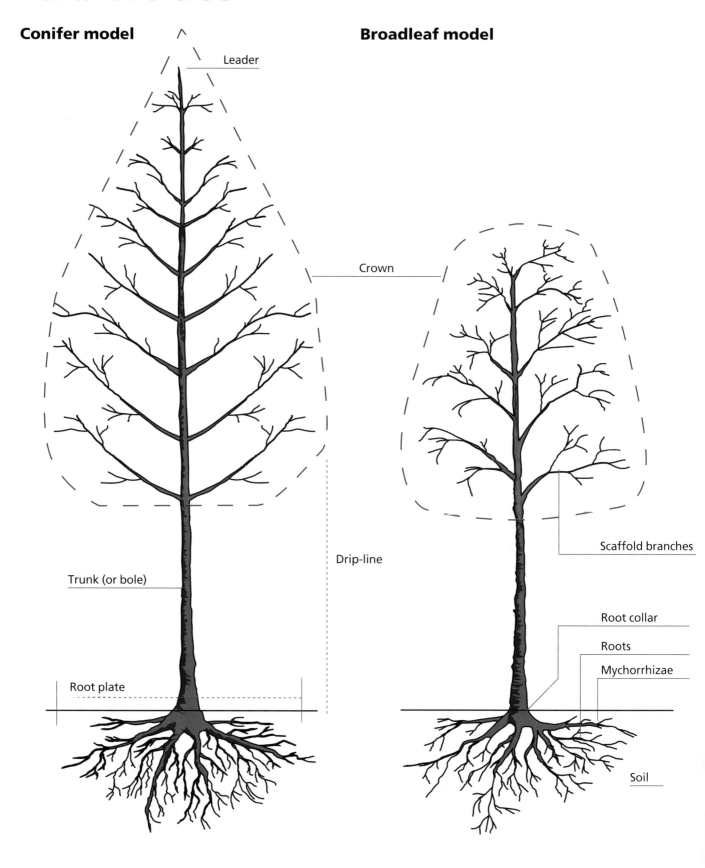

Leader

Crown

Scaffold branches

Drip-line

Trunk (or bole)

Root collar

Roots

Mychorrhizae

Root plate

Soil

Soil: Crucial to the tree's survival but often underfoot and overlooked, the soil is a mixture of organic matter, minerals, gases, liquids and living organisms. For this reason, in a forest environment it can actually be very difficult to differentiate where the tree ends and where the soil begins. In more urban settings, however, the 'soil' may be lacking some of these elements, which will make it difficult for trees to survive and thrive.

Mychorrhizae: Formed of two Greek words literally meaning 'fungus-root', mychorrhizae are the interface between the plant roots and the soil. The tree and the fungus are inseparably linked and are often totally dependent on each other. The fungi get food from the tree roots and the tree is able to access dissolved nutrients from the fungi. Under natural conditions the roots of most plants do not exist independently of the fungus. Therefore, in most cases, nutrient and water uptake by trees is mainly by way of the fungus and not directly by roots.

Roots: Like many plants, trees use their roots to extract water and nutrients from the surrounding area, as well as to anchor themselves securely in the ground. Most of the roots will be found in the top 60cm (2ft) of soil. Although a tree can extend a taproot – a central, vertical tapering root – deep into the soil to exploit water from wells or air from broken drains, deep taproots are not very common.

Many trees can also produce aerial roots which are above ground. The banyan tree (*Ficus benghalensis*) uses these for stabilisation, while in swamps and river estuaries mangrove roots enable the tree to access air while the soil is waterlogged.

In certain circumstances (such as stress) many other tree species will also produce aerial roots. These adventitious roots seek out

The banyan (*Ficus*) is characterised by its aerial roots, which can become thick, woody trunks able to prop up the tree, and allow older specimens to grow over an ever-widening area.

new rooting material to provide nutrients or air for the tree or may sucker to become a new tree, independent of the original parent plant.

Root plate: This is the term given to the main part of the root system closest to the trunk on more mature trees, which is needed to keep a tree wind-firm. It excludes the small outermost roots.

Root collar: A tree's root collar is the area where the roots join the main stem or trunk. The root collar is part of the tree's trunk rather than a part of the roots. Unlike roots, the trunk is not able to resist constant soil moisture, so it's important to have the root collar above the soil level. In more mature trees the root collar may become more flared or buttressed.

Trunk (or bole): The trunk is the main support for above-ground parts of the tree and is responsible for transporting water and other nutrients from the leaves to the roots and vice versa. The trunk is itself made up of several sub-sections described overleaf.

Scaffold branches: These are the main branches of the tree, each of which supports a significant portion of the crown. There is no precise distinction between scaffold and other lesser branches. These are also often called limbs.

Crown: The crown of the tree is made up of all the branches and twigs that grow from the trunk and their corresponding leaves or 'needles'.

Drip-line: An imaginary line that delineates the extremity of the crown, this would be indicated by the crown shedding rainwater.

Leader: This is a dominant shoot whether at the uppermost tip of a whole tree (central leader) or at the tip of a branch (leading shoot).

Trunk cross section

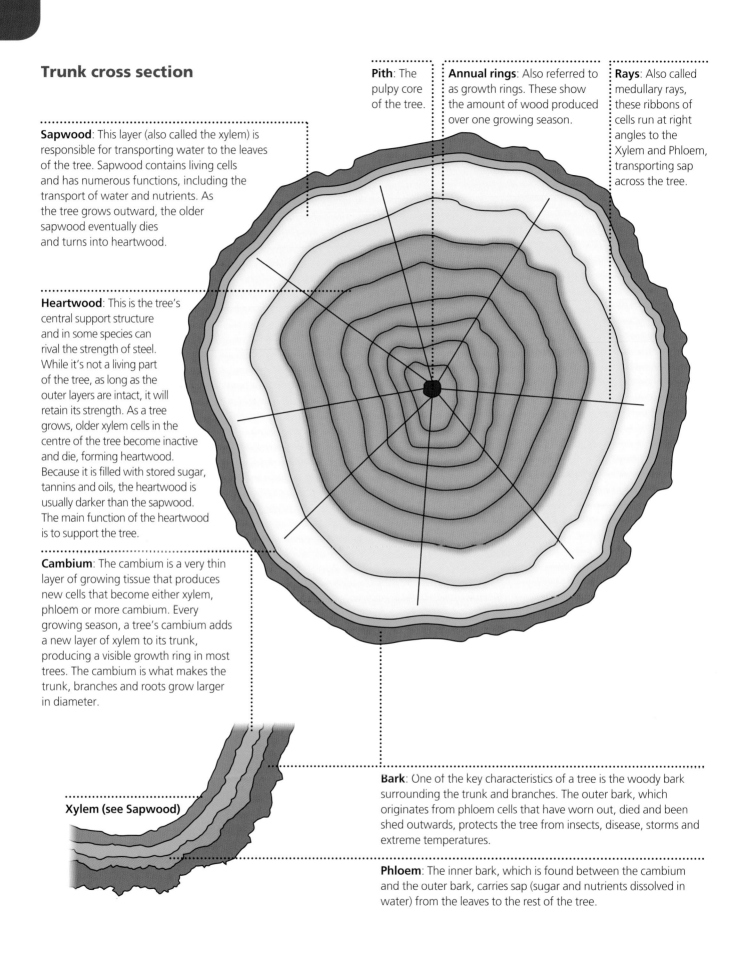

Pith: The pulpy core of the tree.

Annual rings: Also referred to as growth rings. These show the amount of wood produced over one growing season.

Rays: Also called medullary rays, these ribbons of cells run at right angles to the Xylem and Phloem, transporting sap across the tree.

Sapwood: This layer (also called the xylem) is responsible for transporting water to the leaves of the tree. Sapwood contains living cells and has numerous functions, including the transport of water and nutrients. As the tree grows outward, the older sapwood eventually dies and turns into heartwood.

Heartwood: This is the tree's central support structure and in some species can rival the strength of steel. While it's not a living part of the tree, as long as the outer layers are intact, it will retain its strength. As a tree grows, older xylem cells in the centre of the tree become inactive and die, forming heartwood. Because it is filled with stored sugar, tannins and oils, the heartwood is usually darker than the sapwood. The main function of the heartwood is to support the tree.

Cambium: The cambium is a very thin layer of growing tissue that produces new cells that become either xylem, phloem or more cambium. Every growing season, a tree's cambium adds a new layer of xylem to its trunk, producing a visible growth ring in most trees. The cambium is what makes the trunk, branches and roots grow larger in diameter.

Xylem (see Sapwood)

Bark: One of the key characteristics of a tree is the woody bark surrounding the trunk and branches. The outer bark, which originates from phloem cells that have worn out, died and been shed outwards, protects the tree from insects, disease, storms and extreme temperatures.

Phloem: The inner bark, which is found between the cambium and the outer bark, carries sap (sugar and nutrients dissolved in water) from the leaves to the rest of the tree.

Tree shapes and forms

Trees come in a wide variety of shapes and sizes. Some are determined by the tree's natural habit (its genotype), through its interaction with the environment (its phenotype) or through pruning such as with bonsai, topiary and espaliers. The drawing below illustrates the main natural shapes and forms of trees. For trained forms see *Tree pruning*, page 94.

This wind swept hawthorn (*Crataegus monogyna*) in the Yorkshire Dales, UK, has obviously been shaped as a direct result of its environment.

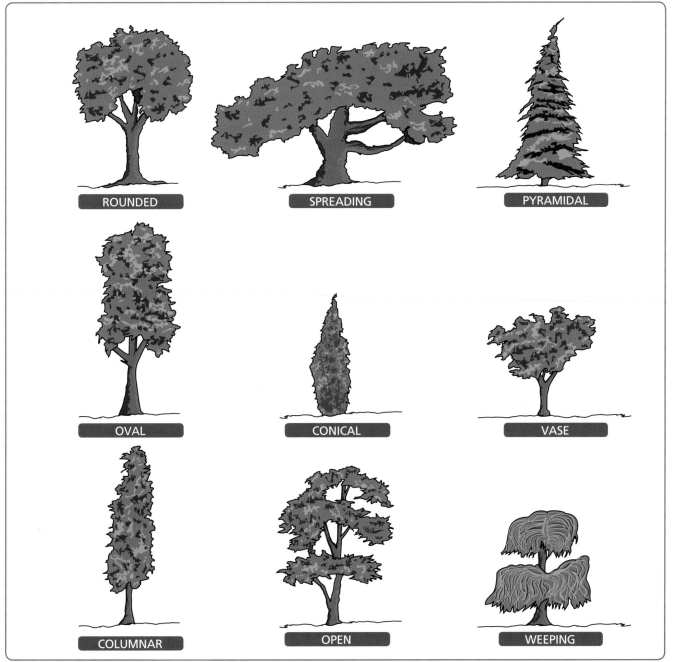

ROUNDED

SPREADING

PYRAMIDAL

OVAL

CONICAL

VASE

COLUMNAR

OPEN

WEEPING

TRANSPIRATION
1 Water absorbed through root hairs
2 Water travels up through the xylem within the tree
3 Water exits through pores in the leaf called stomata

PHOTOSYNTHESIS
1 Chlorophyll in the leaves absorbs energy from the sun
2 Energy used to split water (H_2O) in the leaves into hydrogen and oxygen

RESPIRATION
1 Oxygen is used for oxidation of sugars together with water and hydrogen
2 Carbon dioxide produced and released
3 Sugars (glucose) produced for use in maintaining and growing the tree

How trees work

Trees are complex, dynamic living organisms. This section looks at how trees grow and examines some of their processes. This is important because by understanding what trees need to grow it is easier to spot factors that may be restricting that growth and putting the tree under stress.

Trees have evolved to harness light energy from the sun, while also absorbing water and nutrients from the ground. This process converts light energy to chemical energy to fuel the growth of the tree and to create the organic carbon compounds of its structure.

Almost all of the life on Earth requires energy for growth and maintenance. Because plants can convert energy from the sun to create their own food they are known as primary producers. Everything else needs to consume plants for energy, or will need to eat something that has eaten a plant. Were it not for trees and plants we, and many other creatures, would simply just not be here.

The main processes of trees include:
- Photosynthesis
- Respiration
- Transpiration
- Growth
- Reproduction

Photosynthesis

The foremost function of the leaves and needles of trees is photosynthesis – the use of solar energy to convert water (drawn from the roots along with minerals from the soil) and carbon dioxide (absorbed from the atmosphere through pores in the bark and leaves called stomata) into energy-rich organic compounds (glucose sugars or carbohydrates) that trees need to grow.

In the cells of the leaves, chlorophyll absorbs the energy from sunlight. This energy is then focused on the water molecules harvested by the tree's roots (and transported up through the tree through the transpiration process) and is split into its component hydrogen and oxygen atoms (water being H_2O).

The hydrogen is then combined with carbon dioxide (from the respiration process) to create sugars (the staple of the tree's diet), which are then transported to other areas of the tree to either fuel growth or to be stored for later use. The remaining oxygen and some water is released into the air (see respiration and transpiration, below).

Trees need stored sugar (or starch) to provide the energy needed for various functions, such as to break dormancy in temperate trees, to heal wounds and to have in reserve in order to fight off pests and diseases through fuelling the reactive growth of various tissues.

Respiration

Respiration occurs when glucose (sugar produced during photosynthesis) combines with oxygen to produce useable cellular energy. This energy is used to fuel growth and all of the normal cellular functions. Carbon dioxide and water are formed as by-products of respiration.

Respiration occurs in all living cells, including leaves and roots. Since respiration does not require light energy, it can be conducted at night or during the day. However, respiration does require

Photosynthesis and respiration

Photosynthesis:
    carbon dioxide + water + light energy = glucose + oxygen
Respiration:
    glucose + oxygen = energy + carbon dioxide + water

oxygen, which can be problematic for roots that are in compacted or waterlogged soils with poor drainage. If the roots cannot take up oxygen and convert glucose to maintain cell metabolic processes then the living tissues can die.

Transpiration

While photosynthesis and respiration are chemical processes, transpiration is a physical one, describing the movement of water through the tree. During the process of transpiration, water evaporates from the foliage through openings in leaves called stomata, effectively pulling up all the adjoining water molecules behind it. This pulling action draws water and nutrients up through the trunk and into the leaves.

During the growing season a tree is a constantly flowing wet system that must be maintained. If the process fails to provide water to any point of the tree (such as to a snapped branch) it will eventually die, due to the failure of both water and food requirements that are necessary for life to reach it. Only a small amount of water taken up by the roots is used for growth and metabolism. The remaining 97–99% is released into the atmosphere via transpiration.

Growth
THE LIFE STAGES OF THE TREE
Trees in the temperate zones generally have three phases of life:

1 Juvenile period during which the trunk and the crown increase in size at around the same rate.
2 Mature phase, when the ultimate crown size is reached (generally around 40–100 years). The trunk continues to grow but the rate at which it increases in girth reduces (the annual rings will be closer together).
3 Old age (sometimes also referred to as over mature). This occurs when the tree has exhausted the available nutrients within its rooting zone. Parts of the crown will die back, and this will in turn reduce the leaf area (and therefore photosynthesis), which means the tree's capacity for annual growth will also reduce.

Some trees are able to recover or rejuvenate from stage 3 and go back to stage 2 or even stage 1! Trees such as yew (*Taxus*), oak (*Quercus*), lime (*Tilia*) and cypress (*Cupressus*) may also enter further stages of life and may be classed as ancient or veteran trees:

1 Hollowing, in which the trunk continues to grow, but very slowly, and the heartwood begins to decay, but both the crown of the tree and the trunk remain alive; roots may begin to form inside the tree and recycle the decaying heartwood as it degrades; the hollow tree may begin to break apart and the aerial roots become newer 'trunks' that support the old (or that form a new) tree crown.

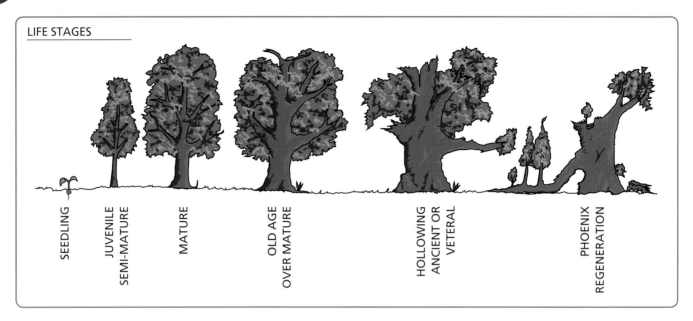

LIFE STAGES

SEEDLING · JUVENILE SEMI-MATURE · MATURE · OLD AGE OVER MATURE · HOLLOWING ANCIENT OR VETERAL · PHOENIX REGENERATION

2 Phoenix regeneration occurs as regrowth in some species (such as willows (*Salix*)). As the tree falls apart the live parts of the crown that come into contact with the ground can take root, with the branches forming new trunks. In limes (*Tilia*), suckers at the base of the tree from the same roots can also become new stems.

These life stages may not happen in every case, but even completely dead trees can be full of life as the decaying wood provides a valuable habitat for insects and fungi.

HOW TREES GROW

Trees grow upwards in height and outwards from the buds (apical growth). Simultaneously, the trunk, branches and twigs thicken and grow outwards (radially) in girth. It's this secondary growth that separates trees from palms and other plants. It's also this secondary growth that enables trees to become some of the largest living things on the surface of the earth.

Very little of a tree's volume is actually living tissue. Around just 1% of a tree is actually alive and composed of living cells. The major living portion of a growing tree is located within a thin film of cells just under the bark (called the cambium) and will normally be only one to several cells thick. Other living cells are located in the root tips, leaves and buds.

Bud (apical) growth

Tree height and branch lengthening begins with the buds. Cells divide and elongate at the base of the bud to create the upward and outward growth at the tips of the branches in the tree's crown. There are three distinctly visible steps:

1 The bud at the tip of the branch opens.
2 Leaves emerge and enlarge.
3 The area between the leaves expands (i.e., the stem grows).

The tree's genetics will cause these buds to grow at determined rates, creating the particular tree species' height and form (this is called the phenotype). However, this form will invariably be influenced by the tree's immediate environment and external

factors such as light, temperature, exposure to wind, competition from other trees and soil conditions.

Many trees will also have lateral (side) buds on the actual trunk and branches. These will grow in the same way, but often these are dormant and do not grow until they react to such activities as pruning, storm damage, increased light levels or when the tree is stressed.

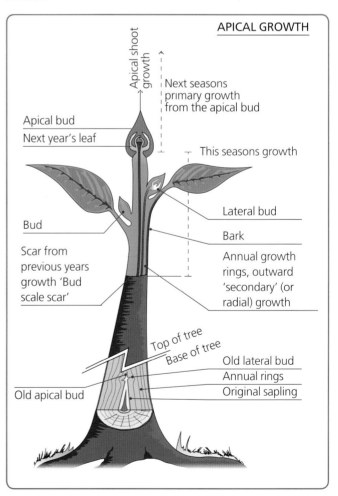

APICAL GROWTH

Apical shoot growth

Next seasons primary growth from the apical bud

Apical bud
Next year's leaf

This seasons growth

Lateral bud

Bark

Bud

Scar from previous years growth 'Bud scale scar'

Annual growth rings, outward 'secondary' (or radial) growth

Top of tree
Base of tree

Old lateral bud
Annual rings
Original sapling

Old apical bud

Bark (cambial or radial) growth

Between the wood and bark is a thin layer of cells called the vascular cambium. The cambium divides, producing new wood towards the inside and bark on the outside. Over time these new cells increase the diameter of the trunk and branches. The new wood cells, called xylem, carry water and minerals up from the roots to the leaves. The old wood in the middle eventually becomes the heartwood. Heartwood, while effectively dead, supports the weight of the tree. The inner bark cells, called phloem, carry sugars and other materials from the leaves to the storage locations of the tree.

Tree trunk growth is coordinated with the increase of tree height and width. When buds begin opening in the early spring, cells in the trunk and limbs get the signal to increase in girth by dividing and in height by elongating. New layers of wood are added each year between the bark and the previous year's wood. These are called growth or annual rings and can be used to age a tree.

Annual rings vary in size and thickness according to the season in which they are formed. Cells that are produced in the spring are larger with thinner cell walls. These are the light-coloured rings, and the wood is called early or spring wood. Cells produced in the summer are smaller, and are termed late or summer wood. Summer wood has a higher density and darker colour, which helps to distinguish the annual rings. Trees in the tropics can grow all year round and may not have early and late wood and therefore no visibly discernible annual rings.

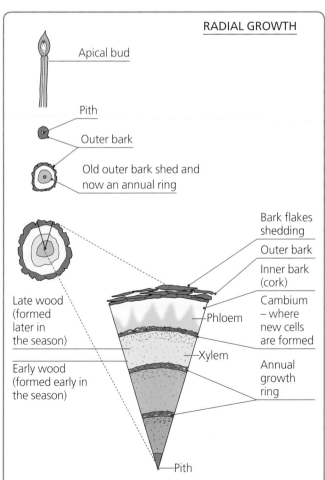

RADIAL GROWTH

Apical bud

Pith

Outer bark

Old outer bark shed and now an annual ring

Late wood (formed later in the season)

Early wood (formed early in the season)

Bark flakes shedding

Outer bark

Inner bark (cork)

Cambium – where new cells are formed

Phloem

Xylem

Annual growth ring

Pith

Bark of the London plane (above) clearly shows the bark plates.

The quick-growing eucalyptus has bark which comes off in large strips (right).

The decorative bark of the birch is a wonderful amenity feature (below).

All woody trees have an outer bark that constantly renews itself and protects the tree from pest attacks and environmental impacts. Some trees have thick bark that is resistant to injury, such as the fire-resistant giant redwoods (*Seqouiadendron giganteum*). Others are easily injured because they have thin bark, such as the beech (*Fagus sylvatica*), which can even suffer from sunburn. As the tree grows in thickness, the outer part has to give, forming ridges and cracks in the bark, and eventually this outer bark is shed.

Growth below ground

Roots also grow in length, diameter and number. At the tip of a root is the root cap. This cap protects the root and must be constantly replaced by the tree as a root pushes through the soil. Root diameter growth is similar to growth in the stem, with the vascular cambium producing wood (xylem) and bark (phloem).

Roots can also grow new lateral roots that form and branch off the main root. Roots grow best in an uncompacted, aerated soil. Generally speaking, around 80% of roots will be in the top 60cm (2ft) of soil. Although some trees can form a taproot, contrary to popular belief they are not common. Roots tend to spread outwards to find nutrients in the upper soil horizons and to provide stability to the tree.

Seasonal variations

Most trees in temperate climates tend not to grow at a steady rate all year round. This is mainly due to the availability of sunlight. Typically, growth will slow as the days shorten. When the weather becomes too cold or dry the tree will enter a period of dormancy. In the tropics, trees can grow all year round.

Lifespan

Just as they have many forms, tree species also have a wide range of lifespans. For example, while birch trees (*Betula*) may only live for 100 years, oaks (*Quercus*) may live for 300 years, cypress (*Cupressus*) 2,000 years or more, and the oldest known trees, such as the bristle cone pine (*Pinus longaeva*) over 5,000 years.

The average urban street tree, however, may only have one-tenth the lifespan of a tree in its natural habitat. This is due to all the stress and pressure from factors common in urban areas, such

Tree roots need to anchor the tree and find water and nutrients, therefore they are more commonly shallow and spreading.

as compacted or waterlogged soil, vandalism and pollution. In some places urban trees are being replaced at great expense every 10–15 years! This is largely due to a lack of understanding about how much room tree roots require to grow, the large variations in tolerance for different species in different sites and because very often trees are undervalued and therefore there is not the money available to care for and maintain them. Often, tree professionals (arboriculturists) are not consulted or engaged in planning for trees, meaning that there is potential for the wrong tree species to be chosen, the design of the tree pit and available soil for the roots is inadequate and that the tree is also poorly planted and maintained.

As with humans, when a tree ages, growth generally slows down. As the tree uses up the available nutrients from its rooting zone it becomes more susceptible to diseases and fungal infection and the top of the tree may start to die back. Even in this state the tree may still live for hundreds of years and, if there were a localised change in the environment (such as availability of nutrients) it could even regenerate. There is an old saying that an oak takes 300 years to grow, 300 years in middle age and 300 years to die. With this in mind, careful consideration to both the tree planting and tree species for the site is a must.

Reproduction

In the natural world trees are generally produced from seeds, which are created from mature trees. In many tree species, pollen from the flower of the male reproductive organs of a 'father' tree fertilises the ovule in the flower of the female reproductive organ of the 'mother' tree. However, for some tree species, individual trees will have both male and female flowers present. In either case this part of the sexual reproduction process is known as pollination.

Pollination results in the creation of a seed that eventually drops (or is carried on the wind) from the tree and hopefully will land on the ground. If the environmental conditions are right, the seed will sprout roots, grow a shoot, and eventually become a small seedling. The seedling will have a genetic make-up that reflects both its parents.

Trees can also reproduce asexually, either naturally, through layering or suckering, or through human intervention such as in the cultivation of cuttings. In asexual reproduction the 'new' tree is genetically identical to its parent.

SEXUAL REPRODUCTION

The fundamental part of sexual reproduction for trees is that pollen must get from the anther of a flower on one tree to the stigma of a flower on a different tree. The basics are also the same for conifers with the aim of getting pollen from one cone to another. In most cases tree flowers or cones will be pollinated either by the wind or by the wing.

Wind pollination

Wind pollination may seem a rather unreliable strategy, as after all, the pollen may not even reach another tree, let alone another flower. But trees produce lots and lots of pollen to increase the chance of pollination. Many of the acers, for example, will produce upwards of 200,000 grains of pollen from just one of its many flowers. When conditions are right and there is wind, trees will shed their pollen so it can drift on the wind until they can settle, hopefully on a female flower or cone.

Many wind-pollinated trees, such as birch (*Betula*) and hazel (*Corylus avellana*) also have catkins, which dangle from the branch so that pollen is easily shaken loose in the wind. Hazel catkins emerge before the leaves, allowing the pollen to travel further away from the parent without the obstruction of foliage.

Wing power

Letting insects and other animals do the wing work is another strategy. These pollinators can be anything from hummingbirds to moths, bees, butterflies, wasps, beetles, flies and even bats. This strategy does require some investment from the tree though. The tree will have to advertise itself as a destination point, using the shape, colour or scent of its flowers in order to attract and reward potential pollinating creatures and insects. For example, the bright flowers of the cherries (*Prunus*) send the message to the insect world that nectar is available. Flowers can also release a fragrance irresistible to bees, butterflies and beetles. The flower has to be just right, with the nectar and the anthers positioned favourably for the pollinator and the right amount of nectar available. Too much nectar and the insect won't need to visit another flower so won't deposit the pollen.

Fruit and seed development and dispersal

Once at the stigma the pollen germinates, fertilises the ovule and finally seed is produced. Soon afterwards the tree might display fruits or nuts ready for dispersal.

Some seeds are encased in a palatable fruit or nut and are either dropped to the ground or eaten off the tree by birds and other animals. Some birds, like the crossbill, have beaks specially designed to crack open conifer cones, thus spreading the seeds. Those that fall to the ground may take root there, close to the parent tree. Or they may be eaten by animals, which will then spread the seeds over a wider area as they move on and defecate. Nuts are often collected and 'planted' by squirrels, who store them for later. Other seeds are wind-borne, much like pollen, and have adaptations to help them glide in the air until they land on a patch of ground further away from the parent tree.

The parrot crossbill (*Loxia pytyopsittacus*) is adapted to break open, eat and disperse pine seeds from their cones.

Pollen grains released from a blue spruce cone on a warm day with a gentle breeze.

The winged seeds of the field maple (*Acer campestre*).

ASEXUAL REPRODUCTION

In asexual reproduction the tree self-propagates (also known as vegetative propagation) from part of its own structure, be that trunk, root or branch. Not all trees are able to self-propagate. Naturally, trees may sucker or layer, and the characteristics that allow this to happen have been exploited by humans for thousands of years to produce greater numbers of trees with desired characteristics (such as larger fruits or more colourful flowers) of the parent plant.

Layering

Layering has evolved as a common means of vegetative propagation of numerous species in natural environments. Natural layering typically occurs when a long low branch makes contact with the ground, whereupon it takes root. At a later stage the connection with the parent plant may be severed and the 'new' tree becomes independent. In some species such as crack willow (*Salix fragilis*), large branches may break off the tree and touch the ground and take root, or, the whole tree may break apart from the trunk and regenerate.

Suckering

Suckers are growths that appear from the root systems of many trees and shrubs. They may appear in borders, lawns, between paving stones or through paths, and can be a nuisance. Poplars, cherries, plums, staghorn sumach (*Rhus typhina*), lilacs and false acacias all sucker freely. Suckers often appear as a response to root damage, resulting from mowing, digging or forking around trees.

Cultivation and cloning

Foresters have been cloning trees for years. This allows them to

A fallen eucalyptus felled by the wind, the old 'branches' now becoming trees in their own right.

produce trees that are genetically identical to the parent tree, which is particularly useful in tree improvement programmes where timber production is often of prime importance.

Cuttings

Cuttings are smaller sections of stems taken from a tree which can be planted in soil. After a time, these stems begin to develop roots and will grow into another tree. As this is a form of asexual reproduction the new tree will be an exact copy (or clone) of the parent tree. Using this method, you can create hundreds of trees from one parent, with each one having identical characteristics.

The False Acacia (*Robinia pseudoacacia*) suckers freely, creating 'new' trees from shoots sent up by roots near the surface. In this way the tree can colonise large areas, leading it to be considered an 'invasive' species.

Microplants of cloned willows (*Salix*) in test tubes with nutrient medium. Micropropagation technology allows the propagation of very small cuttings meaning that hundreds of new trees can be created from a single parent tree.

The benefits of trees

The benefits of trees have, in the main, long been known, even if they have not been fully understood. Trees are fundamental to making better places to live in a whole variety of ways: from the large woodland on the edge of town to the small ornamental cherry in a front garden, all are silently contributing to making our lives more comfortable.

The Victorians, for example, recognised that the plane tree (*Platanus*) filtered sooty particles from the air (trapping them on its leaves and bark), while also tolerating the dense pollution of London at that time. It is through these extensive Victorian plantings and propagation that the tree became known as the London plane (*Platanus* × *hispanica*), the most dominant street tree in both London and New York. Many cities across the globe enjoy a legacy of trees of a similar stature, planted over 100 years ago, in the Victorian era. Yet those planting the trees would have seen little benefit. An even older Chinese proverb nicely sums up this foresight: 'The best time to plant a tree was 20 years ago. The second best time is now.'

What's also quite remarkable is that trees can provide a whole range of benefits affecting both the immediate and wider environment, as well as our own physical, mental, cultural and even spiritual needs. Trees are capable of providing many of these benefits simultaneously and essentially for free!

Torbay was the first town in the UK to measure the benefits provided by the trees of its 'Urban Forest'. In total this was estimated at over £1.5 million every year.

What's more, there is an ever-growing body of research that demonstrates these effects.

Consider a single 'young' 80- to 100-year-old oak, around 10–15m (33–49ft) high and with a crown of the same diameter. It will have somewhere in the region of 100,000 leaves in the summer months. These will convert its base of 113m^2 (1,200ft^2) into some 11,000 m^2 (118,500ft^2) of leaf area, which is larger than a football pitch.

On a sunny day this tree could convert about 9kg (20lb) of carbon dioxide, meaning that around 18,000m^3 (635,000ft^3) of air will have passed through the leaves in its canopy. These leaves will have filtered out bacteria, fungal spores, dust and any other harmful substances that may have been present in the air. At the same time the tree will have drawn up around 200–400l (50–100gal) of water through its roots, evaporating this through the leaves, humidifying the air as it does so. Through the process of photosynthesis, the tree will also produce around 7kg (15lb) of oxygen, which equals the needs of around five people.

The figure overleaf illustrates just some of the 20 or so benefits of trees identified and listed using the Common International Classification of Ecosystem Services (CICES). Ecosystem services

Increased property value and rental value

Attractive high streets
Increase in consumer spending and restaurant patronage

Reduced air-conditioning costs

Improved recovery times from illness

Stormwater attenuation

Evaporative cooling in hot weather

- Summer shade
- UV protection

Noise reduction

Air quality
Pollution filtration

- Reduced surface flooding
- Soil infiltration
- Soil conservation

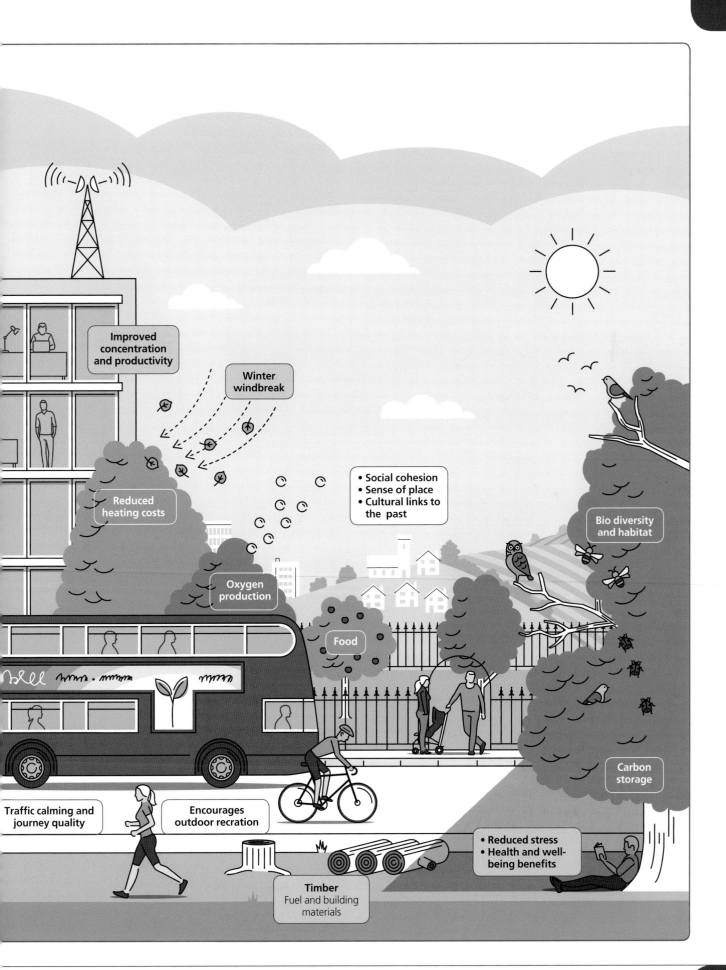

Improved concentration and productivity

Winter windbreak

Reduced heating costs

• Social cohesion
• Sense of place
• Cultural links to the past

Bio diversity and habitat

Oxygen production

Food

Traffic calming and journey quality

Encourages outdoor recration

Carbon storage

Timber
Fuel and building materials

• Reduced stress
• Health and well-being benefits

Amenity value of trees:

A) In this image *(copyright and courtesy of the Trees Design Action Group and Capita)* the substantial visual amenity of this London plane is highlighted by its (digitally produced) absence. The amenity of this particular tree has been valued at over £1.25 million. Yet even this is almost certainly a conservative estimate when the value of the surrounding properties it affects has been taken into account.

B) Trees break up an otherwise stark high street. Shoppers spend a longer time and more money in leafier high streets, while research shows that where there are trees, restaurant patronage is increased by around 15%.

C) Bark of pine (left) and plane (right) creates texture and interest.

D) Light and shade play through the canopy of these plane trees in London, providing places for people to rest, relax and socialise.

is the technical term given to the services with which the natural world provides us and from which we derive benefit. Throughout the rest of this manual we will use the term benefits. We are now going to explain some of these in further detail.

Visual amenity benefits

Perhaps one of the most widely understood benefits of trees is that they look nice. They are aesthetically pleasing, breaking up the straight edges of buildings, while contrasting textures and colours provide visual interest and stimulation. Trees are one of the most useful items in the landscape designer's 'toolkit' for these aesthetic and screening qualities. On many highways networks, tree planting is often planned with the aim of improving 'journey quality', reducing the visual impact of the highway and softening road noise.

Trees also provide a cultural link to the wider environment and the past, with many trees having been present in the landscape for hundreds of years, through many cycles of human generations. Trees also act as a focal point for shared spaces (such as town squares and village greens) and provide a backdrop and navigational aid, framing scenes and viewpoints in our towns, cities, villages and countryside.

However, not only do trees contribute to attractive streetscapes and landscapes, they are also an asset that appreciates, delivering even greater benefits as they grow.

In adulthood, having access to trees and greenery improves our mental well-being and state of mind. Just spending time under tree canopies and in green spaces produces chemicals in the brain that reduce both stress and blood pressure. Public areas and private gardens that include trees provide good spaces to relax and socialise, which can combat depression and improve our general mental well-being. This is important because depressive disorders are the foremost cause of disability in high-income countries and are often precursors for chronic physical health problems.

It should come as no surprise therefore to learn that tree cover is also positively related to longer life expectancy. This has been demonstrated by studies in Canada, the US and in the UK, where healthy life expectancy has been mapped against tree cover (maps showing the extent of the canopies of trees). These studies show that where there is greater tree cover there are higher life expectancies. These differences can be stark too. Some cities in the UK have life expectancies that can differ by several years from the areas of lowest tree cover to the highest. Similarly, in Canada, a study carried out by the University of Toronto showed that having just ten more trees on a city block equated to living up to seven years longer.

Across towns and cities, trees also encourage physical activity, by providing a pleasant environment in which to exercise, with greater uptake of walking and cycling through woodland, tree-lined paths, cycleways and trails. This is an important benefit because across Europe around 1 in 15 deaths is associated with a lack of physical activity. In the UK, for example, only one-third of the population actually achieves the recommended level of exercise.

In Japan, Shinrin-Yoku or forest bathing (essentially walking mindfully through woodland) is a popular activity, and the philosophy is gaining interest in other countries too. Scientists say it reduces stress and blood pressure and boosts the immune system.

If you have ever walked through a conifer woodland after a summer shower and smelled the wonderful fragrance of the trees, then your lungs too will have benefited. These scents are actually

Forest bathing has been a popular practice in Japan since the 1980s but it is now gaining popularity worldwide for its beneficial health and well-being effects.

doing you good! Best known perhaps is the distinctive pine fresh scent, which lightly cleanses your airways with a mild antiseptic effect as you inhale. The chemicals released are also antibiotic. The same chemicals released by the trees are synthesised into many 'pine fresh' bathroom cleaners, and it's no accident that these trees are used worldwide in health spas. In fact, global forests generally exert an antiviral and antibacterial action on moving air masses, quite literally purifying our air.

In some areas of the United States where many thousands of ash trees have been felled due to a particularly devastating insect, the Emerald Ash Borer, there has been both a marked decrease in air quality and relative increase in asthma rates in the areas affected. This is because the tree canopies that would have filtered the particulates from the air are simply no longer present.

Should you be unfortunate enough to end up in hospital, it's worth noting that your recovery time will be positively influenced by views of greenery and trees from your window. A European study on gall bladder operations found that recovery times were significantly improved in wards where there were views of nature. Access to and views of trees and nature are not a magic bullet, but certainly having nature nearby supports opportunities for better mental and physical health.

Finally, there are the medicines derived directly from trees. Most well known, perhaps, is the source of aspirin from the bark of the willow (*Salix*), but there are many other medicinal trees, from the bitter quinine used to combat malaria, a product of the South American cinchona tree, to the smooth, light birch (*Betula*) sap, which has been drunk as a health tonic for centuries in Russia and Scandinavia. Other examples range from frankincense tree resin (the sap of the *Boswellia* tree), grown in Oman and Somalia, which is a natural antidepressant burned in thuribles in churches for thousands of years (and more recently being investigated as a cure for Crohn's disease), to the recent chemotherapy drugs developed from clippings of yew trees (*Taxus baccata* and *T. brevifolia*). In all, it has been estimated that there are in excess of 50,000 medicinal products from trees used around the world. Just listing them all would fill this book, and there are still many more, just waiting to be discovered.

Unfortunately, many of these medicines and products are from trees that have been overexploited or harvested in unsustainable ways. Although extraction of medicine from wild trees can be both sustainable and provide an economic value, without careful

The lacebark pine (*Pinus bungeana*) in Beijing providing shade and improving the air quality by removing particles and gasses through its needles and plate-like bark.

management or with overexploitation, a significant threat to many invaluable trees exists.

Climate benefits

It is now widely accepted that the amount of carbon dioxide in the atmosphere has increased by more than 40% since humans began industrialising, resulting in a gradual warming of the planet over the past century. 'Locking up' carbon is often talked about as a means to reduce or slow the rate at which this important greenhouse gas is created.

Trees and plants take carbon dioxide from the atmosphere and around half of this carbon dioxide is stored in their branches and roots, with large amounts of carbon also stored within the surrounding soils.

This process is known as carbon sequestration and, as long as the vegetation is preserved, it results in an overall reduction of atmospheric carbon dioxide concentrations.

However, the decomposition of dead trees and plants returns carbon dioxide to the atmosphere.

Overall, trees and woodlands take in much more carbon than they return to the atmosphere, but maintenance and management play a crucial role in determining how much carbon they will store. For example, larger, longer-lived trees will sequester and store more carbon in the timber and branches but will also start to store up carbon in the soil too if conditions allow. Looking after existing large or mature trees is particularly important, because they continue to sequester and store large amounts of carbon. Finally, by using/making longer-lived timber products such as tables and furniture, carbon will be locked up for longer than if the wood is used for fuel or paper.

In the UK, urban temperatures are typically 1–2°C (2–4°F) higher than surrounding rural areas. However, during peak summer temperatures this can increase by up to 7°C (12°F). This is known as the Urban Heat Island (UHI) effect. It occurs because the materials used to build towns and cities absorb more of the sun's energy than the natural surfaces (such as grass, trees and hedges) which they replaced.

The UHI effect makes people living in urban areas particularly vulnerable to heatwaves. In 2003 for example, there was an estimated 42% increase in mortality in London during a heatwave that affected large areas of Europe. In Paris that same year over 14,000 people died as a result of the heatwave. In a study carried out by the World Health Organisation it has been forecast that by 2050 deaths from heatwaves could increase by up to 250,000 globally every year.

Climate change is only going to make the threat of urban heatwaves more severe, as the increase in greenhouse gases traps more of the sun's energy, increasing the frequency and severity of heatwaves.

Anybody who has walked in woods and noticed that they are cooler in summer and warmer in winter, will have been witness to the fact that trees create a microclimate under their canopies, with different conditions to the surrounding countryside and built-up areas.

Trees reduce urban temperatures by providing shade and by cooling the air through the process of evapotranspiration. During evapotranspiration, the sun's energy is used to transfer water from the leaves of plants into the atmosphere (see How trees work, page 17 for further details). Essentially this is very similar to the way in which we sweat to cool down, but on a much larger scale. By the process of evapotranspiration trees are able to lower peak summer temperatures by up to 7°C (12°F) during both the day and night. This cooling effect can be felt up to a kilometre away from larger groups of trees. During the summer months trees can reduce the need for air conditioning and therefore energy use in nearby buildings.

Trees also produce direct and dappled shade, providing a degree of ultraviolet (UV) protection. This is a particularly important benefit in children's play areas and community spaces in warmer climes. Trees can act as a windbreak in winter months and are capable of reducing winter heating costs if designed and carefully integrated with the building.

Flooding and water-quality benefits

In both rural and urban areas trees are able to reduce the effects of flooding. In urban areas, the materials used for roads and pavements mean that rain is not absorbed on these impervious surfaces and therefore the water will either remain on the surface or will run off. During periods of heavy rainfall this water accumulates and when the drainage capacity of the area is exceeded, flooding will occur.

In contrast, trees are able to intercept and store water on their leaf and bark surfaces and the water can then re-evaporate into the air after the rain stops. Much of the rain will be directed by the tree's branch structure to run down the trunk to the base of the tree where it can be absorbed into the soil, thereby also reducing the volume of rainwater that runs off. Benefits from individual trees can be further increased if the trees are planted in tree pits or in areas containing non-compacted soils, or where the growth of tree roots is not restricted beneath pavements and roads.

A further consequence of high levels of surface water run-off is that rainwater washes pollutants away from the surfaces it falls onto, transporting them into water courses. This can be detrimental to water quality in streams, rivers and lakes.

Water quality is important for both wildlife and our own health. A recent international study of 300,000 children in 35 countries carried out by the University of Vermont found that incidences of digestive problems and diarrhoea are significantly worse in cities whose watersheds (defined as the area from which run-off resulting from rainfall is collected and drained through a common point) are not protected by enough forest and tree cover.

In many places, climate change is likely to lead to warmer, wetter winters, which will exacerbate existing flooding and water quality issues. Using trees as part of new developments, as well as integrating them within existing built infrastructure, has been highlighted by designers, planners and academics as a cost-effective way of reducing these risks.

Air-quality benefits

Air pollution consists of tiny particles, known as particulate matter (PM), and gases such as ozone (O_3), nitrogen dioxide (NO_2) and sulphur dioxide (SO_2). These pollutants are formed as a result of vehicle and industrial emissions caused by burning fuel wood and fossil fuels.

Fine particulate matter (less than 2.5 micrograms (µg) in diameter, also known as $PM_{2.5}$) can be deeply inhaled into the lungs and is estimated to cause 4.2 million premature deaths per

Trees provide shade and urban cooling

year worldwide (according to the World Health Organisation), primarily from cerebrovascular disease (e.g., stroke) and heart disease (e.g., heart attack). $PM_{2.5}$ exposure also contributes to chronic and acute respiratory diseases, including asthma. The gases can also interact, compounding the problem: while nitrogen dioxide causes shortness of breath and chest pains, when it is exposed to sunlight it can also form ozone, which is linked to asthma and irritation of the respiratory tract. The problem has the potential to get worse: one study forecast that, by 2050, particulate matter could kill around 6.2 million people around the world every year.

Cities and national governments are well aware of the threat $PM_{2.5}$ poses, and they are urgently looking for ways to reduce it. In many UK cities, average levels of NO_2 in the air exceed the legally binding limits set by the European Union. For example, in London in 2017 these annual limits were already exceeded by 5 January!

Trees and shrubs have multiple impacts on air quality. They remove both particles and gases from the air; particles stick to the surface of the leaves and bark, while gases are taken up through small pores on the leaf and bark surface (called stomata). Trees with complex, ridged or hairy leaves, such as pines (*Pinus*), elm (*Ulmus*) and planes (*Platanus*), or those with a larger surface area such as the cypresses (*Cupressus*) and sequoias tend to capture more particles than deciduous trees with broader, smoother leaves. Of course, deciduous trees also lose their leaves in the winter, which further reduces their capability to filter pollution.

Children in schools surrounded by green space have been shown to experience lower levels of traffic-related pollution in their classrooms. Concentration levels are also increased. However, many schools have lost trees, tree cover and playgrounds as sites are developed to cope with increasing numbers of students.

However, the bark will continue to capture and filter pollutants throughout the winter months.

As pollution formation is intensified in the heat of summer months, the trees' cooling effect on the local climate also further reduces the formation of air borne pollutants, especially ozone.

Wildlife and habitat benefits

Our towns and cities are typically considered to host a less diverse range of plants, animals and birds than nearby rural areas. However, green spaces within an urban area can be home to many of the same species that are more commonly associated with rural settings, including those that are rare or threatened. For some species, urban areas can provide a more favourable habitat than intensively farmed countryside, suggesting that towns and cities could actually make an important contribution to national conservation efforts.

Large parks and woodland regions are able to support the widest range of species, and can support more breeding bird species than any other habitat, but even individual trees offer shelter, food and breeding sites and can support a surprising range of plants, insects and birds.

The UK Biodiversity group, for example, recorded 1,500 insect species, 65 bird species and 20 mammal species in a study on trees in hedges. Oaks can support 400 or more insect species, while ash can support more than 200 species of lichen. The early leafing and

Information on ancient trees

In the UK the Ancient Tree Forum keeps an inventory and online map of ancient trees as well as providing opportunities to become further involved in initiatives such as the Ancient Tree Hunt. For more information see www.ancienttreeforum.co.uk

flowering trees (such as apples, blackthorn, hawthorn, maple and willow) provide food in spring for insects, which in turn provide prey for birds and mammals.

Collectively, trees and hedges can also act as 'wildlife corridors', linking together larger parks and providing links to rural areas on the outskirts of towns and cities. This helps the movement of animals, birds and insects between these natural features and prevents the isolation of wildlife by the 'fragmentation' of their habitat.

In the UK, trees form an important habitat for pollinators, such as bees, butterflies and hoverflies. Maintaining a healthy population of these pollinators is vitally important as many flowers and crops (including tomatoes, apples and strawberries) depend upon them in order to reproduce. Pollinator populations around the world are declining so the provision of habitats for these species is very important.

Trees also provide homes for larger mammals such as bats, owls and birds. Ancient and veteran trees are typically older trees that have larger, hollowing trunks full of interesting biological features such as large amounts of dead wood in the crown and cavities on the trunk and larger branches. These are particularly important for providing habitat, having been around for hundreds (and sometimes thousands) of years, slowly building up a community of other flora and fauna and providing unique habitats that are just not present in younger trees.

Economic benefits

All of these tree benefits also provide very real economic impacts. Globally the potential health benefits derived from trees save health care organisations millions of pounds every year – a figure that looks set to increase for the foreseeable future.

Trees make a buffer against climate change at international, national and very local scales, locking up carbon and providing shade, summer cooling and winter warming.

The fact that trees hold up flood water and storm water means that this water does not cause damage to property or enter combined sewerage systems, therefore saving the water companies the expense of treating this water.

Similarly, with air pollution, trees have been shown to remove significant amounts of pollution from the air that would otherwise damage people's health and the very fabric of buildings. A global US study carried out by the Nature Conservancy found that the cost of tree planting is less than every other pollution removal strategy considered (except for 'cool-roof' technologies). Of course, in cases where both pollution concentrations and high temperatures are a concern, the comparative attractiveness of additional tree cover would be higher still. Furthermore, trees near road networks will also reduce noise, lower traffic speeds and can prolong the life of the asphalt itself, compared to roads without tree cover.

Trees also provide products such as apples, pears, walnuts, chestnuts and foliage for floristry. Finally, at the end of their lives, the trees' timber can also be utilised for a whole variety of purposes from fuel wood (logs) or woodchip to the manufacture of everything from wood pallets to fine furniture. Obviously, the better the product or furniture the longer that carbon is locked up.

Trees and their timber have been one of the primary building blocks in the progress of civilisations, used for homes, tools,

Timber in buildings:

Japan) The Kennin-ji Temple, Kyoto, is over 1,000 years old.

US) Timber houses in Michigan with trees in close proximity providing shade and shelter.

Italy) The Bosco Verticale, Milan, is a 'forest skyscraper' over 100m (330ft) tall containing more than 900 trees, 4,500 shrubs and 15,000 plants, which help to clean the air, absorb CO_2 and conserve energy. This vertical forest equates to around 20,000m2 (215,000ft^2) of forest.

UK) The Forum Building at Exeter University. With an area of more than 3,200m^2 (34,500ft^2), the Forum's roof is the largest freeform timber gridshell in the UK.

boats and planes. Trees have provided the structural timber for construction for millennia, from the roof trusses and frameworks of many of our modern homes to the Kennin-ji in Kyoto, a five-storey-high Buddhist temple built in 951, the oldest building in the city. More recently modern timber is now being used for high-rise buildings such as The Tree, a 49m (160ft) tall apartment block in Bergen, Norway, and the 300m (985ft), 18-storey Tall Wood residence in Vancouver.

But it doesn't stop there! Research shows that increased tree cover not only means that people are healthier and happier, but the presence of trees leads to increased property prices and a reduction in crime, while employees with access to green tree-filled spaces experience less stress and are more productive.

Leafier high streets mean shoppers spend more time and therefore more money. Restaurant patronage increases up to 15% on weekends where there are trees and greenery present. There are also significant improvements in school exam results in leafier environments. All of these positive benefits are subject to a growing number of research projects and come with direct and indirect economic benefits.

However, all of this depends on making sure that the right tree species is planted in the right place, as trees can also provide long-lasting and potentially expensive disbenefits, especially if no thought is given to the species, the space it's going to occupy, the size it is going to get to, its purpose (be that for aesthetics, shade, windbreak or timber) and its careful installation.

The disbenefits of trees

So, the benefits of trees are both many and varied, with a very real economic value. However, the catch is that the wrong tree (or trees) planted in the wrong place (as they often are by both private landowners and public bodies) can lead to negative effects or disbenefits.

For example, in some instances, tree canopies can trap local pollution by reducing the ventilation of air. The presence of large trees in narrow streets can obstruct the wind and limit the ability of trees to remove pollutants in these areas.

As well as filtering airborne pollutants, trees can also emit compounds that create ozone and other Biogenic Volatile Organic Compounds (or BVOCs). The release of pollen by certain trees also affects around one-third of the world's population, prompting an allergic response such as coughs, honey fever and skin reactions. It is interesting to note that stressed trees will actually emit more of these BVOCs. When mixed with pollution from vehicle emissions these BVOCs can form ozone. This combination has been cited as the main cause of a higher incidence of reaction to tree pollen in built-up areas than in the surrounding countryside.

Despite being a fabulous pollution-busting tree, even the London plane, for a couple of weeks a year, produces many fine hairs that surround its seeds, and these can irritate the airways. Pollen from many tree species can also induce hayfever, although some studies attribute the rise of these conditions to the mixing of pollen with air pollution, which may increase our sensitivity.

A few trees are also just plain poisonous. Apart from the Himalayan yew (*Taxus wallichiana*), all other yew species are poisonous, with the toxins being present in every single part of the tree, with the exception of the red flesh around its seeds (called the aril). There have been some instances of those working around yew trees in hot summers suffering headaches, nausea and even hallucinations. To put this into perspective though, a worldwide survey of 11,197 records of yew poisoning found that no deaths were reported.

The staghorn sumach tree (*Rhus typhina*) has toxic sap which can burn the skin, while the aptly named headache tree or Californian laurel (*Umbellularia californica*) causes headaches and migraine. In botanical gardens such as Kew, just outside London, exposure to these trees when pruning them is closely monitored in order to reduce the risk.

Poisonous and irritant trees:
A) Laburnum avenue at Nong Prajak Public Park, Udon Thani, Thailand; these are beautiful trees but the wood dust when cut is toxic.
B) All parts of the yew are poisonous apart from the red flesh of its fruit.
C) The fruit of the London plane tree also releases many fine hairs which can irritate the airways and skin.

Laburnum is another example of a tree with poisonous parts. By far the biggest risk comes from children potentially eating the seed pods or tree workers inhaling wood dust from tree works such as pruning. However, instances of poisoning are rare, and instances of serious harm are even rarer. In 'Accidental poisoning deaths in British children 1958–77', published by the *British Medical Journal*, the author, Neil Fraser, found that 'Laburnum is frequently cited as the most toxic and commonly fatal poisonous plant in both children and adults, but there appears to be no report this century of a childhood poisoning death'.

While a shady car parking spot in the summer is much sought after, some trees overhanging these areas can host thousands upon thousands of aphids, who feed on the fluid in the leaves and will deposit a sticky residue (honeydew) on car windows and paintwork.

Ginkgo fruit and leaves.

Tree root damage to pavement in London.

The female maidenhair tree (*Ginkgo biloba*) produces a fruit which when ripe will produce a pungent odour similar to rotting flesh – not very nice!

Similarly, tree roots can create uneven surfaces in pavements and sidewalks and slippery leaves or fruits in autumn can make walking hazardous. Falling leaves also block drains and gutters and need to be cleared to avoid creating localised flooding.

Fallen leaves are also notorious for delaying trains in many countries. In heavily deciduous forested areas like the American Mid-Atlantic, many parts of Europe, including the UK, and Southern Ontario, Canada this problem can arise. In the wet, damp conditions of autumn, fallen leaves build up on the tracks, and are then compressed by the trains and rolling stock into a slippery coating on both the rails and wheels. The wet leaves adhere to the rail very effectively.

As the build-up of leaves under these conditions is not worn away by the passage of trains, this results in slippery rails and a loss of traction. Leaves on the rails also insulate trains from the rails, meaning that the signalling system, which uses electric currents in the track to locate trains, becomes less accurate, causing delays.

Dead trees and falling branches are also concerns, as is the use of public trees by some to hide drugs, train dangerous dogs or engage in other antisocial behaviour. Trees and wooded areas are also perceived by some as being places to avoid, especially at night when they can create anxiety and fear.

Trees planted on the wrong side of a building will block light and also heat (solar gain) from the sun. This will mean heating and cooling costs for your home or office could be increased. In certain circumstances trees can cause direct damage to buildings and drains through root growth, direct contact or through dropping branches. Trees may also cause indirect damage through subsidence, although prevalence is low and only occurs in areas where 'shrinkable' clay soils are present.

Of course, with a little planning, most of these issues can be either managed out, or, with the right tree species selection and planting location, will never actually happen in the first place.

Throughout this manual, methods and techniques will be described that will allow you to get the very best from your tree while minimising any negative disbenefits.

Conclusions

We are at the beginning of what some describe as the Anthropocene age. This new geological epoch represents humanity's impact on Earth. The current epoch, the Holocene, is 12,000 years old. Carbon dioxide emissions, sea level rise, the global mass extinction of species, and the transformation of land by deforestation and development mark this 'new human' geological time.

One of the main challenges society now faces will be in making vibrant, healthy and attractive places to live. This chapter has focused on just one small part of this task: the contribution that trees can make.

Societies across the globe continue to strive to reduce concentrations of particulate matter and other atmospheric pollutants. Governments and corporations are finally beginning to plan for the increased frequency and intensity of heatwaves that climate change will likely bring. Succeeding against the challenges of air pollution, excess heat and other extreme weather events will require an array of different approaches. Can trees play a role in helping to solve the challenges?

The answer from both the scientific community and practitioners appears to be a very definite 'Yes!'. However, in order to achieve any degree of success, the proper planting, care and maintenance of the trees is paramount.

However, with the unabated increase in development, and the current widespread underinvestment in replacing trees lost through old age, vandalism and disease there is a general reduction in the amount of tree cover in both rural and urban areas. For instance, a study by the Nature Conservancy concluded that around 26% of cities globally have a decline in forest cover over the period between 2000 and 2010, whereas only 16% of cities had an increase in forest cover over the same time period.

Your country needs your trees!

Fallen leaves in autumn can block drains and gutters and when wet can be hazardous to walk on.

2 PRE-PLANTING: CHOOSING YOUR SITE AND YOUR TREE

So you want to plant a tree? Before you rush out to your local garden centre or tree nursery, you need to do a little research and preparation. First and foremost you need to find out a bit about the space your tree will be growing into, both above and below ground (a site assessment). Then you should ask if you need your tree to perform any tasks as it grows, such as providing shade or reducing noise. These steps are important as the information you gather will inform what species of tree you choose to plant.

This section also details how to find a good tree at the nursery, what to look for and what to ask for, as well as guides for planting trees to achieve different objectives. Planting is covered in the next section whilst Appendix I gives profiles and characteristics of over 60 tree species. There is a lot to site assessment and so a handy checklist is also included in Appendix II.

Assess your site

Before beginning the process of selecting a tree species for your site it is advisable to carry out an assessment of your planting area to ensure that the conditions are suitable for the tree or trees you eventually choose. All trees have preferences as to site conditions, have many different shapes and forms and grow at differing rates. It is wise to ensure your site conditions match, as near as possible, the requirements of the tree you are planning to plant, or they will not succeed.

Planting sites vary considerably, with conditions ranging from areas of undisturbed natural soil through to compacted building rubble with a thin layer of topsoil. The first place you should start and by far the most important thing to assess, is the soil which your tree will be growing into. Yet all too often this is both underfoot and overlooked!

Assessing the soil

Soil is important because it is key to allowing roots (and therefore the rest of your tree) to grow. The soil provides water, nutrients, oxygen and a steady temperature. When assessing the soil before tree planting we need to consider both the volume (how much soil is there for the tree roots to grow into) and its structure (its chemical and physical properties).

SOIL VOLUME

This is all about the underground space for your tree. Contrary to popular belief, tree roots are not a mirror-image reflection of the above-ground parts of the tree. Generally speaking, tree roots need a soil depth of around 0.6–2m (2–7ft) of soil and will spread outwards to exploit available nutrients, anchor themselves to the ground (so they don't fall over) and search for water. Imagine a wine glass; this is the proportion of a tree in every respect. The goblet that holds the wine is the crown, the stem of the glass is the trunk and the base that stops the glass from falling over is the root plate. This is always worth remembering!

Take care!

In order to reduce the risk of personal injury or permanent damage to yourself or your tree, please read and follow these important precautions. Remember that your tree will grow! Even varieties described as 'dwarf' in some nurseries can grow much larger than indicated on the label. Therefore do not:

- Plant your tree where it will interfere with buildings, overhead utility lines or pavements as it gets bigger.
- Plant your tree within 6m (20ft) of overhead electric wires if your tree will grow taller than 9m (30ft). You should also check with your local electricity network provider as the exact minimum distances will vary depending on your location.

When there isn't enough soil available, the size of the tree canopy will be limited, as the roots will not be able to feed it to grow. As a rule of thumb, for a healthy tree you will need to provide $1m^3$ ($35ft^3$) of rooting space for every $3m^3$ ($106ft^3$) of crown or canopy.

SOIL STRUCTURE AND SOIL TYPE
Structure and texture
What makes up the structure and texture of your soil? Soil structure is the arrangement of the solid parts of the soil and how they aggregate together. Soil texture describes soil classes defined by their physical texture. The type of soil is important because the characteristics of soil determine whether or not a tree will grow well. It is also a factor in deciding which species of tree should or can be planted on any site.

Generally speaking soil types are a blend of sand, silt and clay in varying proportions. The composition and characteristics of a soil depends on the proportion of these three minerals and the spaces between individual particles, which will be filled with either water or air. The relative percentages of sand, silt and clay in a soil are collectively known as soil texture. In different proportions the soil can be categorised into several broad types as illustrated in the soil triangle.

The soil triangle.

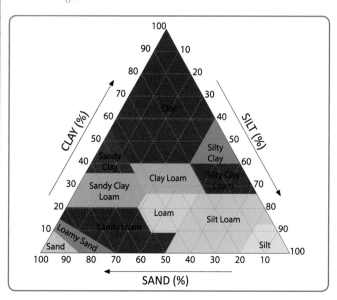

Because of the size of the sand, silt and clay elements it is also possible to determine the texture of your soil by feel, using a simple hand-moulding technique. Take a small ball of soil and moisten it until it just begins to stick to the hand. Manipulate the soil; the extent to which the moist soil can be shaped is indicative of its texture as described in the illustration below.

Determining soil texture.

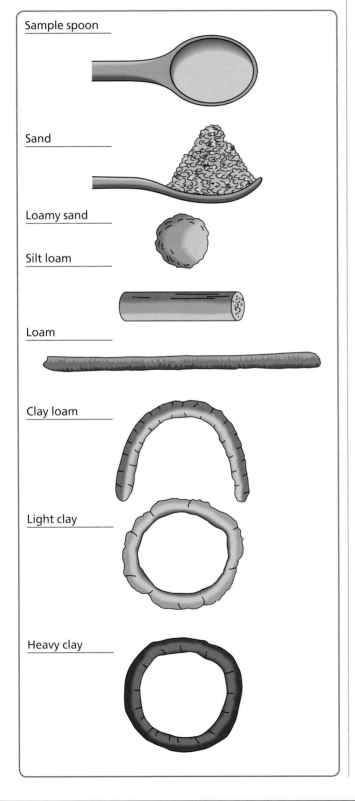

Sample spoon

Sand

Loamy sand

Silt loam

Loam

Clay loam

Light clay

Heavy clay

Soil compaction

Naturally, soil is not solid! It also includes organic matter (partially decomposed leaves, etc.) and around 25% of it will be made up of water and air (spaces). However, in our urban places, the soil will more than likely include a lot of old building materials and human junk including plastics, metals, brick, concrete and glass. A compacted soil is one where the spaces between soil particles have become compressed. Both air and water are effectively squeezed out of the soil and tree roots are unable to develop or penetrate through the soil.

To relieve soil compaction the soil needs to be aerated so that the spaces between soil particles are re-established. In its simplest form, surface compaction can be alleviated using a garden fork and breaking up the surface of the soil. Compaction relief to a greater depth may require the use of specialist equipment such as an air spade. It is important to understand the causes of the compaction and ensure these are not repeated following remedial work. Mulching post-planting will reduce the risk of a soil becoming compacted (for further information on de-compaction of mature trees see page 99 *Management of the root plate*).

Uncompacted

Space for air, water and root development

Compacted

No space

Compacted and un-compacted soils.

Soil drainage

It is also important to assess how quickly water drains from your soil. The speed of drainage is dependent on the soil structure, texture and compaction. Sandy or very light soils with little organic matter can drain too freely, making it difficult to keep young trees adequately irrigated. Poor drainage will potentially cause waterlogging, which can kill newly planted trees very quickly as the roots cannot access any oxygen whilst underwater.

A simple way to assess your drainage is by carrying out a percolation test. This measures how quickly water moves through the soil by gravity. Do this after some rain. After digging a sample hole in an area where you are thinking of planting (this can also be planting pit), tip 5–10 litres (1–2gal) of water into the pit and see how long it takes to drain. If it takes less than two hours then the soil is very fast draining (your tree will need more irrigation during dry weather until it is established). If it takes longer than 18 hours then the soil is very slow draining. Make sure the hole is not filling with water – your tree will drown. In these circumstances planting on a raised mound is recommended.

Soil pH

A measure of the acidity or alkalinity of a soil, pH stands for potential hydrogen. The pH scale ranges from 0.0 to 14.0 with 7.0 being neutral. Values between 0.0 and 7.0 are considered acid and those over 7 are considered alkaline. In the neutral range (between 6.0 and 7.5) more nutrients in the soil become available for uptake by plants' roots. However, tree roots grow best in more acidic soils (5.5–6.5) where there are greater numbers of fungi in the soil.

Most trees will grow successfully within the central range of pH values, but there are some species which have a distinct preference for either acid or alkaline soils. A simple pH test kit can be obtained from any garden centre. Amending the soil pH is possible but a difficult task and it would be better to select a tree species that is naturally pre-disposed to the conditions on site.

Local environmental conditions

Every planting site will have different environmental characteristics. There will be different levels and periods of sunlight, varying levels and duration of shade and variable exposure to wind. All of these may be exacerbated by the proximity of buildings and other infrastructure present in the built environment. All these factors need to be considered and allowed for when deciding on which tree species to plant. Unless conditions are extreme, a simple visual assessment and local knowledge should be enough to ensure an appropriate species is chosen.

FROST POCKETS

These usually occur in low spots within the landscape where frost can also become trapped against walls. Frost can impact on spring bud development, which will mean that your young tree will not grow as quickly. Generally speaking conifers are better adapted to cope with frosts.

WATERLOGGING

In waterlogged soils air spaces become filled with water which impacts on the diffusion of gases between the atmosphere, rhizosphere and roots. Root functioning is impaired, which affects numerous physiological and metabolic processes of the tree. Dependent on the duration of soil saturation this can lead to wilting, chlorosis, abscission, reduced photosynthetic activity, blackening of roots and eventual death. There are some species that naturally grow in wet soil with root systems that are 'designed' to cope with wet conditions. A good example is the swamp cypress (*Taxodium distichum*), which can grow permanently in water.

EXPOSURE

The height, aspect (whether a site faces north, south, east or west) and exposure of your planting site to the elements will also

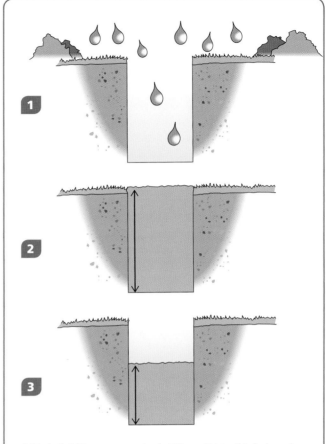

1 Dig hole 300mm square, depth 450mm. Wet soil in hole and 300mm around hole.
2 When near saturation point, fill hole with water and measure depth.
3 After 15 min measure height of water again. Subtract second reading from first.
Multiply by four to get estimate of water loss in one hour.

The percolation test.

The swamp cypress (*Taxodium distichum*) growing directly in water.

have an impact on the growth and shape of your tree. In exposed places you will need to ensure that adequate shelter and staking is in place to prevent the tree becoming windswept or, in extreme cases, falling over completely. In coastal areas (and often at some distance from the sea) trees can be affected by salt spray too, which will also restrict the growth of the trees by damaging the leaves.

URBAN AREAS

Generally speaking, urban areas are not great for trees. Paved surfaces tend to increase the soil temperatures, which can harm trees, whilst walls that reflect and intensify both light and heat add further stress to the tree. Urban areas also contain many impermeable surfaces, meaning that rainwater just washes away rather than being absorbed into the soil for use by the tree.

Wind canyons are created by high-rise buildings where the effect of wind is intensified. Buildings can also reduce the available light to the tree, which will result in slower growth. Street lights and other artificial light can impact the tree's normal growth patterns. The time of leaf fall may be affected in the autumn, and flowering times disturbed. In extreme cases these variations can even be seen on the same tree.

AVAILABILITY OF SPACE

It is easy to forget that trees grow. They grow at different rates, to different sizes and into different shapes. A young tree viewed at the nursery or selected from a catalogue can look attractive and harmless only to become a giant in later life. This can happen very quickly, as with species such as Lawson cypress (*Chamaecyparis lawsoniana*), poplars (*Populus*) and willows (*Salix*), or slowly, over several years. The young coast redwood (*Sequoia sempervirens*) in the tree nursery gives us no clues as to the 100m (300ft) giant it has the potential to become.

Example of mature tree heights.

The giant sequoia requires plenty of space.

Other points to consider

NUISANCE

The tree that you choose, like and may eventually come to love may not be perceived or experienced in the same way by your neighbours or others in your community. It is as well to be aware of this and consult others prior to tree planting if you think they may be impacted. Your tree is likely to be there a long time.

YOUR TREE IN THE WIDER POPULATION

While the individual or group of trees you plant will deliver many if not all the benefits outlined in earlier sections of this book, it must

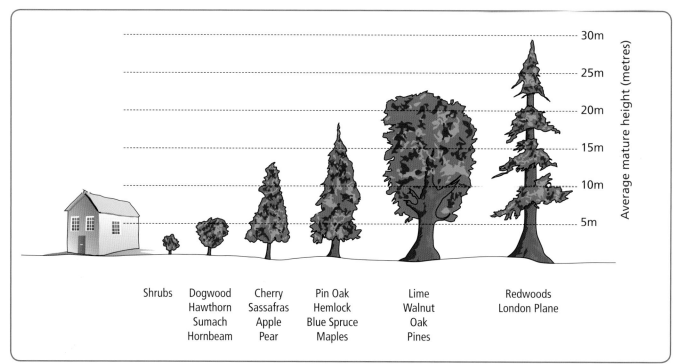

Shrubs	Dogwood	Cherry	Pin Oak	Lime	Redwoods
	Hawthorn	Sassafras	Hemlock	Walnut	London Plane
	Sumach	Apple	Blue Spruce	Oak	
	Hornbeam	Pear	Maples	Pines	

Average mature height (metres): 5m, 10m, 15m, 20m, 25m, 30m

be remembered that all trees are part of a wider tree population. It is the tree population, including your trees, that delivers these benefits. Tree populations are dynamic and change with time. There are many challenges to our trees, including the threat from imported pests and diseases. The sustainability and resilience of the tree population is related to the diversity within that population. The greater the number of species present the more resilient the population is. It is an easy and enjoyable task to observe which tree species are present in your local population, those that are dominant, those that are poorly represented and those that are not present at all. You can then use this information to select a tree accordingly.

What do you want your tree to do?

Trees can be planted for many different reasons. Often it is for their aesthetic beauty alone. There is, however, a bigger picture and trees can (and are) planted with many functional expectations too. Trees can be chosen for their capacity to screen, to produce fruit,

to dampen noise, to hide undesirable sight-lines, to attract wildlife, to stabilise sloping ground and many others. It is wise to have a clear idea of what you want your tree or trees to achieve as this will influence what species you choose and where they are planted.

Planting trees to modify temperature

Where summer temperatures are very high, trees can be used to provide shade and reduce temperatures. Groups of trees can reduce local peak summer temperatures by up to 7°C (45°F), whilst the shade can also provide a useful UV filter. This can reduce the need for air conditioning by up to 50%, saving both energy and money. To have the greatest cooling effect (in the northern hemisphere) medium to large broadleaf trees should be planted close to the property on the west and south-west sides. The leaves will provide their cooling effect throughout the summer but after leaf fall will also allow most of the winter sun to warm the building in the colder period.

Similarly, a planting of evergreen and conifer species on the northern and eastern sides will help to block cold winds and reduce the need for heating. This effect does not produce quite as dramatic a saving but a 17% reduction in heating bills is still a considerable amount. Two or more rows works best if space allows but even a

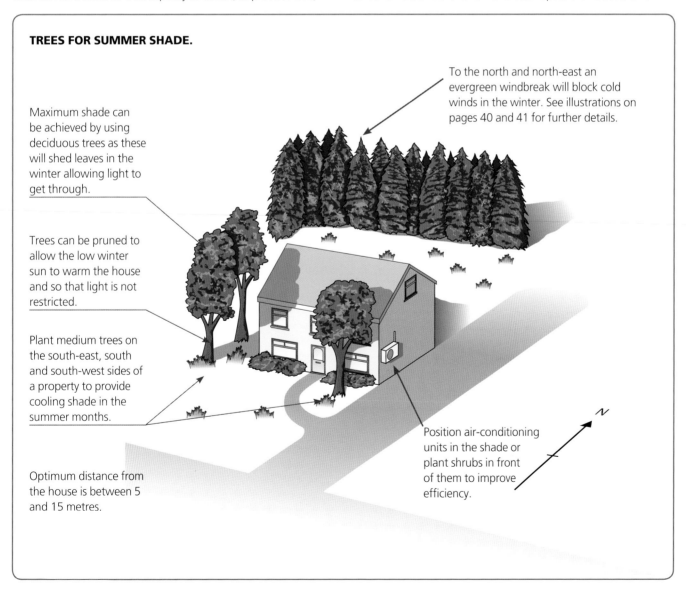

TREES FOR SUMMER SHADE.

Maximum shade can be achieved by using deciduous trees as these will shed leaves in the winter allowing light to get through.

Trees can be pruned to allow the low winter sun to warm the house and so that light is not restricted.

Plant medium trees on the south-east, south and south-west sides of a property to provide cooling shade in the summer months.

Optimum distance from the house is between 5 and 15 metres.

To the north and north-east an evergreen windbreak will block cold winds in the winter. See illustrations on pages 40 and 41 for further details.

Position air-conditioning units in the shade or plant shrubs in front of them to improve efficiency.

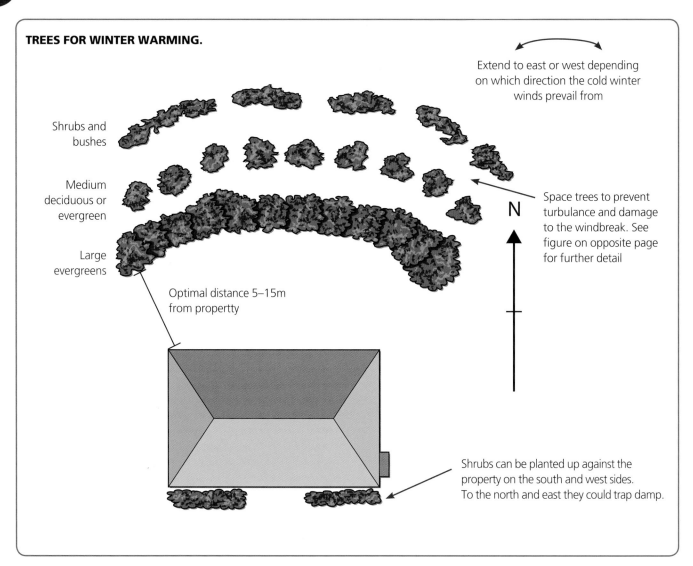

TREES FOR WINTER WARMING.

Extend to east or west depending on which direction the cold winter winds prevail from

Shrubs and bushes

Medium deciduous or evergreen

Large evergreens

N

Space trees to prevent turbulance and damage to the windbreak. See figure on opposite page for further detail

Optimal distance 5–15m from propertty

Shrubs can be planted up against the property on the south and west sides. To the north and east they could trap damp.

---

single row will help. It is important to choose a species with thick foliage that can regularly be pruned back and regrow.

Planting trees for a windbreak

Planting trees for a windbreak is very effective because trees are porous to the wind, allowing it through, so they are much more effective (and nicer to look at) than solid man-made barriers. Solid barriers create turbulence when the wind is forced up and over (rather than through) the obstacle. Trees will reduce wind speeds by 30–50% across an area around ten times their height. On the other hand, however, you will have to wait for these trees to grow. A 5m (16ft) high shelter-belt will ideally need to be around 2–5m (6.5–16ft) wide whereas a high shelter-belt of 25m (82ft) will need to be 10–15m (33–49ft) wide.

As for winter warming, conifers and evergreens are the best choice for this task. Again, those that can be repeatedly pruned without dying back are the best option, otherwise as the trees mature and lower branches die (through natural tree growth habit) the effect will be reduced.

Planting trees to reduce noise

In built-up areas, noise can be a major problem and health issue, as it increases our stress levels. As towns and cities become more populated, reducing and absorbing noise becomes increasingly important. Trees can do this effectively but require a lot of space to form an effective barrier. A noise break, featuring rows of trees around 25m (82ft) wide can reduce traffic noise by around 20dB but even individual trees can have a noticeable effect. Recent research has shown that it is the trunk and woody area of the trees (rather than the foliage) which are critical in absorbing sound. Therefore, it is best to aim for limited spaces between trees (or for individual trees choose a species with dense branching), whilst also trying to choose trees with large trunks. For the best effect the planting should not be regular (no straight lines and rows of trees).

Planting trees to reduce pollution

All plants, hedges and trees play a role in capturing air pollution. Trees do this very effectively, as discussed earlier. Trees closest to the source of the pollution (usually roads) are best, and shrubs and hedges are just as (if not more) important here as they have foliage that is closer to the low-level exhausts of vehicles using the highway.

Conifers with small needles are the best species to choose for filtering pollution due to their finer, more complex foliage (a greater surface area for the pollution to be deposited on) and the fact that they are in leaf all year round.

TREES FOR WINDBREAKS.

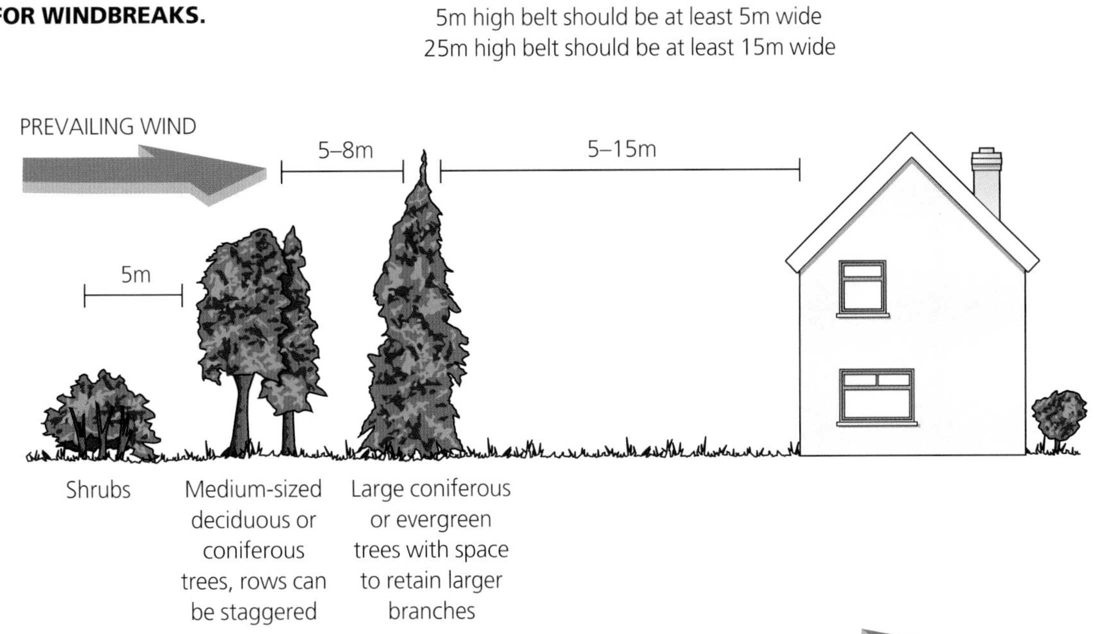

5m high belt should be at least 5m wide
25m high belt should be at least 15m wide

PREVAILING WIND

5m

5–8m

5–15m

Shrubs

Medium-sized
deciduous or
coniferous
trees, rows can
be staggered

Large coniferous
or evergreen
trees with space
to retain larger
branches

Windbreak needs to
be semi-permeable to
the wind to slow and
redirect it.

Turbulance can break
branches and tree tops
or flaten crops

If the windbreak is
too dense, strong air
currents are formed
that can cause damage
to the windbreak trees,
garden or property.

TREES TO REDUCE NOISE.

The wider you can make a noise screen the better. 30 metres wide is optimal.

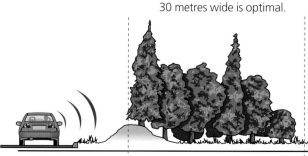 

Even a small bank can help reduce noise.

Evergreen broadleaves with low branches are the best trees for noise reduction.

A visual screen is also provided by trees

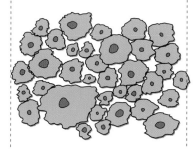

Better noise reduction with randomised tree locations, avoid rows and lines

Randomness in trunk diameters improves noise reduction. Larger trunks are better at reducing noise as are those with larger spreading crowns

Increased effects with increasing depth

TREES TO REDUCE POLLUTION.

Pollution wil be captured on leaves. Conifers are better as they have a greater surface area and needles are generally present all year round.

Pollution is also captured on the bark to a lesser extent.

A thick evergreen hedge is an effective buffer but needs to be tall enough to be effective in reducing pollution on its other side.

Combination of low shrub on hedge and tree (or high hedge) is much more effective for capturing the low level exhaust emissions and higher level drift and resuspension of pollutants.

Choosing the most appropriate tree for your site

All tree species have different genetic characteristics and growth strategies that have been developed to maximise their survival and growth in their natural environment. These characteristics and strategies manifest themselves in different species tolerances, attributes and adaptations. Once you have assessed the planting site and your requirements it is time to choose the most appropriate tree species to plant. For long-term success it is wise to match site conditions with natural characteristics of the tree.

The tree species selection guide in Appendix I will assist in selecting the right tree for your needs. However, there are also some general rules of thumb to bear in mind when selecting trees.

Drought

Drought-tolerant trees will often have small leaves or, in the case of conifers, smaller needles that will have a lower surface area. Drought-tolerant trees often accumulate waxes on their leaves or needles, for example the Judas tree (*Cercis siliquastrum*), holm oak (*Quercus ilex*), sea buckthorn (*Hippophae rhamnoides*) and stone pine (*Pinus pinea*). These waxes reduce water loss through transpiration and reflect light, which prevents the leaf temperature becoming too high. Waxy leaves often appear glossy.

On some species, leaf hairs (called trichomes) do a similar job and appear as a grey or white down on the surface of the leaf. These also reflect light and reduce water loss. It must be remembered that the tree from the nursery has been nurtured in controlled conditions and, although it may be genetically adapted to tolerate drought, it will still need time to adapt once planted.

Waterlogging

Flood- and waterlogging-tolerant tree species often have an ability to generate special adventitious roots and root structures. These root structures are filled with spaces between the cells that aid in the diffusion of oxygen from the lenticels on the lower stem and other bark tissues. Essentially this means that whilst underwater the tree roots are still able to utilise this trapped oxygen.

Some trees have very visible adaptations. A species of alder (*Alnus incana*) produces adventitious roots near the soil surface. Swamp cypress (*Taxodium distichum*) produce clearly defined aerial roots called pneumatophores or 'knees', which are filled with air spaces. Others have genetically adapted to reproduce seed in the spring, at a time when flood waters can assist in seed dispersal. These include willow (*Salix*), poplar (*Populus*), silver maple (*Acer saccharinum*) and Oriental plane (*Platanus orientalis*). All these have a capacity to tolerate varying levels of periodic waterlogging.

Salt

There are no clear and consistent visual indicators as to the tolerance of a tree species to salt damage, which is mainly incurred either through de-icing salt or coastal planting. Tolerances vary, often in the same species, and can depend on whether the salt is wind-blown or present in the soil. Trees that grow only in saline soils are known as 'halophytic' and have distinct strategies for tolerating salt.

Taxodium distichum pneumatophores, also known as 'knees'.

Some have adapted leaves that sequester the salt, storing it before rupturing and releasing the salt back into the atmosphere. Others, like mangroves, have developed a filtration system that collects salts and releases them back into the atmosphere. A useful guide if considering coastal planting is to observe which species are already growing successfully in the nearby environment. Roadside trees that are growing successfully despite seasonal road salt applications can also provide a useful guide.

Soil compaction

There are very few, if any, tree species that can survive when soil compaction is severe. Root development is inhibited, anaerobic conditions prevail, and tree performance is impaired often to the point of eventual failure. Ideally, where soil compaction exists the soil should be de-compacted before planting. However, there are species that can contend with these conditions better than others, such as field maple (*Acer campestre*), hawthorn (*Crataegus monogyna*) and London plane (*Platanus × hispanica*).

Shade

Trees have varying capacities to survive in shaded conditions. Generally speaking, those with darker leaves and denser foliage are better able to tolerate shade. Holly (*Ilex*) and beech (*Fagus*) are good examples of shade-tolerant trees, whilst yew (*Taxus baccata*), western hemlock (*Tsuga heterophylla*) and Douglas fir (*Pseudotsuga menziesii*) are conifers that are able to grow under other tree canopies.

Biosecurity and Plant Health information (UK and US)

There is a full regulatory framework surrounding plant health and the importation of plant material. The fine detail of the regulatory framework is constantly amended. To familiarise yourself with up-to-date information it is worth referring to: https://planthealthportal.defra.gov.uk in the UK and https://www.aphis.usda.gov/aphis/ourfocus/planthealth in the US

There are also useful guidance notes and online practical information produced by the Arboricultural Association available at: https://www.trees.org.uk/Help-Advice/Biosecurity

Range of average annual minimum temperatures for each hardiness zone (courtesy RHS).

Pests and diseases

All tree species are vulnerable to various pests and diseases. However, such vulnerability is normally balanced by the tree's natural defence mechanisms and natural predators found in the wider environment. Ever-increasing international trade, not only of plant material, has resulted in an accentuated vulnerability to imported exotic pests and diseases. Trees have few natural defence mechanisms against 'new' imported pests and diseases and there are few, if any natural predators also. Biosecurity is, therefore, an important consideration when buying and planting trees. Wherever possible it is best practice to source trees from a nursery where the plants have been sourced and grown in the same country, rather than having been imported from overseas. Often this is not always possible, in which case it is worth checking to ensure that any trees that you are buying have been on the supplying nursery for at least one full growing season (12 months) and have been subjected to a full pest and disease control programme with regular monitoring and inspections. In the UK these are carried out by the Department of the Environment, Food

HARDINESS RATINGS (courtesy RHS)

Rating	Temperature ranges (°C)	Category	Definition	USDA
H1a	>15	Heated greenhouse – tropical	Under glass all year.	13
H1b	10 – 15	Heated greenhouse – subtropical	Can be grown outside in the summer in hotter, sunny and sheltered locations (such as city centre areas), but generally perform better under glass all year round.	12
H1c	5 – 10	Heated greenhouse – warm temperate	Can be grown outside in the summer throughout most of the UK while day-time temperatures are high enough to promote growth. (Most bedding plants, tomatoes and cucumbers.)	11
H2	1 – 5	Tender – cool or frost-free greenhouse	Tolerant of low temperatures, but not surviving being frozen. Except in frost-free inner-city areas or coastal extremities requires glasshouse conditions. Can be grown outside once risk of frost is over. (Most succulents, many subtropical plants, annual bedding plants, many spring-sown vegetables.)	10b
H3	1 – -5	Half hardy – unheated greenhouse/mild winter	Hardy in coastal and relatively mild parts of the UK except in severe winters and at risk from sudden (early) frosts. May be hardy elsewhere with wall shelter or good microclimate. Likely to be damaged or killed in cold winters, particularly with no snow cover or if pot grown. Can often survive with some artificial protection in winter. (Many Mediterranean-climate plants, spring-sown vegetables for later harvesting.)	9b/10a
H4	-10 – -5	Hardy – average winter	Hardy through most of the UK apart from inland valleys, at altitude and central/northerly locations. May suffer foliage damage and stem dieback in harsh winters in cold gardens. Some normally hardy plants may not survive long wet winters in heavy or poorly drained soil. Plants in pots are more vulnerable to harsh winters, particularly evergreens and many bulbs. (Many herbaceous and woody plants, winter brassicas, leeks.)	8b/9a
H5	-15 – -10	Hardy – cold winter	Hardy in most places throughout the UK even in severe winters. May not withstand open/exposed sites or central/northern locations. Many evergreens will suffer foliage damage, and plants in pots will be at increased risk. (Many herbaceous and woody plants, some brassicas, leeks.)	7b/8a
H6	-20 – -15	Hardy – very cold winter	Hardy in all of UK and northern Europe. Many plants grown in containers will be damaged unless given protection. (Herbaceous and woody plants from continental climates.)	6b/7a
H7	< -20	Very hardy	Hardy in the severest European continental climates including exposed upland locations in the UK. (Herbaceous and woody plants from continental climates).	6a-1

Hardiness rating notes
1. New hardiness ratings supersede the previous RHS hardiness ratings (H1-H4) which are not the direct equivalents of the new ratings.
2. The temperature ranges are intended to be absolute minimum winter temperatures (°C), not the long-term average annual extreme minimum temperature used for the USDA zones.

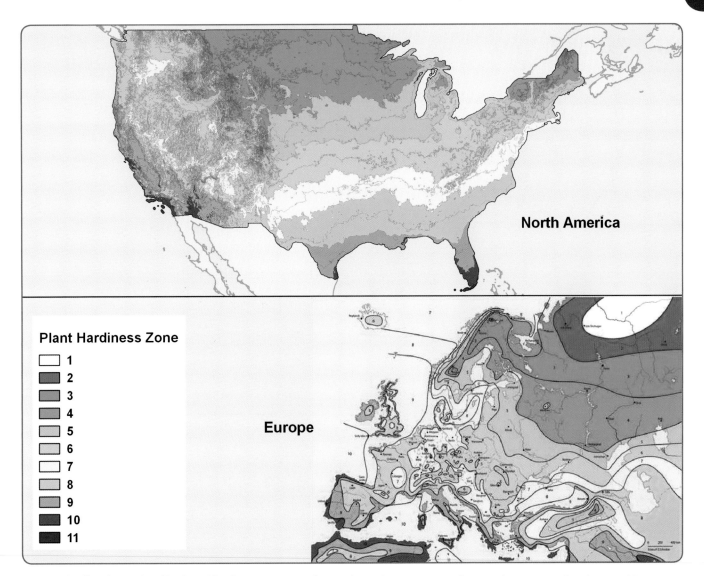

Hardiness zone maps for US and Europe. Based on the United States Department of Agriculture (USDA) Plant Hardiness Zone Map. The map is not an official USDA Plant Hardiness Zone Map

Plant Hardiness Zone

1
2
3
4
5
6
7
8
9
10
11

North America

Europe

and Rural Affairs (DEFRA) and in the US by the Department of Agriculture (USDA).

Hardiness zones

Its important to consider the hardiness zone of your area when choosing trees because many trees will not tolerate lower temperatures than they are used to. Therefore they may not survive the winter if they are planted outside their hardiness zone.

Based on the minimum 10-year average winter temperatures, plant hardiness zones have been subject to ongoing development. Originally created by the US Department of Argiculture (USDA) for the United States they are now also available for the rest of the world.

Essentially the scale defines 13 zones by annual extreme minimum temperature. So a tree described as 'hardy to zone 10' means that it can withstand a minimum temperature of -1°C (30.2°F) to 3.9°C (39.0°F). Suitable hardiness means a tree can be expected to grow in the zone's temperature extremes, as determined by the lowest average annual temperature.

Do bear in mind, however, that these maps are guidelines and do not factor in local site conditions. Also there are other systems in operation in different territories around the world. For example, in the UK the Royal Horticultural Society (RHS)

system is used, which allows for the UK's climate. The USDA zones do not work particularly well in the UK as they are designed for a continental climate and cooler UK summers also have to be considered.

The RHS hardiness ratings are based on absolute minimum winter temperatures (in °C) rather than the long-term average annual extreme minimum temperatures that define USDA zones, whilst in Australia there is a system developed by the Australian National Botanic Gardens.

USDA hardiness zone maps for the UK, US, Europe and much of the rest of the world are available available at: https://www.plantmaps.com

Natural range

The natural range of a species reflects the geographic locations in which that species grows in nature. This is of importance because all tree species have adapted genetically to grow well in particular environmental conditions. The closer these natural genetic adaptations match the site you intend to plant the more likely successful planting and longevity in the landscape is achieved. Some information on natural range is given in the Species Selector section.

Provenance

The provenance will directly affect the tree's ability to tolerate and thrive in the designated hardiness rating. If the parents of the seedling came from particular conditions (such as higher altitude), the seedling will be adapted to the same conditions. A tree species designated as having a cold hardiness rating of 6°C (43°F), which originates in the south, will struggle when faced with more extreme and possibly colder temperatures in the north.

Succession

Succession is the term used to describe the stage at which a species will naturally begin to appear and thrive in a forest/woodland development. This successional status can affect the likelihood of a tree species thriving in any environment. A pioneer species (which might be among the first to colonise a disturbed or cleared area) may struggle to survive in a heavily shaded spot, while a late succession type (which might grow slowly in nature) may struggle in an open, sun-soaked, paved square.

A warm dry mountain slope with a limited soil volume may replicate conditions found in a paved urban environment. Here early succession species such as black pine (*Pinus nigra*), sessile oak (*Quercus petraea*), and golden rain tree (*Koelreuteria paniculata*) are likely to be successful. Similarly, on an urban site fully exposed to the sun, pioneer species such as Italian alder (*Alnus cordata*), Hungarian oak (*Quercus frainetto*), Turkey oak (*Quercus cerris*) and Swedish whitebeam (*Sorbus × intermedia*) are likely to succeed.

Below: The native silver birch, *Betula pendula*.

Below right: An exotic *Betula utilis var. jacquemontii* 'Grayswood Ghost', with similar shape and form as the silver birch, and with excellent bark effect.

Planting trees for their botanical attributes

Having taken all these factors into consideration, it is now time to decide what attributes you would like from your tree – most of these are personal preferences. Spend some time deciding when you would like your tree to be working at its hardest in terms of the ornamental values and qualities that it will give at different times of the year. Some species provide year-round interest. The following are some to help you narrow down your selection criteria.

Native or exotic

Depending on the setting, whether the tree is for a rural or an urban setting will often determine whether a native or exotic species will be selected. In a rural setting, often a native species fits into the planting scheme more easily than an exotic species. In the UK, typically trees like the silver birch (*Betula pendula*), field maple (*Acer campestre*) or rowan (*Sorbus aucuparia*) would be typical species to plant and more suitable for the local biodiversity compared to the following in an urban setting. Himalayan birch (*Betula utilis var. jacquemontii*), Father David's maple (*Acer davidii*) or the Japanese rowan (*Sorbus commixta*) would be alternative choices for an urban setting.

Evergreen or deciduous, conifer or broadleaf?

A simple choice as to whether a deciduous or evergreen canopy is required and if planting a windbreak or screen, or a mixture may be a preferred option. The choice of conifer or broadleaf should also be considered at this stage.

Tree form and shape: vase-shaped, fastigiate, columnar, pendulous, spreading etc.

There are various forms of overall tree crown shapes and the position and space in the garden will be a contributing factor. The more space, the wider the canopy and larger the overall size of the tree at maturity, and an English beech (*Fagus sylvatica*) could be planted. The smaller the space and a tree with a more columnar or even fastigiate habit with a very narrow canopy like the Dawyck beech (*Fagus sylvatica* 'Dawyck') would be a better alternative. If a weeping tree is preferred then the weeping beech (*Fagus sylvatica* 'Pendula') would be a good choice, providing there is enough space as these trees can be wide-spreading when mature. Always think of the tree when it's mature and not the size it is in the tree nursery. Trees grow!

A mature English beech, *Fagus sylvatica* in a large garden.

The columnar Dawyck beech, *Fagus sylvatica* 'Dawyck' in a smaller garden.

A beautiful, graceful weeping beech, *Fagus sylvatica* 'Pendula'.

Bark interest – colour and texture

Trees with attractive bark give all-year-round interest, especially in winter when the leaves have disappeared and the trunk and branches are easily seen. Trees like birches (*Betula*), the paper bark maple (*Acer griseum*) and snake-bark maples like the moosewood (*Acer pensylvanicum*) make the perfect candidates.

Left: Paper bark maple, *Acer griseum*, grown for its attractive bark effect.

Right: The moosewood, *Acer pensylvanicum*, one of the snake-bark maples.

The golden variegation of the tulip tree, *Liriodendron tulipifera* 'Aureomarginata'.

The large, simple leaves of the northern bean tree, *Catalpa speciosa*.

The pinnate leaves of the Chinese yellow wood, *Cladrastris sinensis*.

Leaf shape and colour/ variegation

Leaf shape, size and colour will often determine how much light will penetrate the canopy into the garden below and it is important to choose the leaf type, a simple or pinnate leaf, green, red or yellow. So many choices and an important choice to make, as they will be on the tree for most of the year. Don't forget when they fall you will have to clean them up off the floor and some of the larger, fleshy leaves like those of the bean tree (*Catalpa*) or foxglove tree (*Paulownia*) could be a potential slip hazard if left in the wet.

Autumn/fall colour or not?

If it's special effects in autumn you want, particularly for that tree planted adjacent to a water feature for reflection, then autumn or fall colour will be a good choice. There are lots of tree species and cultivars that show their true colours in autumn, but many are specially selected for this attribute in particular.

All the cultivars of the American sweetgums (*Liquidambar styraciflua*) and red maple (*Acer rubrum* 'October Glory') are good examples.

Left: *Acer rubrum* 'October Glory' living up to its name in October.

Right: The American sweetgum, *Liquidambar styraciflua* in full autumn colour.

The popular Japanese flowering cherry, *Prunus* 'Kanzan'.

The bright red fleshy fruits of the Toringo crab, *Malus toringo*.

The flowers of the Persian ironwood, *Parrotia persica* in late winter.

Flower – size, shape and colour

Flowering trees are trees with a special attribute which can be shown during every season. In late winter and early spring the Persian ironwood (*Parrotia persica*) produces bright red flowers before any leaves are produced. In spring, the choice is endless from the flowering cherries (*Prunus*) to the flowering crabs (*Malus*) and the selection is really down to personal taste in colour, shape, size of flowers and abundance. There are so many to choose from in this category including magnolias, buckeyes (or horse chestnuts) and bean trees to name but a few.

Fruit – colour, ornamental or edible

The choice of fruit or not is a big decision to make, as the fruits

can be messy and a possible nuisance if they fall in the wrong place, like by the front door, because when a wet fruit like those of the Toringo crab apple (*Malus toringo*) drop they can walked into the house all over the carpet, it's going to make a mess. However, they are also a food source for the local bird population

The golden, edible fruits of the persimmon, *Diospyros kaki*.

in autumn. Another decision would be to choose an edible and ornamental fruit like a persimmon (*Diospyros kaki*). Choose wisely.

Rarity value for interest

This selection criteria is a matter of taste for the planter who may purely want to show off with a rare tree from an interesting part of the world and a high conservation status, rather than the bread and butter from the garden centre. These trees are generally available from specialist tree suppliers who will give you good advice on their requirements in the garden.

There are also hard-working trees that tick all, or many of the boxes above and will give us all-year-round interest, which deserve that place in the garden, especially if you only have room for one tree.

Once you have chosen what species of tree you would like to plant, you need to buy it from a nursery or garden centre. The next chapter will help you to understand the terminology used in the nursery trade and what the best size and root system of the tree will be.

A rare tree with no common name, *Meliosma veitchiorum* from China. Rare trees can still have incredible garden attributes like architectural shape and form, and extremely large pinnate leaves with autumn colour.

3 SELECTING AND BUYING A TREE

Trees are supplied by nurseries and garden centres in a range of shapes, forms and types of root systems. Understanding how trees are grown and the terminology used by nursery growers is important if you are to buy what you think you are buying. Rule number one is never to buy a tree without seeing it first, especially if you are investing in extra-heavy nursery stock, which is expensive and difficult to handle.

Choosing the tree is exciting, like buying a car, and shouldn't be missed. It's the start of a long journey for you and the tree. A good nursery person will help you choose and advise on anything you need to know about it. They will welcome you with open arms, providing you make an appointment first, and will encourage you to select the tree you want from the nursery lines and tag it, even if it is just a single tree. Take your time viewing the tree from all angles, check the root crown where the trunk meets the root system for scarring and planting depth in the nursery. If possible, check the root system. This is the engine room of the tree and you would never buy a car without flipping the bonnet to see what lies under it. Have a good look at the crown and make sure that you are happy with what you see. Choose a good, reputable tree nursery or supplier. Remember that you get what you pay for and planting a tree is a huge investment in time and resources.

Understanding tree nursery production methods

Trees are offered for sale at many different types of commercial or retail outlet, from garden centres to large specialist tree nurseries. The one certain factor is that all the trees offered for sale have started life on a tree nursery. Trees can be purchased in a variety of sizes from a seedling to the semi-mature tree. Irrespective of size, all trees will have gone through a nursery production system. An understanding of these production systems will enable you, the purchaser, to ask pertinent questions when assessing the quality of the tree or trees you are intending to buy and plant.

There are three principal production methods used by tree nurseries in the UK. Having a familiarity with these systems and understanding the advantages and disadvantages of each will enable you to evaluate the quality of material being purchased. All the production systems have different features and require a slightly different method of examination to ensure the best possible tree is being purchased, and all can deliver first-class results. They are all based on how the root system of the tree is produced. These production systems are:

- Bare-root
- Rootballed
- Container-grown

Bare-root system

Rootballed system

Container-grown system

Rows of field-grown trees in the nursery.

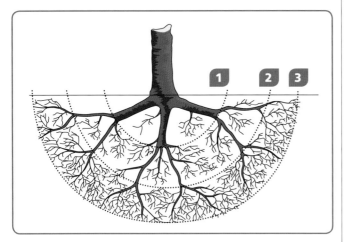

Undercutting: 1, 2 and 3 indicate where roots have been cut to stimulate growth prior to lifting.

Bare-root

These trees are grown in a field with no restrictions to the root system, and are also known as field-grown trees. They are lifted directly from the nursery field and the root system has had all the soil removed from the roots so that it is 'bare-root', with no soil. The roots are exposed to the elements and should be protected as soon as possible after lifting to prevent them from drying out from exposure to the wind or sun. Bare-root trees can be purchased as seedlings, transplants, whips or small standard trees (see page 58).

The most important consideration when buying bare-root trees is that the root system has been protected and kept moist between lifting on the nursery field through to despatch at the nursery retail area. The roots of trees such as beech *(Fagus sylvatica)* and silver birch *(Betula pendula)* can desiccate in as little as 15 minutes if left exposed to the elements on a hot windy day. It is important to specify that all bare-root trees are root-wrapped/bagged following lifting. This is usually done by placing the roots in a poly-planting bag, which is black on the inside and white on the outside to reflect light and heat, keeping the root system cool and moist with some damp barley straw around the roots. This protection needs to be continued through to the planting operation.

Rootballed

These are trees lifted from the nursery field with a portion of the soil in which they have been growing. The rootball is usually wrapped in hessian or a similar material and held together with a wire mesh. The production of a rootballed tree involves either repeated lifting or a process of undercutting. At each stage, the root stem is severed with numerous new root shoots developing. This continues until the tree is finally lifted from the nursery field and wrapped as described above.

Below: Standard trees in the field, rootballed, ready for despatch.

Above: Standard *Betula utilis* and *Betula albosinensis* in nursery rows growing in easy-lift white woven polypropylene bags.

Right: Standard *Betula nigra* growing in Airpots in nursery rows.

Bottom right: An extra heavy standard oak tree grown in a custom-built container.

Container-grown trees

These are trees that are grown in containers. Trees are either lifted from the nursery field and transferred to a container or have been moved from one container to another slightly larger container as the tree has developed. The following are different types of containers that trees can be grown in:

- Rigid plastic containers (the traditional plant pot)
- Polythene bags
- Airpots or Spring Rings
- Easy-lift white woven polypropylene bags
- Custom-built containers for very large trees

Container-grown trees should have been grown in the container for sufficient time for the root growth to have substantially penetrated the growing medium/compost, but not be pot bound. The tree should be growing in the centre of the container, planted at the correct depth, well-rooted and firm with sufficient moisture in the compost. The tops of the containers should also be clean and free from weeds.

Containerised trees

There is a difference between container-grown and containerised trees. The former should have been grown in the container for at least a full growing season before sale, so that a strong, healthy, well-balanced root system has been produced inside the container. A containerised tree is one that has been potted up into a container either from another container, or as a rootballed or a bare-root tree, and sold before they have had a chance to root into the new compost. A good example of this is the Christmas tree that is bought in a pot at Christmas time. These trees are usually dug up from the field and immediately potted up into the container without rooting into the pot. Unsold fruit trees that are generally sold in the garden centre or nursery as bare-root trees with the roots wrapped in polythene are potted up into compost at the end of the winter, before they begin to grow to extend the sales period, but when knocked out of the pot, they become bare-root trees and it will be difficult to establish these successfully.

Advantages and disadvantages of the different production systems

Method of Production	Advantages	Disadvantages
Bare-root	The production process is cheaper, therefore the cost to the consumer is generally cheaper.	Lifting from the nursery and planting is limited to the dormant season, November to March.
	Bare-root trees are lighter and therefore easier to handle and move.	Significant root volume may be lost during the lifting process.
	They are less likely to contain soil-borne pests and disease.	Not all species are tolerant of the technique, particularly conifers.
	This is the best production system for identifying and correcting root defects.	The handling and care of trees between lifting and planting is critical. Roots always need to be protected and kept moist.
		Generally, the larger the bare-root tree within a species, the higher the mortality rate, with survivors slow to recover.
Rootballed	The length of time available for planting is extended beyond the dormant season as trees can be lifted and stored with roots protected by the soil ball.	Rootballed trees are generally more expensive than bare-root trees.
	Trees that have a poor survival rate when lifted bare-root can be successfully planted using this method.	Rootballs are heavy and can be difficult to move.
	Care between lifting from the nursery field and planting is less critical as the soil ball can be kept moist and frost-free.	If nursery practice is poor, then as much as 90% of the root system can be lost on lifting from the nursery field.
		Because the tree roots are never seen, this is the worst system for correcting root problems prior to planting.
Container-grown trees	The root system is entire, undamaged and trees can be planted at any time of the year, although soil conditions can be limiting in the summer.	Root circling in the container is the most serious problem associated with container-grown trees. Roots hit the side wall of the container and continue growing in a circular fashion around the container wall. If left, they have the potential to strangle the tree below ground. This can lead to failure several or more years after planting. The white bags and 'Airpots' prevent this from happening.
	The trees are generally easier to handle and store than either bare-root or rootballed trees.	Container-grown trees are generally more expensive than both bare-root and rootballed trees.
	Trees generally weigh less than rootballed trees as the growing media in the container is usually organic.	Irrigation needs post-planting may be higher because the container compost is organic rather than soil-based.

Practicalities of different root systems

Time of year	The time of year dictates the supply of some forms, e.g. bare-root trees are only available in autumn and winter.
Size of stock	18cm+ trees should always be specified as rootballed or container-grown.
Storage	Container stock will stand for a period with little or no maintenance, unlike bare-root trees.
Handling	Large rootballed/container trees will require handling assistance.
Cost	Large trees may require staking/watering systems and specialist skills, including large plant for handling.
Preparation	Bare-root stock will require a holding area if it is to be stored for a few days. Tree pits may need to be prepared for large trees. Ground preparation is required for whips and containers.
Maintenance	Time of year, supply form and size will all impact on after-care.
Establishment	The expected growth rate of planted stock varies with size and time of year planted and the size of the supplied stock.

How to assess tree quality

Below ground

It is difficult to assess the condition of the root system, especially when you are choosing rootballed or container-grown trees as the root system is hidden from view. You will often have to rely on the reputation of the nursery or go by previous experience.

BARE-ROOT TREES

Bare-root trees can easily be checked, and ideally the root system of a bare-root tree should display three to five principal lateral roots spaced evenly around the main stem. These should have a significant number of small fibrous roots emerging from them. An absence of fibrous root should be a cause for concern. The perfect view of a bare-root system is rarely realised.

ROOTBALLED TREES

As outlined earlier, rootballed trees are the result of a production method that involves either undercutting or lifting and transplanting the trees during the production process over a period of years. The number of times this occurs will depend on the size of tree being purchased. Without breaking the rootball it is difficult to verify whether this production process has been carried out correctly. Ask the supplying nursery for details of the number of times the tree has been transplanted and only buy trees from a reputable nursery.

If the root collar of the tree moves independently of the rootball then there is a reasonable chance that the rootball has not been correctly prepared. This can easily be tested by moving the main stem to the right and left. The rootball should follow the movement of the whole tree. The soil ball will be wrapped, usually in low-grade hessian, and secured with mild steel wire mesh. This should be solid, tight and not collapse when the tree is moved. The rootball should be moist and have been kept in that condition at all stages following lifting from the nursery field.

CONTAINER-GROWN TREES

The biggest single problem with container-grown trees is the potential for the root system to circle within the container. This is caused as the developing roots hit the side of the container and follow a pathway around it. These roots, once they have become woody, will continue this pathway and have the potential to eventually strangle the tree or never send out strong, lateral anchor roots. Tree failure may not happen until

The perfect bare-root system.

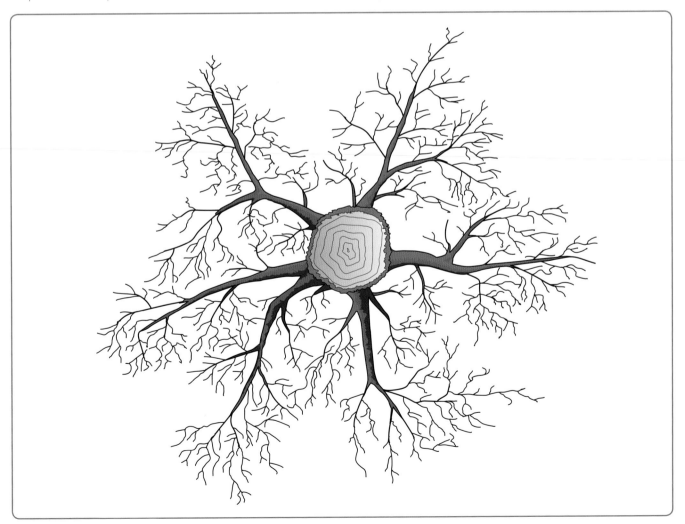

Inspection points on a nursery tree

1. Leaf lesions and/or leaf discoloration: Can be indicative of pest and/or disease or poor nutritional status. Note that when assessing colour, the time of the year must be taken into account, especially the natural variations associated with autumn.

2. Dieback in the crown: Indicates tree is not functioning physiologically as effectively as it should be. Could indicate a problem with the root system, pest and/or disease or poor nursery handling or production practice.

3. Low density and/or small size of foliage: Tree canopy will look sparse and the foliage appears small and lacking in vitality. Indication of poor growing conditions on the nursery, poor nutritional status and poor soil or compost conditions.

4. Reduced length of extension growth when compared to previous years: May not always be apparent because of nursery pruning practices, but this is a useful indicator if possible as to whether the tree is performing as well as it has done in the past.

5. Abnormal adventitious bud development on the main stem: Where young trees have been prepared with a clear stem, abnormal and unwanted adventitious bud development can be an indicator that the tree is stressed and is responding by producing growth nearer the root system.

6. Abnormal flattening on the main stem: Abnormal flattening is only visible on larger nursery trees. When it occurs, this flattening can be an indicator of a problem with the tree's vascular system.

7. Epicormic growth from the rootstock: Many nursery trees are grafted or budded (see page 170). This is apparent at the bud/graft union that is usually visible towards the base of the stem. Growth from the roots will look different from that in the crown of the tree. Such growth can be an indicator of stress, or be symptomatic of a weakness in the bud/graft union, which could lead to failure as the tree develops. It will also take vigour away from the top growth of the tree.

8. Root fibre: Only visible on bare-root trees. Roots should be evenly distributed around the main stem with both structural and fibrous roots visible.

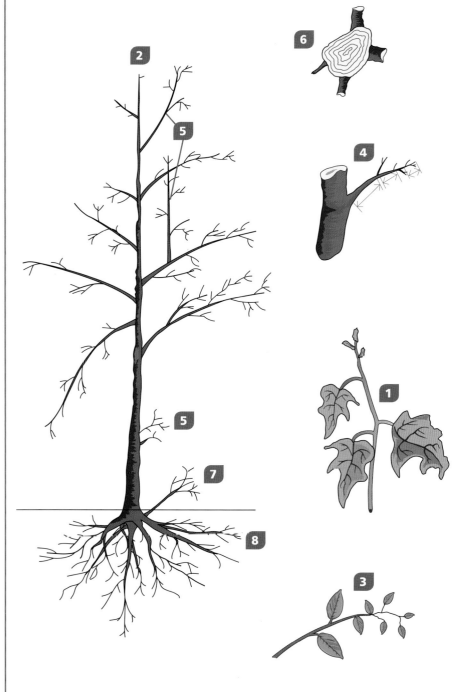

Girdling root on an elm

Circling and girdling roots

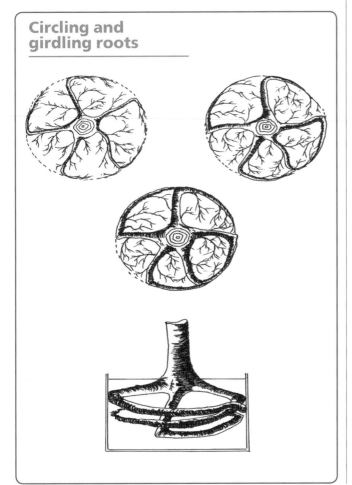

many years after planting. In the nurseries or garden centres where the trees are small enough and growing in rigid plastic pots, knock the pot off and check that the roots aren't circling within the pot. If you see old brown roots with no fresh ones visible and no compost left in the pot, this means the roots are pot-bound. You will also know if the root system looks too small for the tree: can it stand up without support or does it just keep falling over? The latter would indicate that the root system is too small for the size of tree.

Ask how long the tree has been growing in its container. Ideally no small tree should be in the same container for more than one growing season. Beyond this, deformation of some sort is likely to have occurred. Lightly tapping the outside of the container with the foot will give an indication as to the size and thickness of roots present as well as the direction they are taking. Thick roots emerging from the bottom of the container are another good indicator that root deformation is likely.

As with bare-root and rootball the container compost should be moist.

Above ground

This is a visual check to determine that you like the trunk size and straightness and the general shape and that the tree looks to be healthy and in good condition. The crown should be evenly balanced, with good, strong extension shoots and a main leader that looks healthy. There shouldn't be any dead wood or twiggy dieback in the crown and the main branches should be evenly spaced with good lateral branching from the main scaffold. These main branches should be free from algae and moss, as their presence would indicate that the tree isn't really growing well and generally not increasing in size.

How young trees are described at the nursery

Seedlings and transplants

Small trees that are normally available as bare-root plants are graded according to their height. This measurement includes seedling trees, transplants and larger whips. Trees may be lifted once as seedlings and offered for sale or transplanted on one or two separate occasions. The method of describing the age of the plant and the number of times it has been transplanted is numeric. For example:

- 1+0 is a 1-year-old seedling which has not been transplanted.
- 0/1 is a 1-year-old hardwood cutting which has not been transplanted.
- 1+1 is a 2-year-old seedling transplant (1 year in the seedbed, transplanted then grown for 1 year).
- 1+2 is a 3-year-old seedling transplant (1 year in seedbed, transplanted then grown for 2 years).
- 1u1 is a 2-year-old seedling that has been undercut in situ after year 1 and grown on for a further year.

The older the tree and the greater number of times it has been transplanted normally corresponds with a higher cost. These types of nursery stock are usually bought in bundles of 50 and are usually bare-root and range in size between 40cm (16in) and 100cm (39in). This size of tree is perfect for ecological planting for hedges, woodlands and windbreaks.

Whip

These are transplants consisting of only a single slender stem, without any significant side branching. The whip will reflect the natural characteristics of the plant. Some are well-branched from a young age, e.g. silver birch (*Betula pendula*) and common alder (*Alnus glutinosa*), while others will be a single narrow stem or whip. A tree cannot have the laterals pruned off in the nursery to make it a whip. Whips are normally between two and four years old and it is essential that these trees are undercut or transplanted during these early years in the nursery. The size of these varies between 40cm (16in) and 125cm (49in) and they are useful for ecological planting situations similar to where seedlings and transplants are used, such as hedges, woodlands and windbreaks.

Feathered tree

These are trees usually with an upright central leading shoot and a

trunk furnished with evenly spaced and balanced lateral growths down to near ground level, according to species. The nursery can specify a girth size, but they are usually sold by the overall height, up to and between 200cm (79in) and 250cm (98in). Feathered trees are a good tree to buy if you like a low standard tree, as the feathers can be removed as a method of formative pruning to the desired height.

Maiden

This is a low worked, grafted woody plant in which the scion has grown and been trained for one season (see page 171). Usually cultivars and fruit trees are sold as maidens and by their overall height, which will vary greatly depending on the rootstock type and the species. Choosing between a maiden and a standard (below) depends on the overall size and cost that the gardener would like to commit to. A maiden tree is far easier to handle, transport and plant than a standard, is more common in the garden centre and cheaper to buy.

Standard tree

This is a tree with a single, straight trunk, clean of lateral branches and a well-balanced symmetrical crown. The crown can have a central leader or a branched head.

A well-feathered hornbeam (*Carpinus betulus* 'Fastigiata').

A standard oak (*Quercus robur*).

Multi-stemmed tree

This is a tree form with several stems emerging just above ground level, popular with trees grown for their bark effects or flower such as birches (*Betula*) and cherries (*Prunus*). These forms can be produced by cutting off the trunk when they are very young so that multiple stems arise from that pruning point (a minimum of three to develop into the resulting tree).

Larger trees

Larger trees are measured by their stem girth at 100cm (39in) above the ground on field-grown nursery stock or the nursery mark in container-grown trees, and have an industry agreed standard in terms of the expected relationship between the stem girth and the height of the tree when it is sold. These sizes and names of the various grades are illustrated in the diagram below. When visiting a reputable nursery to tag trees, the nursery will usually supply you with a tape measure so that you can check sizes of stem girth without any ambiguity.

An understanding of these grades and sizes is useful if you are not visiting the nursery but ordering remotely or through a contractor's specification. However, remember where possible to visit the nursery and tag your own trees.

A multi-stemmed Himalayan birch, *Betula utilis var. jaquemontii*.

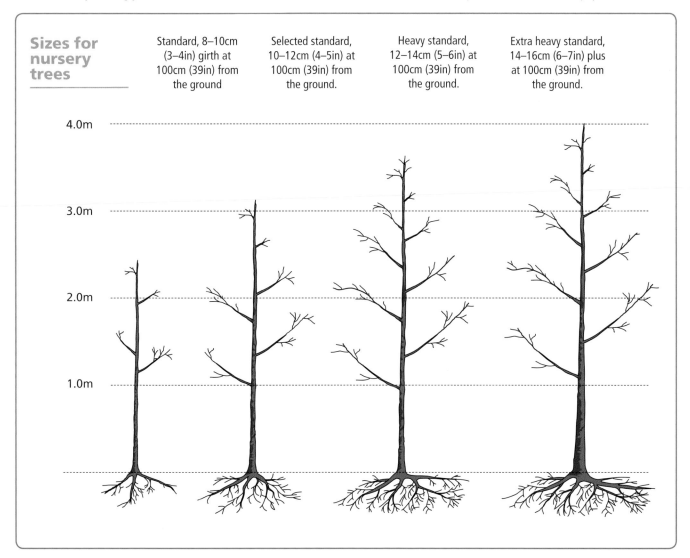

Sizes for nursery trees

Standard, 8–10cm (3–4in) girth at 100cm (39in) from the ground

Selected standard, 10–12cm (4–5in) at 100cm (39in) from the ground.

Heavy standard, 12–14cm (5–6in) at 100cm (39in) from the ground.

Extra heavy standard, 14–16cm (6–7in) plus at 100cm (39in) from the ground.

4.0m

3.0m

2.0m

1.0m

A numbered security tree tag attached to the trunk following the selection in the nursery.

Visiting the nursery to tag up trees.

Tagging your chosen tree

There are no price tags on trees on the large specialist nurseries and, once you have chosen the tree that you would like to buy, it will be 'soft tagged' to reserve it and then measured (following the system described under How young trees are described at the nursery, see page 58). Once the nursery works out a price, either ex-nursery or delivered to your site, and you confirm that you wish to buy it, the tag will be fixed and no one else can buy that tree. If you chose to buy ex-nursery, then you will have to make sure it fits safely into your car, or arrange the transport and add those costs to the tree.

The nursery will provide coloured tags for you to tag the tree that you choose. If it's a large, expensive tree a numbered security tag will be provided by the nursery, which, once fixed to the tree, cannot be removed without cutting off the branch or the tag. When your tree arrives it should still have your security tag attached to it, so you know that this is the tree that you chose on the nursery.

Nursery tree tagged and measured.

Taking delivery of your tree

The branches in the crown will be tied in by the nursery to help with transportation and to prevent any branches being damaged in transit. For the larger nursery stock, this exercise is done over time to prevent the branches from breaking. If you are having your tree delivered, make sure you are ready to receive it; the main task will be getting it off the lorry and the driver will want to move as quickly as possible.

DO:
- Carry your tree by its root package (rootball or container) and not by the trunk. Steady the tree by holding the lowest part of the trunk.
- Use a tarpaulin under the rootball as a sling, making it easier to carry or use a wheelbarrow or sack barrow.
- Use appropriate lifting machinery to lift and transport large rootballed or container-grown trees.
- Take great care of the trunk – even a small wound on a young tree can cause permanent irreparable damage.

DON'T:
- Leave it in a hot vehicle or a heated building.
- Store it lying down on the floor where it can be driven over or walked on.
- Drop your tree.

The branches of the crown being tied in ready for safe transportation.

Storage and aftercare prior to planting

The aftercare prior to planting is determined by the production system of the nursery on which your tree has been grown.

Bare-root trees need to have their roots protected all the time, with exposure to the elements reduced to the minimum. The only time they should be exposed is at the time of planting and then for the shortest period possible. Ideally during storage, the roots should be heeled in. An open trench, large enough to insert the roots into should be dug in the garden, and the roots placed in the trench, then covered with soil to prevent them from drying out. This is a temporary form of planting to preserve the roots until the actual planting operation. Keep them moist until you are ready to plant. They may also be wrapped in either plastic bags or hessian and kept moist. Store trees in the shade.

The roots of rootballed trees are protected within the soil ball. These trees should be stood upright and kept moist until ready for planting. A good, well-developed rootball should have enough soil in the ball to keep the tree growing for a full 12 months if it is kept out of the ground. However, this is not recommended.

The above is also true for container-grown trees, but irrigation needs may be greater as the container compost is likely to be organic and will potentially dry out more quickly than the equivalent rootballed tree.

4 PLANTING: TREE INSTALLATION

Planting a tree is an art and a science brought together and once you have selected the species is the most important stage of establishing a tree in the garden. If the planting is done correctly, following all the guidelines and principles, the tree will establish successfully and give you many years of satisfaction and rewards. In this chapter, we have broken down tree planting into the two different styles that will cover most situations and eventualities.

The engineered approach is a term that we use for planting the larger nursery stock trees, which have a large, well-grown root system that need a planting pit and possibly staking to support the tree until it can support itself. This type of tree planting is usually for the specimen tree in the garden or landscape. Planting larger semi-mature trees or extra-heavy standards needs larger equipment and machinery and an engineered approach, and can be very rewarding but costly to plant and establish to independence.

The ecological approach is a term used for planting the smaller, bare-root trees from seedlings or transplants to whips that don't require an engineered planting pit or a means of support. This method of planting is cheaper, quicker and easier to carry out than the engineered approach and is generally used for planting woodlands, shelter-belts and hedgerows. It can also be used for planting hedges if the nursery stock is small enough and the soil conditions are compatible to this style of planting.

One of the most important stages of establishing a tree is the follow-up or aftercare, including the weed control, feeding and watering which is covered in detail later in this chapter, as is establishing a garden hedge.

The engineered approach

This is a term used for planting larger trees with large root systems, needing a planting pit and possibly staking (for the 'ecological approach', used for bare-root trees, see page 74). Planting a tree is a huge investment in time and money. Give it as much care and attention to detail as possible to ensure that the tree can establish itself quickly in its new home, becoming independent as soon as possible. Most people think that planting a tree is easy, but following a few simple rules makes the difference between success and failure.

The ability of the tree to extend its roots out of the planting hole and into the surrounding soil quickly will help to reduce any environmental or climatic stresses on the tree that may affect it in the future and will enable it to survive with the minimum of aftercare.

The planting operation is a simple exercise with four basic principles to consider, which, if followed, will increase the success rate of your tree planting. Deliver all four of these principles correctly and the tree's establishment rate increases; ignore them

Checking for underground services with a cable avoiding tool (CAT) before starting excavation.

all at your peril as failure will be inevitable. These principles can be used for nursery stock with any types of root systems, including bare-root, rootballed, and container-grown:

1 Choose good-quality nursery stock and ensure that the tree (especially the root system) has adequate protection during the preparation for planting (see previous section).
2 Prepare the planting pit well.
3 Get the planting operation right.
4 Provide good aftercare.

Tools ready for use at the planting site.

Tools and materials

If you have the following tools and materials at your disposal, planting a tree is an easy exercise:

- Tape measure, short post, ball of string and lump hammer for marking out the planting hole.
- Half-moon lawn-edging knife for cutting turf if planting into a lawn.
- Digging spade and fork for digging the planting hole.
- Sharp secateurs.
- Length of straight timber or a rigid garden cane for checking the depth of the hole.
- Board or tarpaulin to place excavated soil on to protect the lawn, paving or other surfaces adjacent to the tree.

If you are using a stake to support the tree:

- Tree stake and tree tie.
- Lump or sledge hammer for banging in the tree stake and a claw hammer and nail if fixing a tree tie.

Timing of planting

With the availability and use of container-grown trees today, planting a tree can be done at any time of the year. However, it is preferable to plant during the dormant period of September to April to prevent extra stress on the tree both during and after the planting operation. Bare-root trees should only be planted during the dormant period.

There are two preferred periods for planting evergreen trees such as conifers and evergreen broadleaves, which are in the autumn between September and November, and in the spring between March and May, when the tree root growth is active and the soil is warm or warming up.

Do not plant any kind of tree if the ground is waterlogged from heavy rains, when there is snow on the ground or when the ground is frozen.

Making the planting pit or hole

We must be cautious when we call the hole a planting pit, as this signifies a deep, pit-like hole, and the planting hole should in fact only be the depth of the root system of the tree to be planted. The ideal diameter of the tree circle is 1.5m (5ft), as this is the optimum size to eliminate any competition from weeds or compacted turf around the tree and will allow for ease of mowing the grass around the tree in future.

1 Mark the centre of the hole with a cane or small post and attach a length of string to it by means of an open loop. The length of the string should be the radius of the tree circle (0.75m/2½ft).

2 Attach the half-moon lawn-edging iron to the end of the string and cut out of the turf a circle 1.5m (5ft) in diameter.

3 Loosen, remove and discard the turf, as there will be no need to incorporate this material into the backfill of the tree pit.

4 The actual tree pit will be square-shaped inside the cut-out circle in the turf, not round, which will create a container underground and lead to circling roots. A square hole has four weak corners allowing the roots to easily penetrate outside of the tree pit. Mark out a cross, using the centre of the hole as the centre of the cross.

5 Where the lines meet the edge of the circle, join the ends up, marking up the square to be excavated.

6 Dig out the soil in the marked-out square to the depth of the spit of the spade, approximately 300mm (12in) deep, or the depth of the rootball. Research has shown that effort is better going into cultivating the width of the tree pit rather than the depth – 'wide and shallow'.

7 If the depth of the tree's rootball is deeper, dig the hole to this depth. This can be pre-measured using a stout bamboo cane and a length of straight timber. Do not fork over the base of the tree pit, as this could lead to further settlement of the soil after planting the tree, which in turn can lead to the tree being planted too deep.

The planting operation

Before planting the tree, prune off any dead, dying or damaged branches back to the parent branch or trunk with sharp secateurs. If no formative pruning has been carried out while the tree has been growing in the nursery there may be a need to do some formative pruning. Further details on formative pruning are given on page 88.

Pruning off a damaged branch from the main stem of the tree.

1 Position the tree in the centre of the tree pit ensuring that the orientation is best suited for the crown of the tree to develop to its best potential. If the tree is one-sided, which can often occur from being grown in a nursery line with insufficient spacing, orientate the crown of the tree to gain the best shape from the most viewed sight line. Once the tree has been given adequate space in its new home, the crown will develop to its full potential.

2 Remove the container and check the root crown of the tree or the nursery mark (clearly identified by a change in colour of bark) to ensure that any compost has not been built up the trunk, burying the root crown in the tree nursery. By rubbing away any compost it will be easy to identify any basal flare and the main root system that will be growing from the trunk. This is the marker that should be used for gauging the accurate planting depth during the planting operation.

3 Check that the depth of the root collar is correct again by using a length of straight timber across the top of the pit from the level of the turf on the outer edge of the circle.

4 Using the soil that was excavated from the tree pit, straighten the tree, ensuring the trunk is upright from several views. Once you are happy, the original soil backfill can be placed into the tree pit and firmed in layers by treading, to ensure that the soil is evenly firm without any air voids that can slump later. Take care with the fleshy rooted species like *Magnolia* and hickory (*Carya*) species, which do not like their roots being firmed too heavily. There is no need to incorporate any planting compost or soil ameliorants at this stage as the addition of organic matter can have a detrimental effect on the establishment of the tree, by causing the soil to shrink, slump and settle after planting, lulling the tree into a false sense of security. The tree must go looking for water and nutrients as soon as possible after planting to be successful and this will be encouraged by using the original soil. Fertilisers can also have a detrimental effect on newly planted trees and should not be added as they will not be used by the tree in its first year of establishment and the nutrients will be leached out of the pit and wasted. There are other branded soil ameliorants such as mycorrhizae (highly specialised root-inhabiting fungi which form beneficial relationships with the roots of trees) that are available for use in tree planting operations, but the jury is still out on the benefits that they provide. Fortunately, they do not cause any damage if used so do not be afraid to try them.

5 Once all the soil backfill is added and the tree pit has been filled, the surface of the rootball should just be visible, which means that the tree has been planted to the perfect depth. Poor rates of growth and actual losses are attributable to planting the tree too deep, so this is one of the most important factors of tree planting. Get this wrong and, even if everything else is right, the tree will not establish.

Trees in a garden centre grown in rigid black plastic pots.

Planting container-grown and containerised trees

The containers may be anything from rigid black plastic pots or the white bag system to Airpots. Keep the container on the root system until the actual planting operation to prevent any roots drying out in wind or direct sunshine. The container can be submerged in a bucket of water to give the root system a thorough drenching before planting. Once submerged, keep the container in the water until air bubbles stop coming out of the rootball.

If excessively girdled roots are found when the root system is taken out of the pot, return the tree to its place of purchase. Girdled roots are a sign of poor nursery practice and the tree has been left to grow in the pot for too long and not moved up into a larger pot at the right time. Root systems on trees like these should not be tolerated as the tree will not thrive and reach its full potential.

Planting rootballed and burlapped trees

If a rootballed or burlapped tree is being planted, the rootball will probably be covered and held together with hessian and wire mesh. These packaging materials are very low grade and, when planted in aerobic conditions, will quickly rot and rust and break down naturally. It is important not to remove this material as it holds the rootball together, preventing the soil from coming away from the roots. If the wire and hessian is removed, the rootball could fall apart, exposing the roots, leaving a bare-root tree,

A large rootballed tree with wire and hessian protecting and holding the rootball together.

which will reduce the success rate of establishment. Once planted and the soil backfilled, any wire close to the trunk can be cut with wire cutters and pulled away from the trunk, but not removed. These packaging materials are your insurance!

Planting bare-root trees

Keep the root system in the planting bag or packaging supplied by the nursery or garden centre for protection until the planting operation. Any fine roots left exposed to wind or sun

Bare-root trees.

for any period of time will dry out and deteriorate extremely quickly, ultimately affecting the successful establishment of the tree. Prior to planting check the root system and prune out any damaged roots.

Mulching

Mulching the surface of the tree pit provides an insulation layer, keeping the soil warmer in winter and cooler in summer, protecting roots from extreme temperatures, which can injure trees. It will help to suppress weeds and reduce the competition between the weeds and the tree's roots. At the same time it will help to retain any moisture in the soil, reducing the amount of watering that will be required through the summer. It will protect the tree from mower or strimmer damage by providing a visible zone that is not to be mown. A good organic mulch will help to improve the structure and fertility of the soil backfill. The mulch should cover all the surface of the tree pit and should be 5–10cm (2–4 inch) deep. It is important **not** to let the mulch come in contact with the base of the trunk or root crown, as this can encourage root collar rot and expose the tree to other invasive fungal organisms like honey fungus. The bark of the trunk is not designed to have soil or organic matter against it. When mulch is applied to the surface, pull any mulch away from the trunk, creating a 10cm (4in) circle of mulch-free surface so that none touches the trunk of the tree.

Do not mulch excessively! There should never be more than a 10cm (4in) layer of mulch over the roots. Too much will prevent the movement of rain and any irrigation water from percolating through the thick layer of mulch and any gaseous exchange getting through to the roots. Once the mulch starts to break down and disappear, it can be topped back up to 10cm (4in) deep.

Tree circle being mulched with composted woodchips.

Close-up of a mulched circle with a clear 10cm (4in) un-mulched surface at the base of the tree.

WHICH MULCH TO USE?

Mulches can either be organic or synthetic. Not all mulches are suitable for all trees and they should be used with care.

Organic mulches:

■ **Bark, shredded or chipped.** This can be from hardwood trees or conifers and has a good ornamental/aesthetic effect, which is long lasting and generally sterile. As bark mulches rot down, it is not uncommon to find them colonised by white fungal growth or covered in a crop of toadstools. Thankfully these belong to saprophytic fungi that are harmless to plants; they are simply breaking down the organic material. No action is required.

■ **Composted horse or cow manure with straw or sawdust.** This is a good source of nutrients, but it is important to compost before applying or it may burn the tree, causing damage to the bark, and it should be mixed with a coarse-textured material like a woodchip.

■ **Mushroom compost.** A good source of nutrients when mixed with soil or other materials, this is high in alkalinity.

■ **Composted grass clippings.** These should be dried or composted before using and it is better to mix grass with other materials to increase the porosity and reduce matting.

■ **Composted shredded leaves.** These are a good source of nutrients but may increase weeds if not composted adequately. Care must also be taken if the leaves have fallen from an infected tree, as some pests and diseases can overwinter on the old leaves and be spread to uninfected trees.

■ **Composted woodchip.** With woodchip, it is good practice to compost it prior to using it on tree circles. There are often questions asked as to whether woodchip robs the soil of nutrients or spreads tree diseases to uninfected trees, but research has shown that trees are capable of dealing with nutrient loss from fresh wood products and, unless the woodchip is from trees infected with honey fungus or *Phytophthora*, it is safe to use.

■ **Pine needles.** Not widely available in the UK but more common in the US, needles should be mixed with other materials unless soil acidity is desired. They are sometimes dyed different colours for different ornamental effects.

■ **Straw.** Coarse-textured so it persists for a long time, straw can blow away easily unless mixed with other materials. Straw is also very clean and prevents soil and soil-borne diseases from splashing onto the tree trunk.

A series of well-mulched tree circles.

A woven geotextile mulch mat.

Synthetic and inorganic mulches and mulch mats:

- **Black plastic.** While stopping weeds, black plastic exposed to the sun also gets very hot in the summer, and the heat can damage fine tree roots. We should also be reducing the amount of plastic that we use in the garden, so it should be avoided where possible.
- **Woven geotextile fabrics.** These are available as purpose-made tree mulch mats. They are usually made in a square from a water-permeable, UV-degradable polypropylene fabric with a slit from the centre of the mat for easy installation around the base of the tree. They can either be dug in with a spade around the outer edge of the tree circle or fixed to the ground with plastic barbed pegs.
- **Stone/Gravel.** Non-biodegradable materials like stone and gravel offer no boost to the fertility of the soil, but they do help to retain moisture and suppress weeds and are very decorative.

While synthetic and inorganic mulches do a good job of holding moisture and blocking weeds, they don't improve the soil structure or add any fertility to the soil. Mats can be detrimental to the soil surface by glazing the surface, making it more difficult for water and oxygen to penetrate. Therefore, they are not recommended for domestic use.

Mulches are best applied directly after planting. Top up mulches in mid- to late spring and autumn, when the soil is moist and warm. It is best to avoid applying mulches in winter and early spring as the soil is too cold, and in summer, when it will be too dry, unless watering is done before application.

Occasionally you will see 'volcano mulching' where mulch is piled up around the base of the tree. This is very poor practice for the reasons described above and the tree will suffer as a result.

Staking

WHY DO WE STAKE TREES?

Some trees will need to be staked so that they remain standing until the roots can grow out and effectively anchor the tree into the soil and take up moisture. Only stake if the tree is unstable, for example if the tree is too large for the rootball, or it has a bare-root system, or if the trunk is bending under the weight of the crown or the planting site is exposed to strong winds. Most trees don't need any form of support or we over-stake, not allowing any movement in the trunk.

HOW TO STAKE

For small trees with a thin trunk, a stout bamboo cane can be used to give some additional support to the trunk, and the tree can be attached to the cane using horticultural tubing or garden twine. For larger bare-root trees, a single tree stake can be used. It should be positioned in the centre of the tree pit before the tree is planted and the tree roots spread out around the stake. The stake should be on the prevailing wind side of the tree, so that the wind hits the stake before the tree. When banging in the stake, always remember that it will have to be removed a year later, so refrain from driving it in too deep or it will be difficult to remove without damaging the tree.

Always use a round stake and never a square one. Square stakes have corners that potentially can rub the trunk of the tree during strong winds. It is also easier to attach a tree tie tightly to a round stake than to a square stake.

The height of the tree stake should be one-third the overall height of the tree and the tree should be attached to it using one tree tie, no more than 3cm (1in) from the top of the stake. Any lower and this will allow the tree to chafe on the top edge of the stake. If a large tree is being planted, fix a nail through the tree tie to prevent the tie from sliding down or around the stake, leaving about 5mm of the nail protruding to allow for easy adjustment during the summer.

Always use a proprietary tree tie made from rubber, plastic or webbing with the supplied buffer between the trunk of the tree and the stake.

Volcano mulching must be avoided or root rot will be encouraged.

A well-positioned tree tie with a buffer between the tree and the stake.

Never use wire, electrical ties or baler twine as these products will interfere with growth and ultimately damage the tree.

For container-grown, containerised or rootballed trees a single stake will not be able to be used as it will damage roots if banged through the rootball.

For these instances, the following can be used: (see figures)

■ **Oblique staking:** this is a round stake used at a 45-degree angle to the trunk and fixed to the trunk at one-third of the overall height of the tree, as with the single stake.

■ **Crossbar staking:** two posts are inserted on either side of the tree circle with a crossbar attached to both at one-third of the overall height of the tree. The trunk of the tree is attached to the crossbar using a tree tie.

Single staking (above), oblique staking (below left) and crossbar staking (below).

Protecting the tree

WHY DOES YOUR TREE NEED PROTECTION?

Young trees have thin bark that can easily be damaged by browsing animals or weeding equipment such as lawnmowers and strimmers (or brush cutters). While mulch can keep mowers and strimmers away from the trunk of the tree as well as keeping the soil moist, it cannot protect the young tree from rodents, rabbits and deer.

Spiral tree guard fitted to the trunk of the tree immediately after planting and the finished tree.

- Spiral tree guards can be fitted to trees after planting to prevent feeding damage or bark rubbing from small deer. These are designed to expand on their own as the trunk increment of the tree increases with age.
- Tree mesh baskets using four posts and small-gauge green plastic mesh are a good way to mark the location of the planting as a reminder for future maintenance and a good deterrent to a number of mammals.

Mesh basket fitted around the tree after planting.

- Tree shelters come in a variety of materials, colours and sizes. The tube should be large enough to allow around 2.5 to 10cm (1 to 4 inches) of clear space around the trunk. It should also be tall enough to prevent browsing by any anticipated problem species: 30cm (12in) for rabbits and rodents, 50cm (20in) for hare, 1.3m (51in) for smaller deer like the roe and muntjac. Bespoke larger tree guards may need to be made to achieve the desired results, such as 1.5m (60in) for larger deer such as red deer and some farm animals. There is always a top and bottom of these guards, which should be identified before fitting to ensure they are fitted correctly, or damage may be caused to the tree. Some types of tree shelter also have the added advantage of providing a microclimate for the tree (like a mini-glasshouse) that will help to increase its growth and reduce exposure to wind and frost. However, this also makes the tree shelter an ideal nesting site for small rodents like voles and mice.

All tree shelters and guards should be inspected regularly, at least annually for:

- Broken or leaning stakes.
- Weed growth inside the tube overtaking and choking the tree.
- Nesting rodents.
- Damage to the tree from the guard or shelter (especially around the top and bottom lip).

Often, in a smaller domestic garden, trees may not need any sort of protection at all.

A standard tree shelter used for establishing and protecting smaller ecological tree plantings.

Maintenance and aftercare of a newly planted tree

Depending on the type and quality of the nursery stock being planted, research has shown that some trees can lose 80–95% of their roots during transplanting, which causes stress to young trees. Symptoms include fewer and smaller leaves, with little extension growth or dieback on the ends of the branches and the leading shoot. It can take up to three years for the tree to settle down and grow out of this shock to the system. The more aftercare and maintenance that is given to the tree the more you will help to speed up the recovery period and allow the tree to grow away in its new home quickly.

Most trees that are planted in the garden are left to their own devices and expected to survive without any intervention, but at some stage of their early life young trees will need some help if they are to survive, especially during hot, dry periods. In the first two or three years following planting, water is one of the most important ingredients to the successful establishment of a young tree.

Watering

Critical to the success of newly planted trees is providing the right amount of water. The first three years are the most critical, but always pay attention to watering needs throughout a tree's life – especially in times of drought.

HOW OFTEN AND HOW MUCH WATER?

There is no hard and fast rule for this, and the amount of water and how often will depend on the soil type, including the drainage (light sandy soils will need more water, more often than a clay loam soil) and the weather conditions. Rather than water for the sake of watering, check the moisture content of the backfill under the mulch by feeling the soil and observe the appearance of the tree's foliage; is it wilting or looking dry? It is best practice to apply water before the tree shows signs of stress, so observance is key to knowing when to water. For the average 3m (10ft) tall standard tree, 90l (20gal) of water once every two weeks is a good guide during a hot dry summer. Because soil type and weather conditions influence the demand for water, amounts and timings of irrigation will vary. Generally speaking, the larger the tree you have planted the more attention you will need to pay to its water requirements.

Do not over-water! Tree roots need access to oxygen; if the roots are waterlogged the tree will suffer stress with the potential for root rots. Watering too much is worse than watering too little as it is much harder to correct. Newly planted trees also need to be given the opportunity to look for water and if we over-water the tree will rely on the planter to give it to them and root growth may be reduced.

Apply water to the entire area of the 1.5m (5ft) diameter tree circle, not just around the immediate base of the trunk.

There are simple watering products available on the market today called Tree Watering Bags. These bags are placed on the soil surface around the trunk by means of a zip, and filled with water. The bag has a fine perforation in the base, which allows the water

to slowly percolate through into the soil over several hours to reach the root zone of the tree.

Weed control

Do not use brush cutters, strimmers and mowers around the base of your tree as they cause bruising to the young, soft bark when they come into contact. This bruised bark will die and when the tree has been girdled (damage to the bark all around the trunk), this may ultimately kill the tree or allow access to fungal pathogens like honey fungus.

Weeds and lawn-grass are very competitive for moisture and nutrients and usually gain access to it before the tree. It is important to remove this competition, allowing the moisture and nutrients to get down to the tree roots. This is the reason why a clean 1.5m (5ft) tree circle should be maintained. We can do this by a variety of methods: manual weeding, mulching or the application of herbicides. Mulching is best done as the tree is planted. For more information see page 68.

MANUAL WEEDING

Manual weeding means regularly hand-weeding the tree circle by hoeing or pulling the weeds out and discarding them. This only serves one purpose and that is removing the competition. Any water held in the soil will quickly evaporate from the soil surface, especially on dry windy days, so there will be a need to increase watering rates after weeding.

HERBICIDES

Chemical weed control can be very effective if done correctly and can have the same effective control as manual weeding and mulching. There are many different herbicides readily available in garden centres and the manufacturer's instructions on the label should be read and followed, including the method of application, the appropriate calibration rate and the recommended protective

Weed control around a tree circle using herbicide.

equipment and clothing. These instructions and precautions should always be carefully read, understood and followed.

Fertilising young trees

Fertiliser is used to maintain the health and vigour of young trees to increase their resistance to damage from pests and diseases, but should only be applied if the tree is showing signs of stress from a deficiency of soil nutrients or following a soil nutrient test. For visible signs of stress and nutrient deficiency in the leaves of the tree, see Troubleshooting, page 125.

Newly planted trees will not need any fertiliser in their first year after planting, but in the following growing season young trees may need a helping hand with the application of a feed. A good tree fertiliser can be organic or compound-chemical based and should be well-balanced in terms of macro- with micro-nutrients. All three of the macro-nutrients should be included: nitrogen, phosphorus and potassium, which are needed for healthy plant growth. It is preferable to use a slow-release nitrogen that will be long lasting and readily available throughout the growing season. A faster-release nitrogen will stimulate fast, weak new growth that could encourage vascular wilt diseases, and soft fleshy growth that will attract feeding insects and make the shoots vulnerable to winds and cold damage.

The ideal nutrient makeup of a good tree fertiliser should be 12% to 30% nitrogen, with 3% to 12% phosphorus and potassium and should be applied at the recommended application rate on the fertiliser bag or container. The ideal time to feed, if needed, is in early to late spring and the fertiliser should be broadcast over the soil surface of the tree circle, preferably before mulching. Applying more than the specified application rate can have an adverse effect on the young tree and the surrounding environment, as it can leach out of the soil. You will also be wasting your money.

Do not apply fertilisers containing herbicides, also known as 'weed n' feed' for lawns as they will seriously damage and even kill a young tree.

Similarly, applying excess lawn feed to trees grown on lawns, especially combination weed killers and fertilisers, will injure trees and put them under serious stress. Remember that weed killers designed for use on broadleaf weeds will also harm broadleaf trees. 'Pre-emergent' herbicides are, however, safe to use near trees.

Other aftercare needs

Tree stakes will need to be checked and removed at an appropriate time, as the tree will be establishing a strong anchor root system and becoming independent. Many tree stakes are left until they finally rot and fall away from the tree, but this is not good practice: the stake and tie should be removed as soon as possible to prevent the stake damaging the tree by interfering with the tree's growth. The tree tie should be checked regularly through the growing season and adjusted if necessary, rather than allowing it to strangle and bite into the tree trunk. As soon as the tree has an established anchor root system, the tree stake should be removed, not cut off at the base. If the tree cannot support itself after the first two years, then there is a problem: the tree has either been planted too deep, is of poor nursery stock, is in anaerobic planting conditions in the tree pit or has had poor staking. There is little that can be done to re-establish such a tree, emphasising the importance of getting it right first time!

The ecological approach

This is the term used for planting bare-root trees that don't need a planting pit, from seedlings and transplants to whips. This approach is cheap, quick and easy to carry out and usually used for planting woodlands, shelter belts and hedgerows. Bare-root trees can only be planted during the dormant period of September to April to prevent induced stress on them both during and after the planting operation. When planting bare-root whips (transplants between 40cm and 100cm (16in and 40in), consisting of only a single slender stem, without significant side branching) or small bare-root transplants with a good fibrous root system, it isn't necessary to go through the whole procedure of engineered planting and we can use the ecological approach. This is the cheapest, easiest and quickest way of planting a tree and is often used for planting woodlands, windbreaks and hedgerows. This approach entails cutting a notch in the soil with a spade by pushing the spade into the soil to the depth of the spit and moving it from side to side, opening up a notch or split in the soil. Holding the stem of the tree, place the roots into the notch and lift the tree up and down, spreading the roots evenly inside the notch. When the root collar is at the correct depth (soil level) and the stem is upright, place both feet on either side of the notch and firm the soil around the base of the tree. Job done! (see page 76)

Choosing a hedge

There are three types of hedges that we must consider before planting, and the choice will depend on what attributes we desire:

- Evergreen and semi-evergreen hedges, which will include conifers such as the Leyland cypress (× *Cuprocyparis leylandii*), Lawson cypress (*Chamaecyparis lawsoniana*),

Evergreen hedge.

yew (*Taxus baccata*) and western red cedar (*Thuja plicata*). Also worthy of consideration are evergreen broadleaves such as *Photinia* × *fraseri* 'Red Robin', common box (*Buxus sempervirens*), cherry laurel (*Prunus laurocerasus*) and privet (*Ligustrum*). This type of hedge can be planted as a single row of rootballed or container-grown trees. The rootballs of each plant should be butted up against the last one for the perfect spacing that will create an almost instant barrier.

A mixed, native, deciduous hedge, well-furnished to the ground.

Unfortunately, common box is now very susceptible to box blight (*Cylindrocladium buxicola*) and box caterpillar (*Cydalima perspectalis*), so without a thorough integrated pest and disease management programme it will be very difficult to grow this as a hedge successfully.

- ■ Deciduous hedges, which include beech (*Fagus sylvatica*) and hornbeam (*Carpinus betulus*). When clipped and kept juvenile, both of these species hold their dead leaves through the winter, maintaining a permanent barrier. This hedge should be planted at equal spacing in a single line, using feathered trees.
- ■ Mixed native conservation hedges are usually made up of native species with the dominant species being hawthorn (*Crataegus monogyna*), mixed in varying ratios with blackthorn (*Prunus spinosa*), wayfaring tree (*Viburnum lantana*) and guelder-rose (*V. opulus*), hazel (*Corylus avellana*), privet (*Ligustrum vulgare*) and dogwood (*Cornus sanguinea*). This mixture of species should be planted in a double staggered row, approximately five plants per metre length.

TIMING OF PLANTING

Planting a hedge is similar to planting a standard tree and the same principles apply. Container-grown hedging trees can be planted at any time of the year, providing good aftercare can be given. As with general tree planting, however, it is preferable to plant during the dormant period of September to April to prevent induced stress on the tree both during and after the planting operation. Bare-root hedging trees should only be planted during the dormant period. If the trees are delivered early and the ground conditions are not suitable for planting (e.g., there is waterlogged soil, snow on the ground or frozen soil), they should be kept in a frost-free building with the roots kept moist or heeled in outdoors (temporarily placed in a trench with the roots covered with soil) until ready for planting.

HOW TO PLANT A HEDGEROW OR HEDGE

The following planting method can be used for both deciduous and evergreen species of hedging plants that are bare-root, container-grown or rootballed. Before you start, make sure you have a digging spade and fork and a string line.

1 First run a string line the length of the proposed hedge and excavate a trench the full length of the hedge to be planted, to the depth and twice the width of the rootballs of the hedging plants, about 60–90cm (2–3ft) wide.

2 Prune any damaged roots off bare-root stock before planting and dip into a proprietary root dip, a polymer-based gel that coats the roots, protecting them from desiccation and drying out before planting.

3 Place the trees in the trench at even spacing 30–60cm (1–2ft) apart with the top of the rootballs or the nursery mark on bare-root trees level with the surrounding ground and backfill the trench with the excavated soil that came out, without any compost. Don't be tempted to plant too deep!

4 Firm the soil evenly around the transplants, ensuring that all the trees are upright.

5 Finally mulch the surface with a suitable mulch to 10cm (4in) to prevent weed growth and where necessary protect the individual plants from rabbits and deer with spiral guards and a stout cane.

For the first two or three years it may be necessary to water the hedge during dry spells and keep the hedge weed free. Today hedges can be bought already established in 1m (3ft) length troughs, grown to varying heights, that when planted at any time of the year form an instant hedge.

For a hedgerow of bare-root trees, it may be more efficient to use the ecological approach of notch planting (see below).

Push the spit of the spade into the ground.

Waggle the spade to and fro to make a notch.

Insert the roots of the tree into the open notch.

Ensure the tree is at the right depth.

Firm the soil evenly around the tree with the heel.

Tree planting complete.

Planting large trees

We have looked at the principles of planting the average-sized standard trees that we can all manage and plant easily on our own without any need for large or expensive equipment or machinery, but it is possible today to plant larger nursery stock, often referred to as semi-mature trees. The term semi-mature is misleading as these trees aren't really semi-mature, but are known as extra-heavy standards. We can buy these specimens from specialist tree nurseries that grow them on, and when they are planted, they can provide an instant effect in the garden or landscape for the impatient gardener.

Many people say that if we plant a young tree and look after it with all the aftercare needed, it will catch up and its growth will overtake some of the larger semi-mature trees that we plant at the same time. This is not true, and a well-grown extra-heavy standard tree that has been transplanted several times during its life in the nursery becomes used to being moved and will establish successfully without too much transplanting shock, provided that you give it the best aftercare, especially water, for at least five years after planting. The range of species available is more limited compared to the smaller trees, but the numbers of different species

Right: A large specimen copper beech, *Fagus sylvatica* 'Purpurea', growing in an Airpot on a specialist tree nursery.

Below: Delivery of several large trees on an articulated lorry, ready to be unloaded on site for planting.

that are being grown today on specialist nurseries is getting larger every year. These large trees are heavy and difficult to handle because of their large rootballs and the size of the tree. Never lift trees using a strop around the trunk. Always lift them by the rootball using suitable, tested lifting equipment and machinery. The right equipment is needed for handling them, and moving them from the nursery to the final planting site requires larger lorries, often articulated lorries, so suitable vehicular access to the planting site needs to be considered before making the relevant purchase. There is nothing worse than not being able to get the trees to the site and not being able to unload them off the lorry.

Many landscaping companies specialise in transplanting these larger trees, and it is recommended that you seek their advice and assistance to carry out this kind of operation. Without the knowledge of how to lift, handle and move large trees or the specialist machinery and lifting equipment to handle them safely, they can be damaged beyond repair and failure is inevitable, with your money, time and a well-grown tree wasted.

Large trees can be moved successfully from one site to another with large heavy machines called tree-spades. These machines have several half-rounded spades which are hydraulically pushed into the ground around the tree to create a suitable-sized rootball in relation to the overall size of the tree. The closed spades are then lifted out of the ground with the tree and the whole lot is transported to the new site where a large plug of soil the same size will have been removed prior to the operation, ready to accommodate the rootballed tree. It is a quick and easy operation, but ideally any trees that are to be moved should be well prepared for transplanting two or three years in advance to reduce any transplanting shock and give them the best chance of survival.

Staking, support and aftercare

When the tree has been positioned in the hole at the correct planting depth, the excavated soil should be returned into the tree pit as backfill without any tree planting compost or other soil ameliorants like fertiliser. During the backfilling, a watering loop,

Planting a large elm tree, *Ulmus hollandica* 'Lobel', with heavy lifting equipment and specialist strops.

A large tree lifted with a mechanical tree spade and ready for transplanting on a new site.

Watering loop prepared and ready for positioning in the tree pit around the rootball.

which is basically a loop of perforated drainage tube, can be installed around the rootball, with the filling point slightly above ground level. This system can be used for watering the tree in the tree pit without any wastage of water. Ideally, position the tube halfway up the rootball as opposed to at the bottom of the hole, so that when the tube is filled, the water seeps out and reaches the root zone in the rootball. If the tube is positioned on the bottom of the hole, the water will be leached away through the base of the tree pit away from the roots.

Trees of this large size, particularly trees with a rounded, burlapped rootball, will need some form of support to hold the tree in an upright position after planting. It will also prevent rotational movement of the root system, which would inhibit the production of strong and fit-for-purpose anchor roots that will support the tree once it is established into maturity. Remember that these trees are heavy, and some may be quite tall with a large crown, so they will need a more substantial means of supporting them than with a small standard tree. A good, experienced contractor will have the appropriate materials and knowledge to carry out this task.

The various systems for support would include: overground guying, underground guying and the use of multiple stakes with appropriate tying materials. As with smaller tree staking, the tree ties will need to be checked regularly and adjusted or removed when the time is right. If underground guying is used to support the tree, the wires should be severed with wire cutters once the tree is established to avoid girdling of the trunk by the wires as the diameter of the root crown increases.

As with standard tree planting, mulch the surface of the tree pit to help these large trees to successfully establish, and a good watering regime is critical for up to at least five years to reduce any transplanting shock and to give the trees enough time to root out and become independent.

Right: An extra-heavy standard pine tree with suitable staking. Note also the watering loop filling point protruding through the ground at the base of the tree.

5 TREE PRUNING

This chapter covers all the aspects of pruning a tree – from the perfect tool selection and maintenance to the correct method of making a pruning cut or removing a branch and creating the final cut. If pruning is carried out correctly and at the right time of the year, it will have the minimum impact on the overall health of the tree and produce a lasting desired effect required by the pruner.

Take care!

Depending on the size of tree and the type of pruning being carried out, pruning can be dangerous work as you will be using sharp pruning tools on living, dynamic plants. Follow these important safety instructions to be sure you are around to enjoy your tree!

Electricity flows through branches and remember electricity can jump a gap: Never prune trees that are within 3m (10ft) of overhead power lines. Distances will vary depending on the voltage of the power line, so contact your electrical network operator or your local utility company when planning to do pruning works near overhead lines. If you are concerned that your trees are in contact with overhead electricity lines or equipment, you should contact the Power Network Operator, who will undertake a site visit to check the risks, offer advice and if necessary arrange for one of their specialised teams to prune the trees.

DANGER OF DEATH

Do not:

■ use ladders. Ladders and trees do not mix. If pruning cannot be done with both feet on the ground then you need to seek professional help and hire an arborist (see page 122). Occasionally step-ladders can be used to make pruning easier; see Hedge cutting, page 96 on purpose-made Niwaki tripod ladders.

■ use chainsaws without the correct training, suitable personal protective equipment and appropriate experience. Hire an arborist instead.

Do:

■ use good-quality, sharp pruning tools that are in good condition and suitable for the task in hand.

■ seek professional help when needed.

Before carrying out any work on a tree always check with the local planning authority to see if the tree is growing in a Conservation Area (CA) or if it has a Tree Preservation Order (TPO) on it. If it has, you will need permission before you can carry out any pruning works on it (see section on Trees and the law on page 120). If the tree to be pruned is growing on a garden boundary or if the tree is growing in a neighbour's garden and you want to remove a branch from it, speak with them first to avoid any potential neighbourly disputes.

Pruning is an important part of tree management with formative pruning in the early stages of a tree's life through to a mature tree and an ancient tree.

If the correct tree selection process has been carried out and the right tree is planted in the right place, then a tree should never outgrow its setting and will require only minimal intervention. However, despite good tree selection, in reality this is never fully achieved and early pruning in the nursery or immediately following planting will help to determine the overall shape and form of the tree. This will also remove any potential future weaknesses in a tree's form. It is important to understand what is required from a pruning operation before starting with the saw or secateurs, as this will determine how to prune, what to remove and where to, ensuring a sound and healthy exercise is done. If the final 'target' pruning cut is made back to the parent branch or trunk, it will ensure that a natural form is made with no need for tree paints, resulting in a healthier, well-shaped tree.

Why do we prune trees?

Pruning is an art and a science brought together in an operation on a tree, which, if carried out correctly, will achieve a purpose without reducing the overall health or aesthetics of the tree. Before starting any form of pruning operation, it is important to ask the question: Why am I pruning this tree? There must be a reason to prune. Many gardeners believe that all trees in the garden must be pruned at some stage of their life, but this is not true: not every tree will need pruning, especially if we select carefully and plant the right tree in the right position. Once we identify what we want to achieve, we then can select the right type of pruning operation to carry out. We need to avoid unnecessary mutilation of trees that achieves nothing for the homeowner or the tree.

This is not pruning, but mutilation, which is unsightly and bad for the tree and must be avoided at all costs.

As with tree planting, there are some key principles to observe that will help the gardener to achieve the right results; they are the **SHARP** principles, which is easy to remember as sharp is what your pruning equipment should be:

S Know the **SPECIES** of tree being pruned
H Know the **HABIT** of the tree when it grows naturally
A Know the **ATTRIBUTES** that are special to this tree, such as flowers, bark, fruit etc
R What's the **REASON** for pruning?
P How will you **PRUNE** it?

The main reasons for pruning a tree are (in no particular order):

- To produce a clean stem, free from branches to make a standard tree, to show off the beautiful bark on the trunk.
- To help the tree to form a well-balanced, strong-structured crown in its early stages of life.
- To reduce any end weight on branches or alter the overall shape of the crown if it's too large or unbalanced.
- To remove the four Ds – dead, damaged, diseased and dying branches, which could also be dangerous.
- To raise the height of the crown, either for pedestrian or vehicular access under the tree, or to allow increased light levels to plantings beneath.
- To reduce the leaf surface, to allow more light into a property or garden, or to lessen the demands on the root system to reduce potential stress.
- To prevent branches from over-extending and interfering with overhead cables or buildings and interfering with sightlines on streets or driveways.
- To encourage flowers; this applies for example to most fruit trees.
- To maintain a safe environment by removing branches that could fail, fall and potentially cause injury to people or damage to property.

Hopefully once you have identified the reason for pruning you can carry out the correct type of pruning operation and the final results will be both aesthetically pleasing and have the correct outcome. Let's not forget that pruning has an effect on the tree. Loss of foliage reduces the tree's ability to photosynthesise to its full potential, potential energy reserves will be lost when branches are cut, valuable energy reserves in the form of carbohydrates are lost to repairing pruning cuts. In addition, epicormic growth can be stimulated, and stressed trees may be further weakened by pruning and made more susceptible to micro-organisms. So to minimise stress to your tree, keep pruning to a minimum, only pruning when needed.

Pruning tools

When pruning trees, it is important to have the right tool for the job and not to improvise with woodworking tools such as saws. Never use a woodworking crosscut saw for pruning.

Secateurs

For small trees and shrubs, most of the cuts can be made with a good pair of secateurs. Secateurs are ideal for cutting any branch up to 10mm (½in) thick. There are various types and makes available. The two most common are the scissor or bypass blade secateurs, and the anvil type. The best secateurs that make the perfect clean and accurate cut when sharp are the bypass type, which are easy to adjust and sharpen. The anvil type tend to crush the branch instead of cutting, especially if they are blunt.

If you try to cut branches that are too thick for the secateurs and exert too much effort into the scissor action, you will damage

Below left: The two types of secateurs: the bypass type (top) and the anvil type (bottom).

Below: A good selection of bypass secateurs with purpose-made leather holsters and diamond sharpening stone.

Close-up of a very sharp tri-edge blade.

A range of good-quality fixed and folding pruning saws, all with tri-edge blades and purpose-made scabbards to protect the blades.

the secateurs and the tree. Any branch thicker than 10mm (½in) in diameter should be cut with a sharp pruning saw.

When not in use, secateurs should always be kept in a suitable, purpose-made holster that can be attached to the belt to keep them clean and prevent damage to the blade if they are accidentally dropped. A good holster will also protect the pruner from the sharp blades of the secateurs. Regular sharpening of the blade, preferably before the cutting edge gets dull, will increase the life of the secateurs, making pruning effortless and leaving clean cuts on the tree. Apply a lubricating oil to the blades then use a sharpening stone or a diamond sharpening stone. A touch of oil or WD40 (a penetrating oil and water displacing spray) will prevent corrosion and keep them in tip-top condition for each important pruning job.

Pruning saws

A pruning saw is specifically designed for cutting green wood; it is not the same as a woodworking saw designed for cutting dry wood. As with the secateurs, there are numerous brands available, but the most popular type is the one with the very sharp tri-edge blade, which has three razor-sharp facets on either a straight or traditional curved blade in various lengths on a wooden or rubber/plastic handle. These saws have revolutionised tree pruning, in that they leave a very clean wound on the tree, which aids healing, but they are ultra-sharp, and care must always be taken when using one.

As well as fixed-blade pruning saws, there are a variety of folding saws with the same type of sharp blades. These are extremely useful to carry around the garden safely in a jacket pocket, so that you always have a good saw with you when you need one. Fixed-blade saws should be kept in a purpose-made scabbard when not being used to protect you, the gardener, from the razor-sharp teeth and the saw from accidental damage to the blade.

Unfortunately, tri-edge blade saws cannot be sharpened, and when blunt, the blades will need to be replaced. If looked after, however, they will give many years of good service in the garden. Cleaning the saw at the end of the day is important; give the blade a good squirt of WD40 to prevent any build-up of sap, conifer resin and gum, and finish off with a wipe with an oily cloth to prevent any rust. See also Biosecurity, page 44.

The perfect comprehensive tree pruning kit that will cope with most pruning needs for the gardener.

The bright red autumn foliage of *Rhus typhina*, which spells danger.

Personal protection

These tools are sharp, and the gardener should exercise the utmost caution and concentration when using them or a finger could easily be lost. Wear suitable thorn-proof protective gloves, not just for protection from the blades, but also from plants with prickles, thorns or spines, especially false acacia (*Robinia*), honey locust (*Gleditsia*) and blackthorn (*Prunus spinosa*). Some plants have toxic saps that can cause skin dermatitis if the pruner is sensitive to them. Such trees include staghorn sumach (*Rhus typhina*), and shrubs include *Euphorbia* and rue (*Ruta graveolens*). Where there is a danger that thorns or parts of the plant may come into contact with the eyes, wear suitable glasses or goggles as a means of eye protection.

To keep yourself safe, ensure you do the following:

- Maintain sharp pruning tools.
- Store all pruning tools in a dry room or shed when not in use after cleaning with an oily cloth.
- Wear suitable protective equipment such as tough leather gloves if inexperienced, especially on the opposite hand to the one working the secateurs or saw.

Pruning principles

When to prune

Most tree species are best pruned during the dormant season before leaf buds open in the spring, or after the new leaves have fully matured. It is also easier to see which branches need to be pruned when there are no leaves present, and to judge where to prune them back to. However, if there is a need to remove a branch that is damaged or needs attention, this can be done at any time of the year.

An exception to this rule are trees in the family Rosaceae, the fruit trees such as cherries (*Prunus*), apples (*Malus*) and apricots (*Prunus armeniaca*), which are affected by a disease called silver leaf fungus (*Chondrostereum purpureum*). These trees should be pruned during the summer months, in July and August, when the disease is dormant and there is less chance for wounds to become infected. If they are pruned at other times of year spores can be spread via pruning.

Some trees are prone to bleeding from pruning wounds at particular times of the year, especially maples (*Acer*), birches (*Betula*) and walnuts (*Juglans*). If pruned in late winter or early spring as the sap flow begins, they will leak copious amounts of sap, which is difficult to stop until the tree comes fully into leaf. This will not kill the tree, but it is quite a disturbing sight and places excessive stress on the tree; the sweet sap also has the potential to attract unwanted insects.

Free-standing bush and standard fruit trees need pruning during the dormant season.

A birch wound starting to bleed because of incorrect timing of branch removal.

The pruning cut

Where the branch is attached to the trunk or parent branch, it is known as the **branch attachment point**. There are two very important visible features that need to be easily identified and clearly understood by the pruner in order to know where to make the perfect final cut. These are the branch bark ridge and the branch collar. The **branch bark ridge** is created at the top of the branch attachment point by the bark of the trunk meeting the bark of the branch at differing angles, pushing up the bark into a clear ridge, resembling a Fu Manchu moustache. Depending on the tree species, this ridge can be more or less pronounced. On the underside of the branch below the branch bark ridge is a swollen area known as the **branch collar**, often marked by concentric rings of bark, which is formed by the two different internal tissues of the trunk and the branch meeting together and swelling to form an area known as the **reaction zone**. This tissue has exceptional qualities of vigorous cells that are resistant to disease and can compartmentalise the zone, blocking off any route into the tree for invasive fungi. At the same time it produces callus cells quickly, eventually healing over the tree wound in a process called **occlusion**.

Branch attachment point showing branch bark ridge and branch collar on birch.

Target pruning

It is important that when we make our pruning cut, we don't cut into or remove the tissue in the reaction zone, so that the tree can heal its wounds quickly without the use of tree paints or wound sealants. Cutting into the reaction zone is known as **flush cutting** and should be avoided at all costs. The tree is telling us where it wants the final cut to be made and we call this **target pruning**.

For the final cut, look for the branch bark ridge and branch collar. Place the saw blade to the outer edge of the branch bark ridge and angle the blade of the saw so that the finished cut arrives at the outer edge of the branch collar. The result should be a small diameter circular wound, at least half the size than if the cut had been made flush to the trunk of the tree. This will heal far more quickly than a flush cut, and the tree's natural defense mechanism will still be intact, keeping the tree healthy.

If there is no visible branch bark ridge or branch collar, which is common on trees with deeply fissured bark, the top edge of the final cut should be just outside the basal area of the branch and at right angles to the branch being removed, so that the final cut is a perfect circle rather than an oval shape.

Now that we understand target pruning, let's look at how to remove a branch.

A fully callused (occluded) tree wound on a beech tree (*Fagus sylvatica*) with the branch bark ridge and branch collar still present on the trunk.

Above: Pruning small twiggy growth back to a smaller lateral branch with bypass secateurs.

Above right: Removing a slightly larger lateral branch back to the parent branch with sharp bypass secateurs.

Right: The final pruning cut made on the parent branch showing a small wound.

Branch removal

WITH SECATEURS

Even with the smallest of branches (a shoot), target pruning should still be followed, ideally removing the shoot back to the parent branch or another shoot or bud. This allows the sap to be pulled back to the end of the shoot and for the wound to heal. If the branch isn't cut back to a growing point or bud, the sap flow will end, and the snag will start to decay; this decay can run back into the parent branch and eventually the trunk, weakening the tree.

When pruning an evergreen tree with secateurs, the pruning cut should be made back to a bud or leaves (node) to create a natural junction where the tree will respond with regrowth, covering up the pruning wound. Again, the smaller the cut the better the response from the tree and the more natural shape will be left.

Pruning an evergreen back to a node with secateurs.

Position of the final cut on a tree with little visible evidence of a branch bark ridge or branch collar.

Removing a lateral branch over 10mm (⅜in) diameter with a sharp pruning saw.

WITH A PRUNING SAW

Since pruning saws are very sharp, they leave as clean a wound as if secateurs had been used. With small, light branches, it may be possible to hold the branch with your free hand and take its weight to prevent it from ripping under its own weight as you are sawing. Such a rip can tear back along the branch into the attachment, which would scar the tree and aesthetically leave an untidy wound that may eventually rot without occluding.

With larger, heavier branches it is best practice to use the three-cut method to avoid the possibility of the branch breaking too early and tearing back to the attachment point. You will still need to prevent the branch from falling to the ground and damaging plants or objects in the garden and by using the three-cut method it can be held safely until it is ready to part company.

Wound dressings and tree paints

Wound dressings were once thought to accelerate wound closure, protect against insects and diseases, and reduce decay, but research has shown that dressings/paints do not reduce decay or speed up wound closure, and they rarely prevent insect or disease infestations. These old paints were usually waterproof black bitumen or latex-based. They often had the effect of concealing micro-organisms behind them, covering up decay in the micro-climate behind. If good target pruning is carried out, the tree can look after itself and heal the wound without any assistance.

Wound dressings are not recommended to be used today but if a dressing must be used for cosmetic purposes, use a thin coating of a material that is not toxic to the plant.

The wrong target for the final cut leaving a snag which will rot back to the parent branch.

The correct target for the final cut on the parent branch.

Small pruning wound left on the parent branch which will heal over quickly.

Three-cut method

CUT 1 The first cut is the undercut, which should be approximately 20–30cm (8–12in) from the attachment point. The depth of the undercut should be one-third to half of the diameter of the branch being removed, or until the blade starts to pinch in the cut.

CUT 2 The second cut is the top cut, which should be made at the branch end side of the undercut, to about one-third of the diameter of the branch. Never try and line up the cuts, as this is almost impossible to do, and it is not necessary.

Once the top cut is made to the correct depth, the branch will automatically snap cleanly off, leaving a step cut on the end.

CUT 3 The third and final cut is to remove the snag that is left, back to the trunk or parent branch. It is important not to leave this snag, as this is not aesthetically pleasing to the eye, will not grow any new branches and will potentially rot back to the trunk, causing further problems later.

Because the weight of the branch has now been removed, it will be easy to hold the snag with the free hand whilst sawing it off and there will be no risk of it tearing back to the trunk.

The final cut will be small, clean and perfectly round for quick occlusion.

The wrong position of the final cut.

A long snag is left from incorrect positioning of the final cut. This will potentially rot back into the main trunk.

Three-cut method: positioning the three cuts for removing a branch safely.

Formative pruning

Definition: *Formative pruning is a pruning operation carried out on young trees to train and encourage a tree that in maturity will be strong and free from any major physical defects and weaknesses.*

Pruning young trees in the early stages of their lives is one of the most important investments of time you can give to a young tree. It will determine the tree's form and will influence the way it grows when planted out in its final home in the landscape or garden. It will also have an influence on the longevity and potential safety of the tree by the use of corrective pruning techniques and the removal of potential weaknesses in later life. Formative pruning has no fixed time frame, but continues until it is firmly established and independent. It is far better to remove an incumbent branch with a sharp pair of secateurs in the first two to five years of the tree's life, leaving a tiny wound that will disappear quickly under callus, than to have to remove that same branch several years later with a pruning saw, leaving a slightly larger wound. However, the latter would certainly be better than having to remove the same branch some 25 to 30 years later with a chainsaw, leaving a much larger wound that may never disappear. Careful intervention with the pruning tools early in the tree's life can prevent the tree from developing a weakness that could have the potential to fail in windy conditions. In addition, a tree that has grown well but produced too much leaf may place an unnecessary burden on a weak branch or branch attachment. Do not be shy with the secateurs.

A tree bought from a reputable nursery will already have had some formative pruning done by a skilled pruner with knowledge of the species and its attributes, but this should continue even after planting. The first rule of formative pruning is to remove the 'four Ds', dead, damaged, diseased and dying branches, so that what remains all has the potential to grow into healthy branches. Next, prune back or remove any crossing branches that are rubbing on other branches or that are becoming tangled and interfering with the internal shape of the crown. For trees that have a distinctive terminal leader such as the larger shade trees – oak (*Quercus*), ash (*Fraxinus*), lime (*Tilia*), plane (*Platanus*), beech (*Fagus*), maples (*Acer*), for example – maintain a single leader. Where there are twin leaders, also known as co-dominant stems, one of them should be removed entirely or one of them suppressed, allowing the other to become dominant. If both stems or trunks are left to grow into maturity, there is

Co-dominant stems on a mature beech tree that could easily split out and ruin this wonderful tree, wasting many years of tree growth.

Before formative pruning.

After formative pruning.

the potential for a weak attachment point to form with included bark, particularly if the union is V-shaped, which could split out in strong winds or inclement weather. Stronger unions are like the wishbone of a chicken and are U-shaped and can be left intact on the tree.

Any branches that are influencing the overall shape and form of the tree should also be shortened or removed at this stage and, depending on the size of the tree, it may be necessary to do this in stages over a period of two or three years to reduce the possible stress on the tree. If a standard tree is required you will need to prune off branches on the trunk to the desired height of the first main branches, but again this may need to be done over a period of years, as the diameter of the trunk begins to thicken. For specimen trees grown for their attractive bark, such as birches (*Betula*), snake-bark maples (*Acer*) and cherries (*Prunus*), the sooner in the life of the tree the lateral branches are removed from the trunk the better. If a larger branch is removed at a later stage, the larger scar will spoil the bark effect.

One tip when formative pruning is to take your time, study the tree and visualise what it will look like after the pruning operation. Look again and again to be sure, before you prune. Once the branches are removed, they can't be put back on! 'Look twice, cut once'.

The attractive, shiny bark of the Tibetan cherry (*Prunus serrula*), with laterals removed early in the tree's life to avoid unsightly scarring to the trunk.

Pruning mature trees

The largest branch that should be pruned by an amateur gardener is about 10cm (4in) in diameter, which is what a pruning saw can comfortably cope with. More extensive pruning and that involving larger branches is a professional, highly skilled operation and only a skilled, qualified and fully insured arborist (tree surgeon) should be used to carry out this type of work. Often ladders and specialist rope access equipment are needed. Never use cold callers or people who knock on your door offering to prune your tree; they are not skilled arborists. They will only cut what they can reach and usually spoil the shape and form of the tree. You will end up with more problems later in the life of the tree, leading to an unsightly, mutilated tree.

Cleaning out and deadwood removal
Definition: *The removal of dead, damaged, diseased and dying branches throughout the entire crown of the tree for aesthetic and safety reasons.*

As trees age and mature, dead wood is naturally produced in a tree's crown and cannot be avoided. This dead wood can be a beneficial habitat for many species of fauna and flora and, in natural areas, should be left as long as there is no risk of it causing injury or damage when it falls from the tree. In more highly populated areas where they can pose a risk to people or property, dead branches can be removed entirely back to the trunk or parent branch, or shortened back to a length that will remain strongly attached to the trunk or branch by snapping them off at their weak point. Any structural weaknesses like split branches should be removed, as should bird's nests, squirrel dreys and climbing plants such as ivy, which is heavy and places considerable stress on branches and can even act as a sail during strong winds. Clearing out of dead wood is usually carried out at the same time as the following tree pruning operations.

Crown lifting
Definition: *Increasing the vertical height of the lower canopy by removing entire branches to the main trunk or a lateral to a main scaffold, whilst maintaining more than 85% of the live crown.*

Crown lifting (also known as skirt lifting in the US) is an operation carried out to achieve greater vertical clearance between ground level and the lower part of the canopy, also known as the skirt of the tree. This may be necessary for improved access for pedestrians or vehicles. This operation could also be done to increase the light levels under the canopy for planted areas such as herbaceous borders. It may be necessary to do this operation over a period of several years to avoid the number of fresh pruning wounds on the main trunk or scaffolds that could place considerable stress on the tree and leave the tree open to infection from invasive micro-organisms. To achieve the desired result, main branches can be removed back to the trunk. The same results can often be achieved by removing pendulous, secondary, lateral branches from the main scaffolds. It is recommended that no more than 15% of the live crown should be removed when raising the crown, with the remaining crown being at least two-thirds of the overall height of the tree.

Crown thinning
Definition: *The selective removal of live branches evenly throughout the entire crown, leaving a well-spaced and balanced branch structure to achieve an even density of leaf area.*

This operation is carried out on deciduous trees, and rarely evergreen broadleaved trees or conifers, as a means of reducing the sail effect on the canopy of a tree and the wind-load on individual structural branches. It allows light to penetrate through the crown to buildings or plantings under trees where there is heavy shading and a need for more light. It should be done evenly on the well-balanced main scaffolds from the trunk out to the tips of the branches, and not just on the inside of the tree, which is easily reached from the main trunk. When thinning is only done in the inner canopy, and the outer tips are left unthinned, this is known as 'lion-tailing', creating end weight and a potential weakness in the canopy. By pruning evenly, no large gaps should be left in the canopy that can open the tree to possible wind damage. Over-thinning or uneven thinning can cause weaknesses in the branches. No more than 30% of the leaf area should ever be removed by the arborist in a single pruning operation otherwise the tree's ability to photosynthesise will be greatly reduced, placing the tree under further stress and inducing epicormic growth. When specifying crown thinning, it should be prescribed in percentage terms, not exceeding 30%, and it may be a repeat operation when needed, especially with tree species that respond with vigorous epicormic growth.

Before crown lifting.

After crown lifting.

Before crown thinning.

After crown thinning.

Before crown reduction.

After crown reduction.

Crown reduction

Definition: *Crown reduction is the reduction in the overall height and width of the crown of the tree by shortening branches back to active growing points such as a strong lateral branch growing in the right direction.*

This pruning operation, also known as drop crotching, is often carried out on trees for the wrong reason, such as increasing light levels to properties or gardens because the tree has outgrown the space – it is possible that the wrong tree was planted. Often crown reduction is carried out when other forms of pruning operations such as crown lifting, or crown thinning, would deliver better, longer-lasting results. Crown reduction should be used where the tree's upper canopy has started to die back and become 'stag-headed'. The tree is failing in health, and dieback has generated dead branches that protrude through the living canopy, resembling the antlers of a stag, hence the term.

Some tree species do not respond to crown reduction and further dieback on these is inevitable. However, if crown reduction is carried out properly and branches are pruned back to strong branches, the overall effect can look more natural, particularly when in full leaf, and the tree can respond to the

cuts by drawing sap to the pruning wounds and occluding. Unfortunately, most reduction pruning is cut back to a stump, which causes further dieback and decay in the pruning wounds. There may only be a need to reduce an individual branch that has over-extended, increasing its end weight; reducing it will lower the risk of possible failure.

Where reduction work is carried out, a plant health care programme should be planned and implemented to overcome the reasons for the original dieback, which is usually a symptom of an underlying problem in the root zone, such as compaction, waterlogging, root disturbance or soil build-up.

Only a skilled, experienced arborist can carry out good crown reduction successfully.

Topping and lopping

Definition: *Topping and lopping is the indiscriminate cutting of major branches/scaffolds to stumps or lateral branches that are not large enough to take on the terminal role. This is not pruning and should be avoided!*

Topping and lopping (also known as heading, stubbing, tipping, hat-racking, dehorning, or rounding over) is crude, heavy-handed, inappropriate pruning, generally done by inexperienced 'tree cutters' to greatly reduce the overall size of a tree that has become too large for the garden, or trees that have become too tall and are posing a risk to the homeowner. However, topping and lopping is not a viable way of reducing the height or the future risk, and in fact has the opposite effect in the long term. Following topping, between 50% and 100% of the tree's leaf area may be removed, placing considerable stress on a long-established mature tree, forcing dormant buds to break and producing the rapid growth of multiple epicormic shoots or suckers on the main trunk and what's left of the scaffold ends. This is the tree's last gasp to survive as it needs new leaves as quickly as possible to produce food, otherwise it will starve and be seriously weakened or eventually die.

An unsightly topped tree with lots of epicormic growth. This is not crown reduction.

A stag-headed sweet chestnut (*Castanea sativa*) in a parkland landscape.

Topping a mature tree will have the following negative effects:

■ Leaves *large open pruning wounds* that cannot occlude, making the tree vulnerable to insect and disease infestation.
■ Leads to *serious decay* from the invasion of wood-rotting fungal organisms through pruning wounds that cannot compartmentalise, weakening the structure of the tree.
■ Causes *sunburn* to the tree due to the exposure of the remaining branches and trunk to high levels of sunlight and heat through the leafless canopy. This will cause bark splitting, cankers and the ultimate death of branches.
■ Disfigures trees, making them *ugly and unsightly,* due to the natural shape and form of the tree being mutilated, and then followed by cloud clusters of foliage on the ends of branch stubs in summer.
■ Incurs *expense*. A topped tree will need lots of corrective tree work later in life and, if it dies, it will need to be removed. An ugly, mutilated tree will have a negative effect on the value of a property, unlike a well-managed tree, which will add to the value of a property.
■ Poses an *unacceptable risk* because of the weaknesses caused to the structural integrity of the tree. Rapid regrowth is weakly attached by overlapping tissues, making it hazardous, and has the potential to fail at any time, which would lead to a finding of negligence in a court of law.

If a tree must be reduced in height or spread, crown reduction should be carried out, reducing large branches back to a strong lateral branch, or removing small branches entirely back to the

Old pollarded limes in a churchyard, pruned for their aesthetic benefits.

parent branch. If it is not possible to do a reduction without producing very large cuts, or preserving the natural form of the tree, then removing the tree may be a better option and replacing it with a more suitable species appropriate to the site.

Pollarding

Definition: *Cutting a tree to encourage the formation of numerous branches arising from the same height on a main stem or principal branches.*

Traditionally pollarding was carried out on trees to produce fodder for livestock and wood to fuel fires for heating and cooking. Today it is done more for aesthetic reasons and to maintain a small-sized tree. Pruning for pollarding is done regularly and started at a young age, preferably as soon as a young tree has become established and must not be confused with topping and lopping mature trees.

It can only be carried out on certain species, as not all trees respond well to this pruning style. Species that respond to pollarding include beech (*Fagus*), oak (*Quercus*), maple (*Acer*), hornbeam (*Carpinus*), lime (*Tilia*), plane (*Platanus*), horse chestnut (*Aesculus*) and willow (*Salix*). This style of pruning can also be done on trees grown for their coloured foliage such as *Catalpa bignonioides* 'Aurea' and *Toona sinensis* 'Flamingo' to encourage more leaf material. The pollard can be started lower down the trunk at around 1m (3ft) to obtain the new, coloured leafy growth at eye level.

Pruning for pollarding should be done in spring, just before the new growth begins. The first cuts of the process should start when the trunk of the young tree is 25–50mm (1–2in) diameter and at the desired height, which will vary depending on the location and access beneath the tree. Once the process has started, the pollard should be maintained by cutting new branches on a regular, cyclical basis, from annually to every two to five years. The frequency of cutting should be decided according to what the management objectives are, the species and condition of the tree. The branches that grow after the initial framework has been created should be cut back in following years with a sharp pruning saw or secateurs to the base of the branch, encouraging the formation of a well-defined 'knuckle' after a number of pruning cycles. This knuckle should be maintained with ongoing pruning and should never be removed, as the shock could lead to physiological dysfunction and decay. If for any reason it is necessary to remove the knuckle, a suitable lateral branch below the knuckle should be identified and cut back to. Rather than wait until the knuckle is too old to maintain a pollard, a shoot originating from the pollard can be left as an extension to the framework and a knuckle formed at the end after several pruning cycles.

A beautiful, well-managed pollard on a London plane in Switzerland. Note the extensions left at the pollards to start a new knuckle and framework.

Pleaching

Definition: *Pleaching is a style of growing trees in a line, usually straight, with the branches of the tree tied or woven together and clipped to form a formal hedge above the clean, bare trunk.*

This is a high-maintenance form of pruning, starting from training newly planted specimen trees, to maintaining an established pleached hedge. As with pollarding, the choice of tree species is very important and trees that will tolerate constant clipping will also lend themselves to pleaching. These include lime (*Tilia platyphyllos* 'Rubra' and *T. × europaea* 'Pallida'), hornbeam (*Carpinus betulus*), field maple (*Acer campestre*) and common beech (*Fagus sylvatica*). A good evergreen that pleaches well is the holm oak (*Quercus ilex*). A pleached hedge can be started from scratch easily, or it is possible to buy an instant, ready-made pleached specimen tree from some specialist nurseries, that can be suitably spaced and planted to join up into a raised hedge.

If starting from scratch, plant selected standard trees in an evenly spaced line and allow them to grow for a year to establish. During the second year after planting, tie the lateral branches onto canes or wire to make levelled tiers. Once the final desired height is reached, cut the leaders back to laterals that are trained horizontally parallel with the lower laterals and prune these annually to keep their box shape. Any branches protruding from the sides should be pruned back to one bud. With some species,

Above: A pleached hornbeam hedge (*Carpinus betulus*) being renovated back to the desired height and width after 20 years of pruning

Right: A homemade jig purposely made to maintain a level top through the length of the hedge.

Laburnum anagyroides pleached and woven to form a tunnel effect of yellow when in full flower.

An established sweet chestnut (*Castanea sativa*) coppice.

include the foxglove tree (*Paulownia tomentosa*), the Indian bean tree (*Catalpa bignonioides*) and tree of heaven (*Ailanthus altissima*).

Coppicing can also be used to renovate or rejuvenate old, overgrown shrubs or hedges. The regrowth from ground level can be thinned to create a new framework on a shrub or left in a hedge to encourage a denser hedge bottom.

The new growth from successful coppicing of *Cornus alba* 'Westonbirt' in the garden.

the branches can naturally graft themselves onto one another, forming a continuing branch network. With pleaching, the trees are prone to producing lots of epicormic growth on the main trunks, which should be removed during the pruning exercise, or rubbed off with the thumb during the year as it appears.

Over the years of pruning a pleached hedge will grow out of shape if it isn't pruned hard enough, and it will need to be renovated every few years to bring it back to a regular size and shape. To maintain a regular shape, a forma or template can be made and moved along the hedge as a guide for the pruner.

Coppicing
Definition: *Cutting trees close to ground level with the intention of encouraging regrowth of multiple shoots.*

Coppicing, also known as stooling, is a traditional pruning operation, usually carried out on a rotational cycle on certain subjects as a means of woodland management to produce materials for the production of woodland products such as hurdles, baskets and trugs. Trees that are generally coppiced in woodlands include hazel (*Corylus avellana*), willow (*Salix*) and sweet chestnut (*Castanea sativa*).

The multiple stems are cut back hard to a coppice stool near to ground level with a handsaw in late winter, and the latent vigour from the established stool generates multiple new shoots from the cut ends. These grow very quickly and straight. In the garden, we can stool ornamental plants like the dogwood (*Cornus alba* cultivars), willows (*Salix* cultivars) and *Acer pensylvanicum* 'Erythrocladum' annually to encourage vigorous new coloured stems. Other trees that can be pollarded to create large leaves

Pruning fruit trees

This is a huge subject and is a book on its own, so we will only cover the pruning of established standards or bush apple and pear trees.

DO:

▧ Take care if using ladders and invest in a tripod ladder for extra safety, which will also make harvesting fruit easier too.

▧ Use sharp pruning tools with holsters attached to the belt for easy, safe access whilst in the tree, including a long-arm or easy-reach pruner.

DO NOT:

▧ Remove too much in one go, as this will encourage more regrowth and generate lots of epicormics shoots, that will not have any flowering buds, defeating the objective. Aim for about 10 to 20% of the crown, evenly pruned around the crown.

WHY DO WE NEED TO PRUNE FRUIT TREES?

1 To establish a strong, open structure, making it easy to maintain and harvest the fruit in the future.

2 To remove the 4 'D's', dead, damaged, diseased and dying branches to keep the tree healthy and strong.

3 To create and develop an open centre in the tree to allow sunlight into the crown to ripen the fruit and reduce the potential for disease by allowing wind movement.

WHEN TO PRUNE?

For apples and pears, winter pruning when the tree is dormant is the best time of year, as there are no leaves on the tree and the overall shape and structure can be easily seen. However, this encourages vigorous regrowth, more new shoots but more flowering buds, which in turn will produce more fruit and require more pruning.

If the fruit tree is large and has reached the maximum size that you can cope with, then summer pruning is advisable. Summer pruning will also be good for dwarf trees or if you want to keep your tree small. If you are training restricted apple and pear forms like cordons, espaliers, fans, step-overs etc., then summer pruning is advisable as it doesn't trigger lots of new growth.

Pruning can be done to the two forms of overall tree shape, first a conical standard with a central leader or a bush with an open vase shape. This is created in the early years as a method of formative pruning from a grafted maiden.

Any tree shape such as a cordon, espalier, fan, pyramid or stepover can be formed by early formative pruning depending on preference and where it will be trained and grown. (See fruit tree forms below.)

It is important before attempting pruning that you understand and are able to identify the difference between a flower bud or growth bud. The latter is smaller and grows against the branch and produces new vegetative growth and no fruit, but a flower bud which is far larger and round with a downy surface growing on a short spur will produce flowers that in turn produce apples or pears.

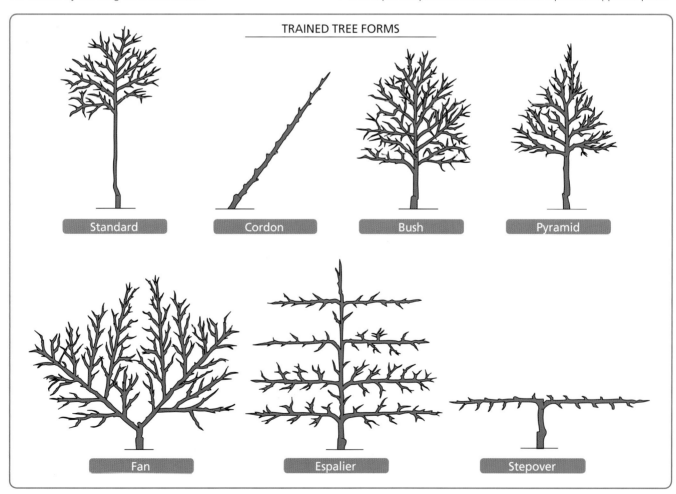

TRAINED TREE FORMS

Standard Cordon Bush Pyramid

Fan Espalier Stepover

A flowering spur on an apple tree. A growth bud on an apple tree.

Pruning above growth buds will help to control the vigour and growth of the tree and by pruning to an outward facing bud rather than an inward facing bud will help to keep a tree with an open centre with outward spreading branches.

There are two types of pruning cuts, *thinning cuts* and *heading cuts*.

Thinning cuts are where entire branches are removed to open up the centre of the tree and are the preferred type of pruning cuts for apple tree pruning. Heading cuts are where a branch is cut anywhere along the length of the branch back to an outward facing bud to encourage vigorous regrowth below the cut which can be used to shape a crown on young trees: a type of formative pruning should be used less on older trees as the crown will be developed.

As with all pruning operations the basic principles remain the same and any large branches should be removed using the 'three-cut method'. Suckers or epicormic shoots (water shoots) are weak and will never bear fruit, merely leafy material, so need to be removed as soon as possible and before the main pruning exercise begins so that the shape of the tree can be seen clearly. Any downward-growing and crossing branches need to be removed to create a tree with a well-spaced branching system, as should any vertical branches that compete with the leader or the open vase shape. Finally, thin out any branches that are blocking the open centre and prune back the upper branches so that they are shorter than the lower branches, but avoid it looking like a bad haircut.

Flowering buds on a spur may need to be thinned out as they can become overcrowded after several years of growth and pruning. Four or five flowering buds will provide good-sized fruit.

As with all tree pruning, there is no need to use tree paints if pruning is done at the right time of the year and pruning cuts are made back to the branch bark ridge or a strong bud.

Sucker removal

Many trees, especially elms (*Ulmus*), poplars (*Populus*), willows (*Salix*), cherries (*Prunus*), staghorn sumach (*Rhus typhina*), and false acacia (*Robinia pseudoacacia*), generate sucker growth from their root system, which can be a nuisance in the garden. Some trees naturally have very shallow root systems and suckers are produced from adventitious buds on these exposed roots, or they can be produced if the roots have been severed or damaged by digging and forking operations around the root plate or by grass mowers

catching exposed tree roots. Suckers can grow some distance from the trunk of the tree and, if these suckers are left, they will grow into mature trees.

Suckers need to be removed from the roots as close as possible to their point of origin, which can be found by scraping away the soil to expose the root. The suckers are best torn off rather than being cut, as this will sometimes deter further regrowth from the root. When planting trees that are prone to suckering, root control barriers can be inserted around the tree pit to discourage any sucker growth; prevention is better than cure. Where suckering cannot be controlled and is beyond being a nuisance, the tree may have to be removed and all the roots excavated, otherwise the tree will continue to sucker for many years after.

On grafted trees, the rootstock can produce suckers, which will grow from below the scion. These need removing as soon as they show. Ideally rub them off with your thumb whilst they are fleshy, before they get woody. Once these suckers lignify and become woody, they can be removed with a sharp pair of secateurs. Don't leave them so long that they need to be removed with a handsaw.

Epicormic growth

Epicormic growth is a shoot growing from a dormant epicormic bud that lies underneath the bark of a trunk, stem or branch on a woody plant, waiting to be triggered into growth. It can be triggered by pruning or by stress, and trees such as eucalyptus and the cork oak (*Quercus suber*) would naturally produce epicormic shoots following fire damage or something similar. In the garden, epicormic growth is usually activated following severe pruning operations, often producing a mass of shoots that need to be removed or thinned out once the tree has reached a balance in its general health. Once the shoots have been thinned or removed, the tree may continue to produce more shoots, and regular pruning may be needed to maintain a clean, shoot-free trunk.

Epicormic growth may be produced on the ends of branches that have been cut back to a blank end. The new shoots can be allowed to form a new framework of branches by thinning them out, leaving an acceptable number to create a new branch structure. This is called crown renovation or crown renewal. Such shoots are usually weakly attached to the trunk or scaffold and it will take several years of growth before they can be classed as part of a new, strong crown.

Sucker growth on the base of a European lime (*Tilia* × *europaea*) in need of removal.

Hedge cutting

Boundary hedges are usually the joint responsibility of both neighbours, and both parties must agree on any major works, including removal and renovation. Hedges can often lead to neighbourly disputes and disagreements. If the hedge is in your neighbour's garden, they own it and you only have the right to cut any part that encroaches over the boundary line into your garden. If your neighbour needs to access your garden to trim the hedge, then they need your permission. Aim to communicate about hedges with your neighbours to avoid disputes and manage the hedge in a way the works for you both.

Under the Anti-Social Behaviour Act 2003: Part 8 in 2005, 'high hedges' were covered in the legislation, which enables aggrieved neighbours to take steps to resolve situations arising around high hedges without having to involve lawyers and to involve the local council if further steps are needed. A 'high hedge' is clearly defined as: 'any hedge or line of two or more evergreen or semi-evergreen trees or shrubs growing over 2m (6½ft) tall that acts as a barrier to light, views or access that harms the reasonable enjoyment of your home'. For further information, read the guidance document 'Over the Garden Hedge' from the Ministry of Housing, Communities and Local Government.

Tools and equipment

When it comes to hedge cutting, it is important to choose and use a suitable working trestle or appropriate, sturdy step ladder that

Pruning cloud trees in Japan using tripod ladders.

will allow you to cut the hedge, especially the top, safely. One of the best step ladders for this job is the tripod ladder.

Tripod ladders are an essential piece of kit for reaching all parts of a hedge, topiary or cloud trees in order to carry out routine pruning or training operations. Whether on the flat or on a slope, you can either work face-on, with the third leg poked into the hedge, or sideways, with the ladder parallel to the hedge. The adaptable three legs give the ladder stability from the wide base and the double rungs give some comfort, allowing the gardener to access every part of the hedge safely. They are also ideal for fruit-tree pruning, where, thanks to the single back leg, you can get right into the crown of the tree. They're also very wide at the base, have a telescopic back leg, which is vital on sloping ground, and are exceptionally light and easy to use.

Hedge-cutters, also known as hedge-trimmers, come in a variety of types and power sources, which all have their advantages and disadvantages. There are three types used for cutting hedges:

- **Mains electricity motor:** These are useful for the smaller domestic garden as there is a need for a fixed power source. Usage is limited to the length of power cord or extension lead. Use an RCD safety trip as it is easy to cut through the power cord whilst cutting the hedge.
- **Cordless rechargeable battery powered motor:** These are becoming more popular with higher voltage and higher capacity lithium-ion replacing Ni-Cad batteries. It is useful to have a spare battery to ensure cutting can continue during the charging time.
- **Petrol:** These are usually powered with a two-stroke fuel mix and are heavy and noisy, but can be used anywhere without limitation. They are also more powerful and have the ability to cope with cutting thicker stems. Definitely better for the mixed native hedge.

Cutting a yew hedge with a hedge-cutter on an extendable handle.

When using any of these powered tools, wear suitable hand, ear and eye protection and ensure that the cutting blades are sharp and well lubricated.

Blade length, double-sided cutters and tooth-width gap should all be a consideration when choosing a hedge-cutter. The wider the tooth cut, the thicker the branches that can be cut. Some models have extra-long reach-adjustable cutting heads that will reach the tops of most hedges.

Hedge shears, also known as hand shears, are useful for smaller hedges or more delicate clipping on species like common box

A well-clipped yew hedge with a slight batter on the sides.

Trimming a topiary yew pyramid with hedge shears in the autumn.

Trimming a topiary yew pyramid with petrol hedge-cutters.

(*Buxus sempervirens*) and Japanese holly (*Ilex crenata*). Secateurs can be used in a hedge to cut back strong woody growths that are too large for hedge-cutters or hedge shears.

When to prune a hedge

Never prune hedges during the bird nesting season (March to August) as it is an offence under Section 1 of the Wildlife & Countryside Act 1981 to intentionally damage or destroy the nest of any wild bird while it is being built or in use.

DECIDUOUS HEDGES:
- Hornbeam (*Carpinus betulus*) and beech (*Fagus sylvatica*): prune once in mid to late summer.
- Hawthorn (*Crataegus monogyna*): prune twice in autumn and summer.

EVERGREEN HEDGES:
- Box (*Buxus sempervirens*), privet (*Ligustrum ovalifolium*) and Wilson's honeysuckle (*Lonicera nitida*): prune twice or three times during the growing season.
- Holly (*Ilex aquifolium*): prune once in late summer.
- Cherry laurel (*Prunus laurocerasus*): prune twice during the growing season.

CONIFER HEDGES:
- Lawson cypress (*Chamaecyparis lawsoniana*) and Leyland cypress (× *Cuprocyparis leylandii*): prune twice in spring and summer.
- Yew (*Taxus baccata*): prune twice in summer and autumn.
- Western red cedar (*Thuja plicata*): prune twice, once in spring and again in early autumn.

Cutting the hedge with mechanical hedge-cutters should be done from the bottom to the top in long sweeping movements, pushing the cut pieces away from the cutting blade as you go. It is important to retain a batter on the hedge to prevent the hedge from falling apart at a later date; a batter means that the hedge is slightly wider at the bottom than the top. A forma can be made to ensure consistency of shape along the length of the hedge. Cutting the top of the hedge should be done using a taut garden string line or surveying poles as a guide to maintain a level, flat top. Don't be afraid of using a spirit level to confirm that your lines are correct.

Topiary
Definition: *The artful form of pruning ornamental features into formal or stylised shapes in the garden.*

Topiary forms come in a variety of shapes and sizes, from simple balls to boxes and pyramids. Plants traditionally used for topiary are usually evergreen for year-round interest and include box (*Buxus sempervirens*), yew (*Taxus baccata*), holly (*Ilex aquifolium* and *Ilex crenata*), Delavay privet (*Ligustrum delavayanum*) and Wilson's honeysuckle (*Lonicera nitida*). Topiary will need to be trimmed annually in midsummer with hand hedge shears or mechanical hedge-cutters, and it may be necessary to trim established faster-growing topiary features twice or more in a year to keep them in shape.

Once a specimen has been neglected, evergreen trees such as holly, box and yew can respond to hard pruning in early or mid-spring, but will need to be followed up with feeding and watering during dry periods. After two or three years with some light trimming, the desired shape can be reformed and then clipped annually again.

'Niwaki': A beautifully well-balanced cloud-pruned tree.

Cloud pruning

Definition: *Cloud pruning is a Japanese art of training trees into organic shapes that resemble clouds.*

Cloud pruning is also known as 'Niwaki', which in Japanese translates as 'garden tree'. Cloud-pruned trees are beautiful art forms and full of character, with no two looking alike. Generally, evergreen species of trees are used for cloud pruning to give year-round interest. Box (*Buxus sempervirens*), yew (*Taxus baccata*), Japanese privet (*Ligustrum japonicum*), Japanese holly (*Ilex crenata*), green olive tree (*Phillyrea latifolia*) and pines (*Pinus thunbergii* and *P. parviflora*) make good, well-behaved specimens. Pre-trained cloud trees can be bought from specialist nurseries to save time and hard work, but take several years to grow to a sizable plant so will be expensive to buy. When starting one from scratch, patience is paramount, but it is worth having a go. To keep an established specimen in good shape, trim it annually with secateurs or hand shears in early to late summer. Keeping a cloud-pruned tree in shape is a high-maintenance job that needs to be done year after year, so bear this in mind before you take one on.

Other tree management techniques

Propping

Occasionally, due to strong winds, waterlogging or trees generally becoming top heavy, they can start to lean and will eventually collapse. However, it may be that the retention of such a tree is important for the garden, perhaps for the flower or fruit which it produces, the character that it possesses or its cultural history.

A good example of trees that tend to lean towards the end of their life are mulberries, particularly the black mulberry (*Morus nigra*) and magnolias (*Magnolia*).

Young trees may begin to lean from the effect of strong winds, creating rotational heave of the rootball in the soil. If there is no damage to the root crown, and if the tree is small enough, it can be pulled back to a relatively upright position and then propped to hold it in place until it develops new anchor roots.

Whether trees will ever be able to support themselves again without assistance is up for question, but if the tree is valuable enough in terms of rarity, floral or fruiting attributes, then a prop for life is a small price to pay and it can be made into a feature to look in keeping with the setting. With trees where there are large, over-extended scaffolds, which could be susceptible to failure, props can also be used to preserve them in a similar way to leaning trees.

Any type of material can be used as a prop, providing it is strong enough to support the weight of the tree. However, determining that weight is very difficult to do and must be guessed with best judgement. A natural wooden prop cut from a large shade tree with a strong, durable timber, such as an oak or sweet chestnut, works well.

Cut a fairly straight section of scaffold bearing a natural fork on the thinner diameter of the scaffold, preferably with a U-shaped fork rather than a V-shaped fork to rest the trunk of the leaning tree onto. The U shape is naturally stronger. The leaning tree can be jacked slightly higher using 'acrow' jacks and

A natural wooden prop on an old, but pretty leaning magnolia in spring.

A well-engineered tree prop supporting a large over-extended scaffold on an oak tree.

the prop pushed in place with the base dug into the ground, preferably resting on a paving slab or layer of bricks to prevent it sliding away under the weight of the tree and at the same time to slow down the potential rotting process to the base of the prop. Some form of rubber padding should be placed between the prop and the trunk to afford some protection to the bark of the leaning tree, which may rub against the prop on windy days.

With large, valuable trees, a more engineered approach can be taken by having a blacksmith or engineer make a purpose-made prop that can be adjusted as needed. This method can be quite expensive and will need technical resources to design, make and install. Cables can be used like guy ropes to prop the tree, but they often look unsightly, restrict access in the garden and need specialist equipment and expertise to install and adjust.

The props will need to be inspected regularly with the tree to ensure there is no deterioration, especially when natural wooden props are used.

Management of the root plate

Imagine a standard wine glass on a table; this is the perfect comparison for the general proportions of most trees. The 'bowl' that actually holds the wine is the canopy of the tree, the 'stem' is the trunk, which is firmly attached to the bowl at the top and the 'foot' at the base. The 'foot' that keeps the glass upright on the table is the root plate. It should be wide enough to support the glass when at least half full and is generally the same width as the bowl (or the drip-line in the case of a tree). These proportions are generally the same for trees, with the average depth of temperate tree roots being about 1m (3ft).

Much as we would like to believe that the root plate is a mirror image of the canopy, as we are sometimes told, it is in fact relatively shallow. This can be a problem for many trees in gardens or urban situations where vehicles, livestock and pedestrians regularly travel over this root plate, causing compaction to the soil around the roots. This compaction makes it difficult for tree roots to penetrate the soil and therefore grow. As the pore space reduces, so does the amount of water and oxygen available to the tree, and the aeration becomes critically poor (tree roots need oxygen just as the leaves and branches do).

Compaction also leads to the loss of organic matter and nutrients in the soil, which, in turn, reduces the amount of

mycorrhizal fungi and soil organisms. The tree will then become stressed and hungry. This can lead to a rapid decline in the tree's health with the symptoms not actually showing at the point of cause. Thinning of the crown, smaller than normal-sized leaves and dead wood of varying dimensions produced in the upper crown are typical symptoms. In a natural woodland, this occurrence wouldn't happen, with the woodland floor being rich in organic matter, regularly topped with fallen leaves, redundant fruit and twigs. Invertebrates, mammals and birds would help to work this material into the soil surface whilst searching for food, which the mycorrhizal fungi would break down, giving some to the tree in return for it being a host to the beneficial fungi.

Ideally, we need to prevent this compaction from happening in the first place, by eliminating the cause, such as by removing or reducing the amount of foot and tyre traffic over the tree's root plate. This can be done in a number of ways, including:

- Fencing the root plate around the drip-line of the tree to create a physical barrier to vehicles, pedestrians and livestock.
- Creating a planted shrub or herbaceous border around the tree.
- Removing a close-mown grass sward, which is seriously competitive with trees.
- Replicating a woodland floor by mulching over the root plate out to the drip-line to act as a deterrent to people walking on the root plate, whilst at the same time feeding the tree and keeping the soil structure open for air and moisture movement.

In the garden, we can mimic this natural woodland situation artificially by a process of de-compacting the soil in the root plate or root zone with specialist de-compaction equipment whilst at the same time incorporating organic matter and preventing

Natural root plate mulching. If we can keep these leaves where they fall rather than raking them up, they will help to prevent compaction, encourage worm activity and de-stress the tree.

re-compaction by mulching and/or fencing around the drip-line. We are often too tidy in the garden and like to rake up all the leaves for composting and to maintain an almost sterile, manicured landscape. If we can capture these leaves, keeping them on the root plate, natural de-compaction will take place without any intervention with air tools (see below).

De-compaction can be carried out on a small tree without any specialist equipment simply by pushing a garden fork into the compacted soil and rocking it backwards and forwards to open up the soil structure. On a large mature shade tree, this would be a daunting task so you are likely to need to hire an arborist with the right equipment.

Air cultivation tools and processes

An arborist will bring in air cultivation tools like the Air Spade, Air Lance, Soil Pick or Supersonic Air Knife and carry out a process called air cultivation. These tools are hand-held and produce a stream of air at high velocity through a 1.2m (4ft) long lance with a supersonic nozzle on the end. This operation penetrates and dislodges most soils, reducing the bulk density and strength of the soil, and encouraging root development without damaging any of the existing roots, buried pipes or cables. Three types of remediation work include vertical mulching, air cultivation and radial trenching/mulching. Another system of de-compaction can be achieved by using a machine called a Terravent, which injects compressed nitrogen into the soil, shattering any compaction. It can also be used to inject nutrients and soil conditioners.

VERTICAL MULCHING

This simple process involves pushing the air tool into the soil to a depth of about 30cm (12in) and pulling the tool out. The high-velocity air shatters any compacted soil, as the air must move through the soil and it cannot exit the same way that it went in. The lance is inserted at even intervals around the trunk of the tree out to the drip-line.

Vertical mulching with the Air Spade.

AIR CULTIVATION

This is the most common process, where the soil around the base of the tree at the trunk is broken up with the air tool, followed by large segments within the drip-line. Organic mulch and any nutritional

Air cultivation using the Air Spade.

supplements are spread over the surface and then mixed and integrated into the soil with the air tool. When completed, the surface of the root plate is top-dressed with another layer of mulch.

RADIAL TRENCHING/MULCHING

A series of trenches, 20cm (8in) wide and 30cm (12in) deep, are created, radiating from the trunk out to the drip-line like the spokes on a wheel. Once the soil is broken up, it is mixed with organic matter and put back in the same trenches. Once completed, the surface is mulched with about 5–10cm (2–4in) of organic mulch. The tree roots will then grow into this de-compacted trench, taking advantage of the open, fertile soil.

A tree de-compacted and mulched with composted wood chip out to the drip-line.

Removing a tree

There are many reasons for removing a tree in the garden, including poor tree selection – 'wrong tree in the wrong place' – or the tree has outgrown the situation, or the tree is dead, diseased, dying or dangerous. Trees may be legally protected, however, and unauthorised work on a tree, including felling, may be a criminal offence that can lead to prosecution (see Trees and the law, page 120). It is also the owner of the tree's responsibility to ensure that protected wildlife is not harmed, so before felling a tree, it is important to check one or two things:

- First and foremost, do you own the tree?
- If the tree has a trunk diameter greater than 7.5cm (3in) at 1.5m (5ft) high, check that it doesn't have a tree preservation order (TPO) on it.
- Are you in a Conservation Area? You can check this as well as the TPO with the local planning authorities.
- Do you need a felling licence? If the tree is in your garden then you don't need a felling licence (see the Forestry Commission website for details of felling licences).
- Do you have permission to take it out?

A good, professional arborist will always want to see evidence of written permission before carrying out any work on the tree and will help you to get the necessary permissions if needed. It is very rare for a tree to be felled as an entire tree in a garden, due to the possible restrictions of space, the proximity of the tree to buildings and garden features, and the overall size, shape and balance of the crown. Most trees in a garden need to be dismantled in stages safely with ropes, beginning with the upper crown, main scaffolds and then the trunk, which is called 'rigging down'. This is a highly skilled job that involves working at height with chainsaws and specialist rigging equipment, and it should only be carried out by a skilled arborist who has the training, experience, insurance and appropriate equipment (see the how to hire an arborist section, page 122).

Disposal of arisings

Arisings from a tree include leaves, twigs, branches and timber from the tree trunk, even the root plate, following a tree pruning operation or the removal of a tree, which you may need to dispose of. Do not burn any tree-related arisings, as it is illegal to burn garden waste at home or in your garden in a 'smoke control area'. Burning waste can be a nuisance to neighbours, particularly on windy days, and can also pollute the air by releasing harmful chemicals into it. It is not environmentally sound!

If an approved contractor is doing the tree work for you, ensure before agreeing the final price that the cost of the job includes taking away and disposing of all the arisings. If you intend to dispose of them yourself, the following methods can be used legally, which are environmentally sound as well:

- Where there are small pieces of twig or prunings from hedge cutting, it is viable to cut the pieces into smaller pieces with loppers or secateurs and compost them with other green garden waste in a suitable compost bin. The resulting compost can then be used as a soil improver or mulch around the garden.
- The woody arisings can be reduced greatly in volume if shredded or chipped using a suitable machine and then the shreddings or chips can be used as a mulch around young trees in the garden. Most domestic petrol shredders can deal with branches up to 55mm (2in) in diameter and can be hired from a local machinery hire shop. They are easily transported around the garden, have a variable waste chute, are auto-feed once the branch is loaded and will take leaves and branches at the same time. Most contractors use heavy-duty chippers that will take larger-diameter branches with ease. Remember to use the recommended personal protective clothing with ear and eye protection.
- Smaller branches can be left at their full length and made into dead hedges, which can be used to compartmentalise the garden. These are great wildlife habitats for insects, birds and the smaller mammals such as mice and voles. They are easy to create by banging two parallel lines of stakes into the ground at a spacing of 0.5m (20in), either in a straight or a curved line. The longer branches are then woven between the posts like a hurdle and the smaller offcuts, leaves and twigs are packed in between the woven sides. The internal parts of the dead hedge will compost down, and can be topped up annually or when prunings become available.

A fully packed dead hedge.

Above: An example of a large ecology pile, also known as a loggery.

Right: An example of standing deadwood; an important habitat for biodiversity.

Below: A domestic ecological log pile that can be made at home.

- The larger branches or logs can be cut into suitable manageable lengths and neatly stacked into **ecology piles** somewhere in the less formal parts of the garden. Over time the logs will decay and start to break down, providing homes for a variety of biodiversity, including fungi and insects.
- If the garden is large enough and the tree trunk is strong and sound, it can be left as **standing dead wood**, making the best habitat for many insects, including stag beetles, fungi, birds and mammals including bats. If left standing, these tree trunks should be inspected regularly for safety, as with any living tree.
- Many local authorities have a **green waste wheelie-bin scheme** and the smaller arisings can be cut up with a saw, loppers or secateurs and placed in these bins for weekly or fortnightly collection.
- Minimal amounts of woody waste can be cut up to manageable lengths and taken to a **local community recycling centre** in the car, where it will be taken to a green waste processing plant and converted into compost for the landscape or garden.
- If there is too much waste material to dispose of by yourself, a **Certified Waste Contractor** can be used who will dispose of the material through the correct channels. Always ask to see the waste carrier's licence and remember that you are responsible for that green waste until it arrives at the green waste processing plant.

Removing a tree stump

When a tree is felled, it is important to kill or remove the remaining stump, as it can produce suckers that will be a problem in the future or act as a host to numerous diseases that can infect and potentially kill other trees in the garden. These diseases include honey fungus (*Armillaria mellea*) on a range of tree species or the giant polypore (*Meripilus giganteus*), particularly on beech. There are various means of killing or removing a stump.

DIGGING OUT THE STUMP BY HAND OR MECHANICALLY

When felling the tree, the trunk attached to the root should be left intact to about 1.3m (4½ft) high rather than cutting it off at ground level. This trunk can later be used as a lever to help loosen and pull the stump over when all the roots have been severed. Dig a trench around the rootball either by hand or using a mini-excavator to expose the radial anchor roots, which can then be severed using an axe, mattock or an old pruning saw. Once all the roots are severed, the roots can be loosened by rocking the remaining trunk, either by hand or with a winch. If you don't own a winch, they can be hired, provided that you have the experience to use one safely. Once loosened, the stump with the attached trunk section can be rolled out of the hole and disposed of.

GRINDING OUT THE STUMP WITH A MECHANICAL STUMP GRINDER

Stump grinders come in a variety of sizes from large mechanical grinders to small pedestrian grinders that can access gardens through narrow entrances and tight gateways. These machines have a large exposed wheel containing fixed tungsten teeth driven by a motor that spins quickly. When placed in contact with the stump, they literally grind away the root plate, turning it into woodchip. These machines can be hired, but they are heavy and dangerous and should only be used by experienced and qualified arborists. It is worth grinding the root plate out to the depth of the roots, approximately 30cm (12in), rather than just taking the top

off the stump. If you leave the root plate in the ground will settle as the remaining roots rot down over time. Once the grinding is completed, the woodchip should be removed from the hole and composted or disposed of to prevent the soil from settling as it rots down, and to eradicate any potential disease that will be harboured in the woodchips. Remember to scan around the stump with a cable avoiding tool to check for any underground services before attempting any stump grinding.

KILLING THE STUMP WITH CHEMICALS AND STARTING A ROT TO BREAK DOWN THE STUMP

There are many proprietary stump and root killers available in the garden centres that contain the active ingredient glyphosate or triclopyr. When they are used, it is important to follow the maker's recommended instructions and wear the appropriate personal protective clothing. The best time to treat tree stumps is from late autumn into winter when the stump is drying out and no sap is running, as the sap will push the chemical away. Immediately after the tree is cut down to a stump when the exposed surface is fresh, the top can either be scored with a chainsaw in a criss-cross pattern, or several 12mm (½in) diameter holes can be drilled around the outer edge where the live tissue is, to a depth of approximately 60mm (2¼in). This drilling or scoring is done to hold the liquid chemical or granules and prevent it from running off the top of the stump into the surrounding soil. Once treated, the stump should be covered with a black plastic sheet that is dug into the soil around the base of the stump to avoid the chemical diluting in the rain and to keep pets away from any contact with the chemical.

A new product available for effective stump killing all year round is the Ecoplug, which uses glyphosate as the active ingredient. It is safely stored inside a sealed plug, which, when banged into a 12mm (½in) diameter hole in the stump, is released and translocated to the entire root system. The holes are drilled at 75mm (3in) intervals into the live tissue around the outer edge of the freshly cut stump.

A large tree stump being ground out with a mechanical stump grinder.

6 MAINTAINING TREE HEALTH

A healthy tree is much more likely to be able to resist attack from pest and disease. This is because it will be performing at its optimum level and will be producing surplus energy, which it can store in reserve. These reserves can then be used to heal the tree by growing over and around lost or damaged areas or by strengthening its tissues to resist attack.

As with humans, ill health in trees is often associated with some form of stress on the tree's system. Tree health can be very difficult to determine because, in the early stages, there are often no visible signs that a tree is actually under stress. By the time visible signs appear, such as dying branches or the presence of fungal fruiting bodies, a significant amount of damage could have already occurred.

Incidental and regular checks on your tree need not be exhaustive and may help you notice problems as they appear. An arboriculturist can then be consulted to provide a diagnosis and treatment if required.

Essentially, trees need access to light, a soil that is not compacted, key nutrients, water and finally the space to grow into (above and below ground). Anything that impedes these will of course put stress on the tree's system.

By understanding how trees grow and what they need to grow (see How trees work, page 17), the potential for stress in trees can be reliably deduced from observing the immediate environment, as this will certainly be impacting on the tree's health. Furthermore, stressed trees will often come into leaf a little later than those that are healthy, and the leaves will often be paler in comparison, so surrounding trees can also be a good guide.

In smaller, newly planted trees health issues are sometimes easier to identify and treat by the homeowner. New trees will have been stressed by the planting process and are unlikely to have reserves as they will be putting all their energy into establishing their growth. Therefore, health issues are likely to be more acute in younger, more vulnerable trees.

In larger, older and veteran trees health issues may well be more complex and professional opinion from a qualified arboriculturist may need to be sought to diagnose any signs of ill health and the implications for management of the tree. Holes and cavities in the tree may not necessarily be a sign of stress, but they are an indicator of previous damage that may need the attention of an arboriculturist.

Recognising signs of stress in trees

Having established that a tree is under stress the next question that should be asked is, why? Normally this will be due to either:

■ The tree's growing environment and other physical factors (called abiotic, or non-living, factors).
■ A living agent, such as bacteria, fungi or mammal (biotic factors).
■ Both of the above, as often stress from the tree's physical environment can lead to an increased susceptibility to attack by a secondary agent.

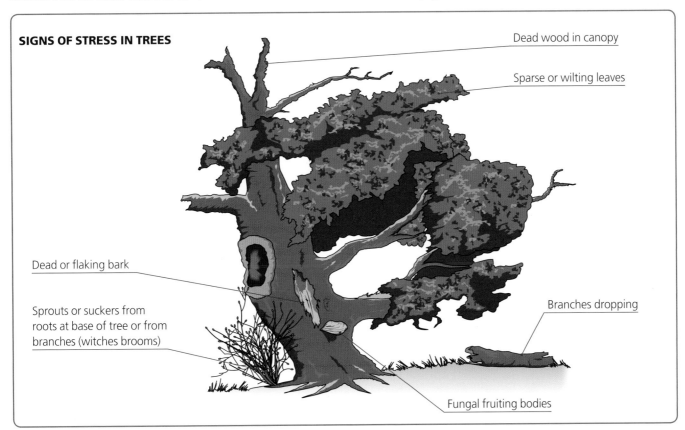

SIGNS OF STRESS IN TREES

Dead wood in canopy

Sparse or wilting leaves

Dead or flaking bark

Sprouts or suckers from roots at base of tree or from branches (witches brooms)

Branches dropping

Fungal fruiting bodies

Adventitious roots heaving paving slabs.

Diagnosing the reasons behind the stress or ill health in the tree may therefore be complex but, in the first instance, before inspecting the tree (or arranging for a professional to do so), a great deal of information can be ascertained from looking at the surroundings in which the tree is located.

Often the constraints on the tree posed by physical features will lead to a stress that can leave the tree more prone to a secondary

Mangroves are adapted for growing in tidal water. Many other trees are not!

attack by pests and disease. So even if a given pest or disease is identified and treated there may be a further underlying cause that is attributable to the site conditions. Recognising the physical features around the tree may help to answer this question and professional advice can then be sought to confirm the cause of stress and the best course of treatment to take. Some of the main causes of potential site-induced stress are explained below.

Lack of available soil rooting volume

Underground but often overlooked, arguably the biggest cause of ill health in trees is that posed by a lack of available soil for rooting. Without room for the roots to grow, the tree essentially becomes pot-bound and exhausts the nutrients in the rooting area available to it. The tree will try to respond by sending roots out over the exhausted area to find new areas to root into. Species such as cherry (*Prunus*), poplar and aspen (*Populus*) and London plane (*Platanus x hispanica*) will often do this. Lifted paving slabs and heaving tarmac around the base of the tree are tell-tale signs, but roots may also be visible along the ground too. The tree may show a small but very dense crown, which also contains a lot of branches that have died back.

Action: In most cases it is often more cost effective to remove and replace the tree with a smaller stature species that is more appropriate to the space, or to re-engineer the planting pit for a larger soil rooting area.

Waterlogged soil

Waterlogged soil will deprive tree roots of oxygen. Tree roots need to breathe (or respire) just like the above-ground parts of the tree. Newly planted trees that have been in the ground for less than five years are more prone to suffer in waterlogged areas as their root systems are less expansive than those of established trees. If an area becomes regularly waterlogged for extended periods (anything over five days), then severe damage or death can occur. Poorly designed tree pits can also become sumps for water, killing the very trees they were meant to home.

Action: If a newly planted tree is waterlogged it is important to dig drainage channels and get the water away from the root system. Mound planting is also an option for new trees: the tree is planted on an artificial mound to position it above the waterlogged soil. However, willow (*Salix*), elder (*Alnus*), poplar (*Populus*) and swamp cypress (*Taxodium*) species are very tolerant of waterlogging and, once established, can survive for several months in waterlogged soil.

Weed competition

Below ground, tree roots will compete for available nutrients and moisture. In newly planted trees, which are likely to be suffering a degree of stress from the planting process, competition for available nutrients can be intense. Although competition seldom causes tree death, the stress that results can leave the tree more

Mulching can work on big trees too such as this oak in Torbay.

prone to other pest and disease. In this instance there may not be any physical signs that the tree is under stress but slower growth is often observed in younger trees.

Ideally a tree, being a forest organism, should be growing in a medium (soil) that is similar to that in which it would be growing under natural conditions. All too often, however, trees are planted within areas of grass. Grass is very efficient at competing with trees for nutrients because grass has a bacterial association with the soil whereas trees are used to forest soils, which have a fungal association.

Using the bases of trees to heap up grass clippings will have the same result as weed competition. As the grass decomposes the chemical reaction will remove vital oxygen from the soil. The increased temperature can also get hot enough to damage fine tree roots near the surface too. Don't heap up grass cuttings around the bases of your trees!

Action: Mulching around the bases of affected trees helps to suppress weed growth. Using a bark-chip mulch will also replicate a forest soil and stimulate fungal associations in the soil that many trees are used to. This method can also be used on larger trees, with the mulch layer spread underneath the entire canopy of the tree.

Compaction

Soil compaction occurs through repeated weight bearing down on the soil such as from footfall, traffic, storage of materials and even flooding. The compaction reduces the volume of the soil and the spaces in between the soil particles (pores) can no longer store water or air. The tree roots can no longer access these for the production of energy and so stress results.

Action: The soil can be aerated over time through natural processes or this can be done mechanically using a fork. On larger areas an Air Spade may be a viable option (see page 100, or your arboriculturist will be able to advise you). Unfortunately the aeration boots that can be worn for lawns will probably not penetrate deep enough to help any but the smallest trees.

Light and temperature

Light is important as it is a fundamental part of photosynthesis, used to generate energy for the tree. Lack of light can therefore put stress onto the tree as it will be unable to produce enough energy to maintain itself. Some trees (normally those with darker leaves) are better able to cope with shade than others. Species such as holly (*Ilex*), laurel (*Laurus*), yew (*Taxus*) and beech (*Fagus*) are what are classed as shade-tolerant species, able to grow and survive in lower light conditions.

As a general rule, trees should not really be planted under the canopy of another tree. In the urban environment tall buildings can also cast shade over large areas for long periods of the day. Buildings can also reflect heat, which, up to a point, can be

beneficial, but can also lead to increased stress in the tree during the summer months when the increased heat is combined with lack of water.

Action: If the tree in question is shaded by other trees it may be possible to prune or remove these to give the desired tree better access to light. Shade from buildings may be more problematic and it may be more beneficial to remove and replace the tree with one more suited to low light conditions.

Using an Air Spade to de-compact the soil around a tree.

Other environmental factors to consider

■ Dust deposits from nearby traffic, construction or industry can build up on the leaves, reducing photosynthesis. It may also be directly damaging to the tree, acting in the same way as chemical damage. This is particularly problematic in drier conditions as there will be no rain to wash off the deposits.

■ De-icing salts and other harmful chemicals can be washed onto the soil or under the tree canopy from adjacent roads and walkways. These will interfere with the tree's uptake of water and nutrients, resulting in stunted or deformed growth and, in severe cases, the death of the tree. Interestingly, some trees produce their own harmful chemicals that are injurious to any other tree species that may take root in the vicinity. Walnut (*Juglans*) and laurel (*Laurus*) are two notable examples of this phenomenon called 'allelopathy'.

■ Drought means that the availability of water to the tree will be greatly reduced and in turn there will be a reduced uptake of minerals, and the process of photosynthesis will be hampered. The tree may shed leaves to conserve water and, in severe cases, the bark may also crack. Heat and drying winds can exacerbate the stress caused by drought. For newly planted trees in their establishment phase, watering is essential during drought periods provided there are no local regulations prohibiting the use of the domestic water supply.

■ Frosts and winter cold can freeze the living tissues of the tree and as the water within them expands it will rupture the cells. This will kill the cells. Damage can be severe in younger trees where frosts and cold lie low on the ground.

■ Snow and ice can freeze parts of the tree in the same way as frosts can but they can also build up a weight on the stems and branches of the tree, which can be enough to snap them. Coupled with the effects of wind in blizzards and ice storms, the effects can be catastrophic. In young

trees snow needs to be regularly cleared to avoid the deformation of the tree's desired form.

■ Lightning can completely shatter trees, whilst less powerful discharges can fissure the trunk of the tree. When lightning strikes, the electricity conducts through the water in parts of the tree, instantly turning the water into steam.

■ Physical damage to trees can take many forms. The presence of a nearby road, pavement or building could indicate that roots may have been severed in the past. If roots have been severed there will often be corresponding dieback within the branches in the crown. Very common is the damage that can be inflicted upon trees through mowing and strimming activities. Vandalism can also be problematic where trees border public spaces.

■ Street lighting can increase the length of the growing season for trees in close proximity to them and this growth, late in the year, can then become damaged by autumn frosts.

■ Winds can take moisture away from the leaves faster than it can be replaced by the tree and so can cause drought effects in the tree. In evergreen trees this can be problematic in the winter months too. Winds also cause direct damage to trees, breaking branches, stems or toppling the whole tree. Where trees are not toppled however, there can be a beneficial effect from the wind rocking the tree as it aerates the soil and stimulates the growth of reactive woody tissues, which will make the tree more wind-firm.

Some of these factors are likely to be present and to affect a tree. However, if none are obvious then the next step is to inspect the tree itself. A record sheet is included in Appendix II. This will be useful to note and observe change over time and to provide as evidence of inspection (covered in the Tree Inspection chapter).

Tree safety

Managing risk is seemingly an ever-increasing priority. Planning for and worrying about things that, one hopes, will never happen seems to take a large amount of time out of our busy lives. Of course, some of this is arguably both prudent and necessary. The likelihood that the average driver of a personal motor vehicle will be involved in a car accident at some point in their driving career is pretty high. Taking suitable precautions before embarking on a car journey is necessary: filling tyres to the correct pressure, replacing worn out bulbs, wearing a seat belt and so on. Taking out a car insurance policy is, therefore, not a waste of time.

Figures from the UK-based National Tree Safety Group (NTSG) from 2011 show that the likelihood that you will be attending the local hospital's emergency department as a result of being injured playing football (around 260,000 hospital attendances each year), a children's swing (around 11,000 hospital visits) or even

the average wheelie bin (over 2,000 hospital visits) is significantly higher than being injured in a tree-related incident. One has to be exceptionally unlucky to be injured badly enough to require hospital treatment following an incident involving a tree, with just over 50 hospital attendances each year. However, unfortunately around six people every year in the UK do lose their lives in tree-related incidents.

Generally speaking, people don't worry about the risks from trees, and justifiably so, given the statistics set out above. This can be seen in people's behaviour on any average, sunny summer's day in your local park. People gravitate to trees, taking advantage of the shade in the noonday sun to sit and have a picnic or take a nap. They don't tend to look up to assess a tree's condition before doing so, and the benefits of avoiding the sun, at least in the hottest part of the day, far outweigh the associated risks (sunburn, headaches and, at the extreme end, skin cancer) from sitting out in the open.

However, it is very likely that someone at some point in the recent past has assessed the tree that provides the shade for safety and made a record of their findings. The next section explains tree inspections in greater detail covering what they are, if one is needed at all and how to make an inspection.

Tree inspection

Regular tree inspections are important as they will allow you to observe changes in the tree's condition over time and can alert you to potential issues or pest and disease outbreaks in good time, allowing you to proactively manage the issue before it gets out of control.

You may need to identify the reason for a decline in the tree's health or to diagnose a problem or symptom with the tree, such as an area of dead bark, wilting leaves or premature defoliation for example. Trees should also be inspected as part of a tree owner's duty of care. This is generally only applicable to larger trees, and even then, trees are normally only inspected where the whole tree or part of it is publicly accessible, or where it could affect any third party (including people and property), such as a tree adjacent to a road, footpath or a neighbour's house. For this purpose it is important to keep some form of record that the trees have been inspected and a form for this is in Appendix II.

It is widely acknowledged that the risk of being killed or injured by a tree is very low. However, tree owners still have a duty to take fair and sensible care to avoid a 'reasonably foreseeable' risk of injury or damage. For the most part, the inspection of your trees should be something that is reasonable and proportionate to the risk posed. In the vast majority of cases – for trees in gardens – an inspection will simply not be required.

The National Tree Safety Group (NTSG) advises that inspections can be categorised into three broad areas:

- informal observations
- formal inspections
- detailed inspections

INFORMAL OBSERVATIONS

Informal observations of trees are essentially nothing more than the day-to-day observations of trees made during the course of your daily life and work. Whilst not going out of your way to make an assessment of the condition of the tree, you will nonetheless be aware of it and any changes that may occur over time. In some circumstances, informal observation may be considered reasonable and appropriate with regard to assessing the tree's health and any structural weaknesses that may pose an imminent threat to public safety.

This type of informal inspection may be undertaken by the homeowner or tree enthusiast, but they must have good local knowledge and be familiar with the nature, shape and characteristics of the tree. Whilst these people may not be tree specialists, they will be closely associated with a property, such as the owner, gardener, other employee or agent, so will understand the way the property is used (areas most and least frequented) and the extent of any danger posed by the tree, should it be found that it is clearly structurally unsound. These informal observations contribute significantly to public safety, being important for deciding when action is needed and when more formal assessment is appropriate. They are generally ongoing and undertaken as a given part of daily life on a site with trees and public access.

FORMAL INSPECTIONS

According to the NTSG, a formal inspection occurs when a specific visit to a tree is made with the sole purpose of performing an inspection that is not incidental to other activities.

Simple formal inspections take the form of ground-level, visual checks. These inspections should provide good value for money, with any clear and obvious signs of structural defects or tree health problems quickly identified by the experienced eye. Formal inspections should target any future action, including tree surgery works or a more detailed inspection.

Formal inspections may be carried out by the homeowner. However, the person undertaking the inspection must have at least some knowledge of 'normal' tree growth and form for the locality. If the tree inspection is for the purposes of determining the level of risk posed by the tree for health and safety purposes then it is recommended that this is carried out by a suitably insured and qualified arboriculturist. This is because in these situations the ability to recognise a broad suite of tree health and structural defects is required. The tree inspector must also have the ability to assess approximate tree height (being competent in the use of special measuring equipment) and falling distance from the tree to any area of use (or potential 'target'), as well as when to next inspect the tree or when to proceed to a detailed inspection, a process that also requires considerable tree knowledge.

Types of formal inspection include survey work to take a tree inventory for those who own a large number of trees, such as on an estate or large garden on the broadest scale, to carrying out risk assessments or tree health and condition assessments and detailing works programmes for a tree care professional to price against. 'Drive-by' inspections may also be acceptable in the first instance for larger landowners. Initial drive-by inspections can assist in targeting future action, such as where further tree management, walk-over or detailed inspection by a tree care professional might be necessary.

Carrying out a formal tree inspection

Once the need for a formal inspection has been identified it is important to carry it out in a structured way. One of the outcomes of evolution and tree design is that it is possible to apply a similar approach to the inspection of almost every tree species one comes across, regardless of where in the world it comes from.

Once a structural defect, stress symptom or physiological issue with a tree has been identified it is important to find out why this has occurred and, even more importantly, what action might be necessary. It may be possible to implement control measures or prescribe tree surgery works in order that the significance of a defect or health issue can be lessened. If the issue is serious and presents an unacceptable risk to persons or property, it may even be necessary to fell or remove the tree.

So, a formal tree inspection will help in identifying not only the symptoms of tree health issues or defects but also any underlying cause. A tree inspection is something of a puzzle and can be a very enjoyable and rewarding task. It is therefore important to take enough time over an inspection of the tree and its surroundings for a successful diagnosis to be made. However, it may be that the inspection is inconclusive and further investigation by a specialist is required in order to successfully diagnose the problem.

Equipment for a formal tree inspection

For a small or newly planted tree not all this equipment will be necessary, and neither will it be necessary in each and every case. However, it pays to be prepared if planning on undertaking tree inspections from time to time and to have what you need to hand. Clearing debris or cutting samples, which can then be studied at the desk by an arboricultural professional or which may need to be sent away for further analysis, provides a useful additional element to diagnosing tree health problems. Below is a comprehensive list of the tree inspection equipment it is useful to own:

- Hand lens – (8x or 10x magnification). Some fungi and pest insects are very small!
- Binoculars (8 × 40, 10 × 50 or similar all-round binoculars are fine). Useful for looking into the crowns of larger trees and picking up detail that can't be viewed with the naked eye.
- Pruning knife or secateurs – for taking small cuttings or paring away small areas of bark.
- Pruning saw – for removing climbing plants or other vegetation.
- Trowel – for removing soil and leaf litter around the base of the tree.
- Notebook and pencil.
- Camera (or smartphone) – for taking pictures of anything of interest.
- Plastic bags for samples that you may want to send away for identification.
- Tree inspection form (one is provided in Appendix III).

Starting the inspection

The inspection form included in Appendix III will help you to make a systematic appraisal of the tree from top to bottom and all around.

The best time to inspect trees (especially larger specimens) is with a good level of natural light and when they are in leaf. Allow time for the inspection and try not to rush the process as some of the signs or clues to tree health problems or structural defects can be difficult to spot. As always, if in doubt, contact an approved and qualified tree care professional or arboriculturist.

Whole tree

Tree defects or health problems are often divided into physiological and structural categories. Physiological problems affect the normal functioning of the tree system (i.e. its working network of vessels, fibres and so on) in some way. Of course, structural damage may also affect the way in which the tree functions, but the primary concern will be the integrity of the tree's structure.

Before getting involved in the minutiae, take time to consider the tree in its surroundings. Your experience and prior knowledge of the site should inform you of changes in the recent past; for example, the widening of a road or the felling of a large tree nearby. Such change may help you to determine the possible causes and significance of any tree defects you come across.

What to look for: As you approach the tree, start at the top of the tree and appraise the general condition of the crown and tree

Tree inspection equipment.

An arboriculturist carrying out a formal tree inspection.

Mower damage to tree roots.

Bark-included junction in liquidambar, ash and split in Lawson cypress.

A good branch union which is more stable and less likely to break than more acute branch junctions (below).

structure first. Pause to consider the overall condition of the tree crown and, if possible, compare it to nearby trees of the same species. Are its characteristics normal compared to how it has behaved in the past and when compared to similar trees nearby? Is there a significant amount of dead wood in the crown? Is the foliage thinning or going brown (taking account of the time of year, of course)? Does the tree (or any of its stems if it is a multi-stem specimen) lean significantly from the vertical and is this out of the ordinary? Are there any broken, hanging limbs?

As you get closer, look at the ground surrounding the tree. Are there any changes in soil level or waterlogged areas? Is one side of the root plate raised and the opposite side potentially sunk in the ground? Are there exposed roots that have been damaged by strimmers, brush cutters or mowers, or by the action of trampling livestock or people?

Foliage

Tree leaves will often be the first part of the tree where visible signs of stress can be observed. For those leaves higher in the canopy it will be useful to use binoculars, or it may be possible to inspect leaves that are growing closer to ground level.

What to look for: Check for wilting leaves (often a sign of drought stress), browning leaves out of season (which could be due to salt spray or wind scorch), or dark necrotic patches on the leaves. Also look at the underside of the leaves for woolly aphids and other pests. A list of the most common leaf problems is given in the Troubleshooting section.

Branches

Moving forwards then, as you get closer to the tree, consider the larger branches and branch junctions, where two similarly sized stems or branches are joined or where smaller branches attach to a larger branch or stem. You will probably have to move around the tree, altering your position frequently to gain a good view of all branch junctions. Have a look to see how the design of the junctions (or forks) differs around the tree.

What to look for: One of the most important aspects to look out for is a bark-included branch junction, as this is a common failure point in trees. This is an acutely angled fork where the bark of the

Poor pruning practice includes stogs, tears and flush cuts.

Young fruiting body of *Laetiporus sulphureus* (also known as chicken of the woods) on the stem of an old willow. *L. sulphureus* is very slow to degrade the heartwood of the host tree, eventually leading to snapping or wind throw of the affected part.

two branches is in contact. The most likely cause of its formation is as a result of a lack of movement at the point where the branches meet. The failure at such a junction is by no means guaranteed, however, and the individual circumstances of each will have to be considered in terms of its environment. More stable, stronger unions form with a cup- or U-shape at the base of the junction. These unions have been exposed to greater forces, enabling the tree to form a better, stronger design.

Also check to see if any previous pruning has been carried out on the tree. Unfortunate as it may be, it is often human intervention that introduces potential defects into the structure of the tree. Almost always, this will not be the intention of those undertaking the pruning works but all pruning involves making a wound and we are thus exposing the internal workings of the tree in an unnatural way. Therefore it is important to prune correctly as this gives the tree the best chance of healing over the wound (see page 86).

In your inspections, poor pruning practice can be identified by flush cuts (where the pruning cut is too close to the stem of the tree, see page 85), long tears down the trunk and stogs (where the pruning cut has been made too far away from the stem of the tree). These practices will often result in the tree not being able to properly repair the damage and grow over the old wound. This is a process known as occlusion.

Other things to look for include the presence of fungi. The presence of a fungal fruiting body on a large stem or branch is likely to be noteworthy and may alert you to the need to look into things further, especially if the affected part overhangs something of value! At this point you should engage the services of a tree care professional who will be able to advise you on the significance of the fungi and any remedial action required. More detail on some of the more commonly encountered fungi and their significance is given in Troubleshooting, see page 137. The significance of wood decay fungi can vary considerably depending on the host tree species.

Axial (along the grain) cracking often occurs in large, lateral limbs, in particular where there is an acute bend in the limb. Variously known as hazard beam splits and cracked or split elbows,

Daldinia concentrica (also known as King Alfred's cake) on a failed ash stem. *D. concentrica* is a useful indicator of decayed, potentially brittle branches, as it only colonises wood that is already dysfunctional and dried out.

Fruiting body of *Inonotus hispidus* on the stem of an apple tree. *I. hispidus* eventually destroys wood completely, causing distinctive, sunken cankers. Decay can eventually cause fracture of the affected part.

Crossing branches.

Trunk cracks.

Tree crack failure.

they are not definite signs of imminent failure. If such cracked limbs do fail, often they will remain at least partly attached. Quite often, these type of cracks will be repaired by the tree and, eventually, come to be as strong as before. If in doubt, consult a tree care professional.

Trunk

Once at the trunk of the tree walk around and inspect the entire trunk if possible. Often older trees are on boundaries and become surrounded by fences, junk heaps, grass clippings, etc. Trunks also may become completely obscured by ivy and this will need to be cleared from the trunk in order for it to be inspected.

What to look for:

Cracks (especially in the main stem extending deep into the tree) are one of the signs of imminent tree failure. Be careful though, as superficial cracks appear in the bark of a number of tree species and are of minimal significance. For example, young European ash trees (*Fraxinus excelsior*) often display significant axial expansion cracks in the bark as they grow. During prolonged drought, some species also display axial cracks in the bark of stem and branches. What you're looking for are cracks that extend into the wood beneath the bark. Cracking in what is often termed the shear plane at the base of the tree is very likely to bring about whole tree failure. Cracks have been described as 'fungal super highways' as they make it easier for the spread of decay fungi through wood. For all these reasons, it almost goes without saying that cracks should be of great interest to the tree inspector, no matter how experienced he or she may be.

Cankers (also known as bleeding cankers or stem bleeds) can sometimes be found around the stem or on the buttress roots of trees, but are equally common on stems and branches (they may also appear further above ground on smaller limbs). Stem bleeds may indicate the presence of a wood decay fungus (for example honey fungus), which destroys or alters the cambium layer beneath the bark.

Bleeding canker of horse chestnut.

Strimmer damage.

Certain fungi (e.g. *Nectria*) cause target cankers on stems and branches, which may be unsightly but are largely an aesthetic problem. Sometimes smaller twigs are killed off, but this is very unlikely on larger branches and stems.

Boring insects can also cause stem bleeding as they create galleries (feeding and breeding tunnels) beneath the bark and exit holes as they enter or emerge from the tree. These can be hard to spot in trees with bark that is deeply fissured. Examples include the great spruce bark beetle (*Dendroctonus micans*), which affects only spruce trees.

Damage to tree from stake left in place too long.

Ash canker.

Bacteria may also cause bleeding cankers. One of the most prevalent affects the horse chestnut (*Aesculus hippocastanum*). The disease, imaginatively called bleeding canker of horse chestnut, causes extensive bleeding cankers and patchy bark necroses (areas of dead bark). Canker of ash is caused by a closely related bacterium that results in odd-looking bark cankers that rarely bleed but that can be quite alarming if they are widespread. However, canker of ash is largely an aesthetic issue. There is much variation between species in terms of susceptibility to water shortage and drought damage, which can also cause patchy stem bleeds in broadleaf trees, sometimes quite extensively.

Wood-boring insects are becoming an increasing threat to tree health in towns and cities across the globe. It is not their activities that generally cause a significant problem to tree populations,

An alder (*Alnus glutinosa*), which suffered in the long hot summer of 2018, displaying stem bleeds late on in the season. Premature defoliation throughout the crown was also observed in association with this stress.

Asian long-horned beetle.

Underneath the leaf litter black bootlace strands of honey fungus mycelium move along this fallen trunk searching out more live wood.

but more that they may carry a disease. For example, the native large elm beetle (*Scolytus scolytus*) is the primary vector for Dutch elm disease, which has killed millions of trees worldwide. With the increase in global trade, it becomes more likely that pest species will be imported to a country or region in which they were previously absent. Such exotic pests can quickly cause serious damage, and history is littered with stories of the damage introduced species can do in a new ecological setting (such as with rats and ground-nesting birds or humans and the dodo). As the name suggests, wood-boring insects bore into trees. Wood-boring insects will leave entry and exit holes as, generally speaking, they enter the tree as grubs and exit as adults. In terms of insect identification, they can be very hard to spot, and such things are easily missed at certain times of year. It is probably more likely then, should a tree be affected by wood-boring insects, that you will come across the entry or exit holes, with the exit holes sometimes having characteristic frass (minute wood shavings).

Stem wounds, also around the base of the stem or on large, lower limbs – and perhaps caused by pruning, mechanical damage or livestock – create an opportunity for decay to take hold. Wounds that expose the functioning xylem vessels beneath the bark can act as entry points for the spores of fungi and allow the wood to dry out, creating a burden on the tree's energy reserves to defend itself.

Some idea of how wood properties vary between species is useful, as some trees are more resistant to decay than those without. Trees will also (to a greater or lesser extent) seek to repair the wound, adding new growth at the periphery. Younger, more vigorous trees will close (or occlude) the wound more quickly, much the same as for a properly executed pruning wound.

Large, old wounds may not occlude at all, and develop into an open cavity. Cavities where the top of the roots meet the stem base are of greater significance, potentially introducing decay and future instability at this point. So essentially then, the relative size and age of the wound and the wood properties of the tree influence the significance of a stem wound.

Loose bark will often indicate an area where the important cambium layer beneath has been compromised in some way. Dead bark may conceal decay. Where it occurs at the base of the tree you should continue to investigate the extent of the issue below ground too. If the dead bark can be prised away from the main trunk of the tree, fungal mycelium (in simple terms a sort of fungal equivalent of a root) may be present. Another possible cause can be from mechanical damage to the tree in the area above or below the dead bark. The extent of the area of dead bark in relation to the amount of sound wood and overall health of the tree will determine the significance and whether any remedial action is required. As a general rule of thumb it is useful to remember the rule of thirds (an accepted principle in nature), whereby in most instances if the area of infection (or damage, or missing material) is less than a third of remaining healthy material then it is not yet significant. Although it must be remembered that as trees are living, dynamic organisms this situation can change in time.

A hollow tree does not necessarily spell trouble. Some of the most ancient trees are hollow, and these trees can remain structurally

Hollow trees can still be structurally sound.

sound for many, many years. It all depends how much sound wood there is left in comparison to the hollow area and the weight that the hollow trunk has to support. Appraising how much sound wood is enough to support the upper parts of the tree crown in its current condition requires a good degree of expertise, and professional opinion should be sought.

Odd bulges in the trunk are another factor to look out for, and could indicate that the tree is trying to compensate for some form of internal defect or weakness (such as a crack or decay) by putting on excess growth around the area in order to strengthen its structure. A fairly uniform bulge around the base of the tree may indicate where a tree had originally been grafted and, if the graft was poor then the tree may be liable to snap at this point, especially if decay has set in. This is particularly common in beech (*Fagus*) and cherry (*Prunus*), but is not limited to these species.

Around the base of the tree and the roots

So, now you have arrived at the base of the tree. You can now take a look at the roots and root collar. As they are below ground, roots are difficult to investigate and are often ignored. However, with some examination and perhaps a small amount of digging, a good deal of information can be obtained from the upper part of the root system.

What to look for: Girdling roots often arise following poor nursery or planting practice where the young tree has been left too long in the pot before being transplanted. As a result, roots are likely to deflect around the inside of the container or pot (see Selecting and buying a tree, page 50). In older trees, girdling quite often occurs at the root collar, where a larger diameter root passes over and constricts a neighbouring root. This can often be seen with little to no excavation whatsoever. Girdling roots can

Above: Bulge in stem; poor grafting.

Below: Girdling root on an *Alstonia scholaris*.

Above: *Ganoderma applanatum* (also known as the artist's fungus) fruiting bodies at the base of a dead tree stump.

Above right: *Meripilus giganteus* (also known as the Giant Polypore) forms very large fruiting bodies consisting of multiple layers of fronds at the base of trees, often associated with common beech (*Fagus sylvatica*), as seen here. Advanced decay by this fungus is feared amongst arboricultural professionals as it can bring about whole tree failure.

Right: A fruiting body of the fungus *Inonotus dryadeus* is seen here at the base of a mature holm oak. This is a common wood decay fungus which persists for many years before becoming an issue. Most often associated with oaks.

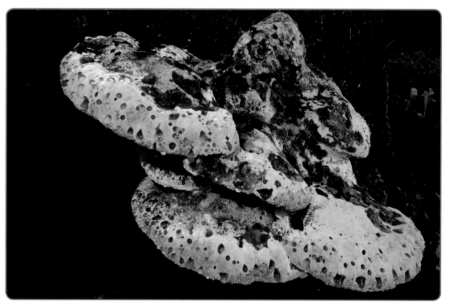

cause implications for tree stability in mature trees, potentially restricting the radial spread of roots and increasing the likelihood of failure.

Returning to fungi again, many species produce fruiting bodies around the base of the stem or at ground level. Some are perennial and the fruiting bodies will be present year round. Some are annual (possibly unreliably so) and the fruiting bodies may be present only for a brief period at around the same time each year.

Identifying fungi is something of a specialism and takes both knowledge and experience to achieve. Further to this, and as a note of caution, the ways in which decay fungi affect the structure of the tree, and how this differs between species of fungi is a large subject. Even the tree care professional may be lacking some knowledge on specific fungal–tree interactions and will often refer to other published texts to investigate further before making a diagnosis.

Some images of the most commonly encountered wood decay fungi are included on pages 137–143. For reliable identification, it may be necessary to employ a more experienced eye. Alternatively, it may be necessary to take samples and send them for laboratory identification.

DETAILED INSPECTIONS

Detailed inspection of a tree should be applied for individual, high-value trees giving high-priority concern in areas well used by the public. Therefore it will not normally be relevant for the vast majority of garden trees. A detailed inspection is normally prioritised according to the level of safety concern by a tree care professional. A detailed inspection will be led by the initial, visual inspection from ground level, undertaken by a competent practitioner who will appraise the tree for defect symptoms, some of which may be subtle.

In a small number of cases, further detailed investigations may be required, involving one or more of the following: soil and root condition assessments, aerial inspections of upper trunk and crown, or other procedures to evaluate the nature of suspected decay and defects, including using specialist diagnostic tools. In many cases, however, a risk management decision is obvious and straightforward. Detailed inspections are therefore unusual, typically reserved for trees that present a special value – for their heritage, amenity or habitat, for example.

A detailed inspection may only be carried out by an appropriately qualified, experienced and insured arboricultural specialist. When commissioning a detailed tree inspection, you should be satisfied as to the arboriculturist's qualifications, as well as the level of insurance cover they hold (both professional indemnity and public liability). A specialist involved in conducting a detailed tree inspection should be able to demonstrate a reasonable basis for allocating risks according to priority, and identify cost-effective ways of managing those tree-related risks.

Detailed arboricultural inspections are nearly always commissioned as a result of the findings of an informal observation or formal inspection. However, if the tree has previously been identified as having special value and is in an area of high public access, detailed inspections may be undertaken on a scheduled basis, especially if a structural defect has been identified that (whilst it may prevent an acceptable risk) requires more frequent monitoring.

As a tree owner, then, it is only the informal and formal inspections that you will be undertaking, leaving detailed inspections up to the arboricultural professional. For details of where to find such specialists see Hiring a tree care professional (page 122).

A detailed tree inspection may entail climbing the tree to access parts of the tree that cannot be seen in detail from the ground. This may be due to the presence of open cavities, old pruning wounds, fruiting bodies of decay fungi or possible cracks in the upper trunk or main scaffolds. There are many species of fungi that can cause internal decay (see section on wood decaying fungi on pages 137–143), which are often hidden behind sound timber on the outer rings of the trunk (the residual wall). The presence of these fungi is an indicator to the arboriculturist that the tree will be decaying internally and further means of inspection is necessary to assess the levels of decay and determine

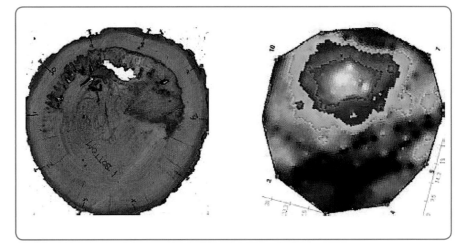

A PiCUS tomogram with the cross section of the tree showing how the decay is expressed in colour.

the risk that the tree poses. This can be done using specialist, non-invasive equipment.

The PiCUS sonic Tomograph

This works on the principle that sound waves passing through decaying wood move more slowly than sound waves passing through solid wood. Sound waves are sent from a number of points around the tree trunk to the same number of receiving points; the relative speed of the sound can be calculated and a two-dimensional image of the cross section of the tree (a tomogram) can be generated. The arboriculturist can then determine the levels of decay and the thickness of the residual wall from the tomogram and give a verdict and recommendation on what mitigation works will be needed

PiCUS sonic tomography being carried out on a plane tree.

to preserve or condemn the tree. These examinations are more often recorded on the main tree trunk at ground level than at height in the tree. However, the tomograph will need to be carried wherever the position of the decay is on the trunk.

The resistograph and Resi-F microdrill

This is an electronic high-resolution needle drill resistance measurement device used for inspecting trees to find internal defects, and to determine wood density and growth rates. A long, thin micro-needle is drilled into the wood of the tree trunk whilst measuring the electric power consumption of the drilling device. This is recorded and printed, providing a high linear correlation between the measured values and the density of the penetrated wood. The resistograph or Resi-F microdrill is often used to back up the results from the PiCUS and is much preferred by the arboriculturist as it is quicker and easier to use.

The fractometer

The fractometer is a hand-held device for measuring the physical properties of wood on site. It measures failure load and the compression strength of wood cores. Wood cores are extracted using an increment borer and placed through an aperture of the fractometer. With a corresponding fractometer table it is possible to quickly determine and compare the wood quality.

A print-out of the results from the use of the Resistograph microdrill.

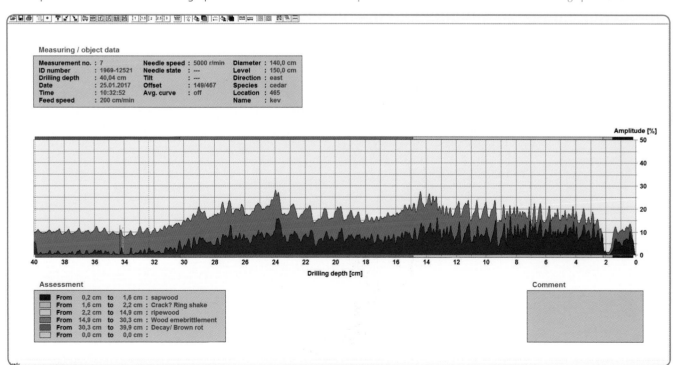

Trees and the law

A basic knowledge and understanding of the laws relating to trees can help to protect trees and guide your decisions. This section gives an overview on the subject covering the tree owner's duty of care and other legislation that has an impact on trees. In general, the principles set out in this section of the book are for the UK. Therefore, advice should be sought from a tree care professional for any other territories.

Tree ownership

There are generally no restrictions on what owners of a property may plant or allow to grow on their land. Tree owners do, however, have a duty of care to both people and property that could be affected by tree roots or branches.

Dangerous trees

The safety of trees is nearly always the responsibility of the owner of the land on which they grow; but there are some exceptions, such as when a rental agreement requires the tenants of a property to manage the trees. The tree owner or manager has a common law duty of care to: 'take reasonable care to avoid acts or omissions which they can reasonably foresee would be likely

A mature Eucalyptus gunnii fallen and damaged a building]

to injure their neighbour', and has a duty under the Occupiers' Liability Acts to take reasonable steps to ensure visitors or trespassers on their land are safe.

In practice, this means that if a tree fails and causes damage to a person or property then the tree owner may be liable. The chances of making a claim, however, would usually depend on whether the owner had been negligent; for example, if the tree was obviously unsafe through damage or disease, and the owner failed to act to prevent the incident occurring.

Therefore, if you own trees it is sensible to have them regularly inspected, and this is best done by a competent arboriculturist. In the UK a list of Registered Consultants is available from the Arboricultural Association. For the rest of the world the International Society of Arboriculture is a good place to start. Contact details are given in the reference section.

The best way to deal with a dangerous tree on neighbouring land is to write to the tree owner as soon as possible politely expressing any concerns you have and asking them to have the tree checked by an arboriculturist. If you still can't reach a satisfactory conclusion then it may be helpful to ask a third party who is known to both of you to mediate before relationships break down completely. As a last resort it may be possible to obtain a court injunction requiring the owner to deal with the tree or, in limited circumstances, the local council may be able to help using their discretionary powers under the Local Government Miscellaneous Provisions Act 1976.

Overhanging trees and encroaching roots

It is generally best to discuss your concerns with the tree owner beforehand, but under established common law, you should be able to prune branches and roots that grow over your boundary, with or without the owner's consent. You also have a legal duty, however, to take reasonable care whilst undertaking the works, and you may be liable if you damage your neighbour's tree, or cause it to become unstable. It is therefore unwise to undertake works without first consulting an arboriculturist. Any of the parts cut off from the tree remain the property of the tree owner, so they should be offered back.

If overhanging trees or encroaching roots have caused damage to your property then you should contact your building insurer for advice. Your insurer will usually contact the owner of the trees asking them to abate the nuisance and will arrange for any repairs to be undertaken. If damage has not yet occurred, but you believe there is a foreseeable risk that the trees will cause damage in the future, then you should discuss your concerns with the tree owner and write to them asking them to have the trees inspected by an arboriculturist. You should keep copies of any letters sent as they prove that you have highlighted your concerns should damage occur in the future.

Trees overhanging the highway

One of the requirements of the Highways Act 1980 (the Act) is that a public highway should be kept clear of obstructions. Trees are living and growing organisms that can extend, in time, over a highway and impede the movement of pedestrians and vehicular traffic. Specifically, section 154 of the Act gives the highway authority powers to require the removal or cutting back of trees, shrubs and hedges that obstruct or endanger highway users.

While no specific guidance is given in the Act, it is generally accepted that the minimum clearance should be 2.4m (8ft) over a footpath and 5.05m (16½ft) over a road (measured from the centre line). As a guide, these minimum clearances should be sufficient to allow a 2m (6½ft) person with an umbrella up to walk unimpeded along a footpath and a double-decker bus to travel along a road without hitting any overhanging branches.

Provided that only the minimum amount of pruning is being carried out to comply with the requirements of the Highway Act 1980, in other words the pruning is directly required to maintain adequate clearance over a footpath or road, then a formal application (for trees that are subject to a tree preservation order) or a Notice of Intent (for trees that are growing in a conservation area) is not required. This exemption applies irrespective of whether the highway authority has served notice on you to carry out the clearance work. The pruning should also be carried out to currently acceptable arboricultural standards.

Tree roots and foundations

The threat of root damage to building foundations is a very real concern for many people, but in fact much of this concern is unwarranted. Trees can only really cause subsidence where there are shrinkable clay soils. Increasingly, insurers are recommending that tree owners fell trees that may possibly be damaging a building even before any detailed investigations have been carried out.

It is reasonable for a tree owner to ask to see evidence showing that the tree is the cause of the damage. Such evidence should usually include any reports by structural engineers or arboriculturists. The tree owner or their insurance company may then decide to appoint experts to corroborate or challenge these findings. Unfortunately, even if the tree has stood for hundreds of years and a new nearby building suffers damage, the tree's owner could still be liable, despite the fact that with better foundations the damage would, in all likelihood, not occur.

Many trees grow in close proximity to buildings without causing damage. However, in cases where they are found to be causing subsidence, often the best course of action is to remove the tree or underpin the building.

High hedges

Part 8 of the Anti-social Behaviour Act 2003 created new procedures to enable local authorities in England and Wales to deal with complaints about high hedges. It is clearly better if disputes can be settled between the parties concerned but, where negotiation fails, a complaint can be made to the local authority who can assess the case, acting as an independent and impartial third party. If they think it is justified, the authority can order the owner to reduce the height of their hedge. But there is no general requirement that all hedges should be kept below a certain height. In particular it is not illegal to plant Leyland cypress (× *Cuprocyparis leylandii*), and it is not illegal to have a hedge more than 2m (6½ft) high.

The council will charge a fee for this service, and you have to pay a fee just to make a complaint. Sounds unfair? Maybe, but that's the way it works. Fees are set locally and vary from about £100 to more than £600. Some councils give discounts, some don't.

The High Hedges Act (Scotland) became law in 2013. In Northern Ireland the High Hedges Act (Northern Ireland) 2011 applies. Although the English law applies in Wales, the way it is interpreted may be different. Consult your local council to find out what the situation is in your area.

Tree protection

There are a number of ways that trees can be protected by law within the UK. These include Tree Preservation Orders (TPOs), Conservation Areas, the Felling Licence system, restrictive covenants, and planning conditions within the planning system. It is important to find out from your local council whether any legal restrictions apply before you undertake work on your trees as you may be liable to prosecution if permission is not first obtained.

TREE PRESERVATION ORDERS (TPOS)

TPOs are administered by your local council in its role as the Local Planning Authority (LPA) and are made to protect trees that provide a significant amenity benefit to the area. All species of tree can be protected (but not hedges, bushes or shrubs), and a TPO can protect anything from a single tree to all trees within a defined area or woodland – but no species is automatically protected by a TPO.

A TPO makes it a criminal offence to cut down, top, lop, uproot, wilfully damage or wilfully destroy a tree protected by that order, or to cause or permit such actions, without the authority's permission. Anyone found guilty of such an offence is liable to prosecution, and an unlimited fine can be imposed for destroying or removing a protected tree without consent from the LPA. To make an application to carry out works to a protected tree you will need to complete an application form and submit it to the LPA.

CONSERVATION AREAS

If a tree is within a Conservation Area you have to give six weeks' prior written notice to the LPA (by letter, email or on the LPA's form) of any proposed work, describing what you want to do. This gives the LPA an opportunity to consider protecting the tree with a TPO. Normal TPO procedures apply if the tree is already protected by a TPO. You do not need to give notice if the tree is less than 7.5cm (3in) in diameter (measured 1.5m (5ft) above the ground) or 10cm (4in) in diameter if the work involves thinning to help the growth of other trees.

FELLING LICENCES

Felling Licences are administered by the Forestry Commission. They are required if you intend to fell (though not prune) trees over and above 5m^3 (175ft^3) in volume (this equates to approximately 20 telegraph poles). There are, however, certain exemptions and you do not need a licence to fell trees if: they are located in gardens or orchards; they are dangerous; they are below 7cm (2¾in) diameter at 1.3m (4¼ft) from the ground; the trees need to be felled to allow for a permitted development or are for statutory works by public bodies; the felling is needed to prevent a danger. For trees outside gardens, however, you may need to apply to the Forestry Commission for a felling licence, whether or not the trees are covered by a TPO.

RESTRICTIVE COVENANTS

A restrictive covenant is a promise by one person to another (such as a buyer of land and a seller) not to do certain things with the land or property. It binds the land and not an individual owner. This means that the restrictive covenant continues over the land or property even when the current owner(s) sells it to another person. Covenants or other restrictions in the title of a property or conditions in a lease may require the consent of a third party prior to carrying out some sorts of tree work, including removing trees and hedges. This may be the case even if TPO, Conservation Area and felling licence regulations do not apply. In such cases it may be advisable to consult a solicitor.

Trees and the planning system

Under the UK planning system, LPAs have a statutory duty to consider the protection and planting of trees when granting planning permission for development. The effect of development on trees, whether protected (e.g. by a TPO or Conservation Area) or not, is a material consideration that is taken into account when considering planning applications.

The amount of information required to enable the LPA to properly consider the effects of development proposals on trees varies between stages of the planning process and in relation to what sort of development is proposed. Table B.1 of British Standard 5837:2012 Trees in relation to design, demolition and construction – Recommendations provides advice to both developers and LPAs on an appropriate amount of information that will need to be provided either at the planning application stage or via conditions (see next column).

PLANNING CONDITIONS

Planning conditions are used by LPAs as a means of securing the retention of trees, hedgerows and other soft landscaping on sites during development and for a period following completion of the development. If planning conditions are in place then anyone wishing to undertake work to trees shown as part of the planning condition must ensure they liaise with the LPA and obtain any necessary consent or variation.

WHAT DOES A TREE/ARBORICULTURAL OFFICER DO WITHIN THE PLANNING SYSTEM?

The Tree Officer is usually an employee of the local council. Their job, like any other council employee, is to serve the interests of the public. In the case of the Tree Officer within the Planning Department this is achieved by maximising the many and varied benefits that trees provide to the council's administrative area, through input into the development management system.

The benefits of trees are many and varied (see chapter 1), but importantly the retention and planting of trees on new developments significantly improves the quality of life of the people who subsequently occupy the development, work within it, or visit it. The Tree Officer will carefully consider development proposals in order to determine whether the retention or removal of trees is sustainable and in keeping with the relevant planning policies. If only small changes to planning proposals are required, it is sometimes possible at this point for developers to amend their plans in order to retain trees that would otherwise be removed.

After considering the proposals the Tree Officer will give their advice to the Planning Officer for consideration within the wider planning context. Part of this advice will often focus on whether a tree preservation order (TPO) should be made, or whether tree-related planning conditions should be imposed if the application is to be granted consent. The Tree Officer will often also be the officer who considers soft landscaping and tree planting schemes for new development.

Within the TPO system if an application is made to carry out works to trees protected by a TPO then it is normally the Tree Officer who makes the decision whether the works should be permitted or refused. If the tree is located within a Conservation Area then the Tree Officer will decide whether the works can go ahead, or whether a TPO should be made to protect the tree.

Hiring a tree care professional

Arborists and arboriculturists

Throughout this manual we have often suggested that the reader engage the services of an arborist or arboriculturist. What is an arborist? Essentially an arborist is more commonly known as a tree surgeon. What is an arboriculturist? An arboriculturist is a specialist in the science of trees.

People who are able to care for your trees are generally either consultants (arboriculturists) or tree surgeons (arborists). Consultants are able to advise on tree safety and risk issues, diagnose problems and ill health in trees, deal with trees in relation to construction and the law and to specify works. Tree surgeons are those who will be able to carry out those works, be that planting, pruning or more complex tree surgery operations, such as crown reductions, sectional felling or stump removal.

CHOOSING YOUR ARBORIST

Tree work (arboriculture) requires a high degree of technical competence, supported by training and experience. For these reasons tree work should only be undertaken by well-trained, competent arborists experienced at the type of work being undertaken.

Anyone can call themselves a tree surgeon (arborist), and place an advert in a phone directory or online. Obviously, an advert does not guarantee quality of work or that it will be carried out safely. It is therefore recommended that you use an approved contractor who is part of an industry scheme; for example, the Arboricultural Association's Approved Contractor scheme in the UK and the International Society of Arboriculture's Certified Arborist scheme for the rest of the world.

Competent arborists will have certificates that show that they have been trained and assessed. They will often have other academic qualifications in arboriculture and will use safety equipment to protect you, your property and themselves. Reputable tree care companies will be pleased to supply copies of their insurance, qualifications and professional memberships and will work to nationally recognised standards.

When engaging the services of an arborist or arboriculturist (the contractor) you should also consider the following points:

■ **Quotations:** Always ask for a written quotation. Reject the contractor if they are not able to supply one. A reputable arborist will always give a positive response. It is advisable to get more than one quote and to remember that cheapest isn't always best. Don't be guided by price alone and never pay in advance! Other questions to ask that should be stated on the quotation include: When will the work be started and completed? Who will be responsible for clean-up? What is the hourly rate for additional work? What will happen to the timber and brushwood? What will happen with any tree stumps? Is VAT included? Who will be responsible for obtaining permission if the trees are protected? What steps will be taken to protect you and your property (and will a risk assessment be undertaken)?

■ **Insurance:** If an arborist is uninsured, as homeowner you could be held responsible for damages and injuries that occur as a result of the tree work. Request certificates, and contact the insurance agency to verify details. Ask if the entire job will be performed by employees of the tree care company bidding for the job. If not, ask for insurance certificates from all independent contractors as well. Contractors should be insured for Employers' Liability and Public Liability with a recommended minimum of £5 million in the UK and in the US around $1 million per occurrence, $2 million aggregate for property damage insurance and workers' compensation insurance of $1 million.

■ **Standards:** Ask if the work is carried out to a standard. If yes, which one? The British Standard is BS3998: 2010 Tree Work – Recommendations. In the US it's the American National Standards Institute standard for tree pruning, which is called ANSI A300. In Australia look for AS 4373—2007 Pruning of amenity trees.

■ **Qualifications:** Ask what qualifications the staff hold (and ask to see copies).

■ **Trade accreditation:** Ask if the contractor is a member of a professional organisation. Membership won't guarantee work standards but does show a degree of commitment to stay current on techniques and information. The Arboricultural Association in the UK run an Approved Contractor scheme and it is recommended that you use a contractor which has passed the criteria for inclusion on this scheme. Similarly, in the US look for ISA Certification. Other UK organisations include the Consulting Arborist Society (CAS) and Institute of Chartered Foresters (ICF); and in the US the International Society of Arboriculture (ISA), Tree Care Industry Association (TCIA), and American Society of Consulting Arborists (ASCA).

■ **References:** Additionally you may want to ask if the contractor can provide you with the phone number of a referee who can either show you some of their work or who you can speak with about it.

■ **Necessary permits and licences:** Some governmental agencies require contractors to apply for permits, a licence, or both, before they are able to work. Be sure that contractors comply with any local, state, provincial, or national laws.

Finally, be very wary of door-to-door sales. These are especially common after storms. Know that good arborists perform only accepted practices. Any mention of either 'lopping' or 'topping' means steer well clear!

Competent arborists and arboriculturists

In the UK there are two recognised schemes certifying the competence of arborists through examination and regular reassessment or Continuing Professional Development (CPD). The ISA should be the first point of contact for the rest of the world.

The Arboricultural Association (AA) maintains an online directory of quality-assured tree surgery businesses and consultants. They are regularly assessed for their health and safety procedures, office and business practices, including customer care, as well as their quality of tree work. They will display either the AA Approved Contractor or Registered Consultant logo. Check the contractor's approval is current on the AA website www.trees.org.uk via the 'Find a Professional' link.

The International Society of Arboriculture (ISA) assesses the individual for their knowledge and ability. Certified arborists will display the ISA Certified Arborist logo. Check with the Society that the arborist's approval is current, through the ISA website www.isa-arbor.com.

Other arborists may be equally competent even if they do not subscribe to either of the above schemes, but you should take more care to follow up the advice contained above.

7 TROUBLESHOOTING

There are many pests, diseases, human activities and disorders that have the ability to affect the way in which trees function. The relative impact of these on the host tree varies significantly from being nothing more than an aesthetic issue to rapidly bringing about tree mortality under the right conditions. Many factors will influence the potency of the pest or disease in interrupting the tree's normal processes and functions, not least of which is the ability of the host tree to resist or limit the spread or effectiveness of the pest insect or bacterium. Many pests and diseases are limited to a specific tree genus or perhaps just one species. However, some pests and diseases may be generalists and are not limited to a single species or genus of tree.

Soil pH directly affects nutrient availability in soil. However, unless the pH is at the extreme ends of the scale for soils (less than 4 in acidic soils or more than 8 in alkaline soils), the effect on tree growth is minimal. Different nutrients will be more or less available to plants at different pH values. There are other possible causes of nutrient deficiencies in soils, of course, but as a general rule, a soil pH of around 6.5 is good for most nutrients to be available to plants.

In this section, we will look at the different structural parts of the tree, describing the signs and symptoms that may indicate the presence of a pest or disease that needs to be addressed. There are also some recommendations for dealing with the potential problem, which may be easily resolved or may require the advice of a specialist. Fungal fruiting bodies are dealt with in a separate section within this chapter. Determining the precise cause of a symptom, however, can be very difficult, and often involves the elimination of a number of possibilities prior to arriving at a conclusion (often with less than 100% conviction!).

Importantly, there is simply not enough space to list all the potential pests and diseases of trees, and the reader is directed to Guy Watson's excellent field guide to the most commonly encountered tree pests and diseases, which is available from the Arboricultural Association (see Resources, page 167).

As a general rule, maintaining healthy trees as a means of reducing the impact of or preventing a disease from taking hold is always a good policy. If in doubt consult a tree care professional.

Tree part: foliage

A tree's foliage can give away much about its condition and will often indicate the presence of a fungal blight or insect damage and also the nutritional status of the tree.

Symptom: Yellowing leaves

Inter-veinal or whole leaf chlorosis (yellowing of normally green foliage) in broadleaves; whole leaf/needle yellowing in conifers. Leaves possibly smaller than normal. Parts of the tree potentially dying back. Possible causes are soil pH too high (alkaline soils; high lime content) leading to iron, zinc or manganese deficiency; soil pH too low leading to nitrogen deficiency; generally poor, nutrient-deficient soil; chemical application to soil or drift in the air (may be accompanied by other leaf symptoms).

Action: Determining precise cause of leaf chlorosis is key and specialist input is possibly required. Soil testing to determine soil pH and nutrient status. Application of appropriate fertiliser to soil at the right time of year (not late in the growing season) may improve nutritional status but repeated application probably necessary to be effective. General soil improvement (aeration, mulching) may help.

Symptom: Leaf necrosis (death)

Marginal/scorched leaves; possibly whole leaf death in young leaves. Possible causes are nutrient deficiency: potassium (marginal scorch), magnesium (inter-veinal necrosis) in mature leaves; in young leaves: molybdenum, possibly zinc or boron; generally poor, nutrient deficient soil; chemical application to soil or drift in the air (may be accompanied by other leaf symptoms, e.g. stunted or curled leaves); de-icing salt damage (often patches of foliage lower down) or sea spray (patchy, windward foliage only affected). Susceptible species may be affected by the water mould *Phytophthora ramorum*, which causes progressive dieback of leaves, shoots and branches as well as extensive stem cankers.

Dieback of young leaves on ash.

Action: Determining precise cause of leaf necrosis is key, which may require further laboratory testing. Specialist input possibly required. Soil testing to determine soil pH and nutrient status if other causes ruled out. Application of appropriate fertiliser to soil at the right time of year (not late in the growing season) may improve nutritional status but repeated application probably necessary to be effective. General soil improvement (aeration, mulching) likely to be of help.

Symptom: Patchy dieback in lower crown

There may also be patchy dieback of foliage in discrete areas of the crown, normally in the lower layers (chemical spray); dieback throughout crown, possibly whole tree mortality (contaminated soil). Various chemicals can be accidentally blown or evaporate onto foliage. This is particularly

Bags of salt stored around the base of a young tree.

prevalent in urban or industrial areas or adjacent to roads. De-icing road salt, blown onto foliage by the wind or vehicles, is common and also leaches into soil around trees. A host of other chemicals may find their way onto trees and shrubs, causing dieback or deformation of the leaves. It may be very difficult to determine the precise cause.

Action: Where sea spray or de-icing salt damage is strongly anticipated, and you are choosing trees to plant, species tolerant of contaminated soil and/or salt spray can be specified. Otherwise, prompt removal or dilution of other chemicals is the best way to limit the effect. However, the presence of chemicals and contaminants might not be discovered for days or weeks after a spillage. General soil improvement (aeration, mulching) is likely to be of help. Specialist advice should be sought.

Symptom: Leaf rusts, scabs, spots and blotches

A whole host of insects, mites, fungi, viruses and bacteria cause various spots, blotches and other deformations of a leaf. At the least, they will reduce the photosynthetic area of the leaves and their ability to essentially feed the tree. Singling out the precise cause is not easy. Small, sometimes numerous spots appear on the surface of the leaf. They are not bounded by the leaf veins but do have an abrupt edge around them. The distinct, black tar spot on sycamore is bordered by a thin yellow line. Possible causes are bacteria or fungal infection, e.g. tar spot (*Rhytisma acerinum*) on sycamore leaf. (See photo below).

Action: Whether or not action is required will depend on the precise cause. Often, as with tar spot fungus, the issue is largely

Tar spot fungus on sycamore leaf.

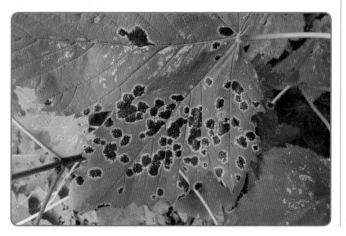

an aesthetic one. Gathering and burning the leaves in the autumn should reduce the likelihood of reinfection in subsequent years. However, this prevents the recycling of valuable nutrients. Widespread infection may require the advice of a specialist and perhaps application of a topical fungicide.

Symptom: Leaf mines

A number of insects spend part of their lifecycle feeding on and living in or on the leaf, often at the larval stage. Leaf miners create chambers or 'mines' in the leaf, often between the leaf veins. They cause damage to the structure of the leaf and in sufficient numbers significantly reduce the photosynthetic area. Horse chestnut leaf miner (the moth *Cameraria ohridella*) is very widespread and, whilst it is not fatal on its own, it may cause additional stress to the tree which, in concert with other pests or diseases, will potentially bring

Holly leaf miner.

about tree mortality. Holly leaf miner and beech leaf-mining weevil both cause minimal, aesthetic damage.

Action: Gathering and burning the leaves in the autumn could reduce the likelihood of reinfection in subsequent years as adults emerge from leaf litter in spring. However, this does potentially remove any natural controls and prevents the recycling of valuable nutrients.

Horse chestnut leaf miner.

Powdery mildew on oak.

Symptom: Powdery mildews

A number of genera of fungi cause powdery mildews on the leaf surface of mainly broadleaf tree species. Most common on oaks, apples and maples. Leaves become coated with a fine, powdery, often white mould. This is sometimes associated with stunted or mis-shaped leaves. Premature defoliation is common.

Action: Treatment in the early stages with a topical fungicide may help prevent spread although this isn't really warranted on amenity trees. Fruit trees may require treatment as production may be affected.

Symptom: Galls

Insects and mites are nearly always to blame for these little (or sometimes not so little) abnormalities, although certain fungi, viruses and bacteria also induce abnormal growth responses in a tree. Galls come in all shapes and sizes and are caused by the action of the insect or mite in inducing abnormal growth in the plant cells of the host. Examples include bud galls, which make the bud swell or prevent it from flushing properly; some nail and spangle galls cause odd-looking protuberances on the leaf surface; cynipid wasps cause a variety of galls, including the common spangle gall and cherry gall on oak leaves, the artichoke gall on the buds and the knopper gall, which causes a distinct acorn abnormality.

Action: No effective control measures are available. As the effect on the host trees is generally very minimal, any efforts to prevent or remove galls would almost certainly be a waste of time.

Symptom: Vascular wilts (fungi)

These are wilts that are caused by a disruption to the plant's ability to transport water. Most notable are the fungi that cause Dutch elm disease, verticillium wilt and silver leaf. Dutch elm disease is always fatal to the affected tree, although, as the name suggests, it affects only elms. Patches of leaves, whole twigs, branches and eventually the whole tree die off. Verticillium wilt is most notable on maples although lots of shrubs are also affected. It is not always fatal but does, at the least, cause patchy dieback of the affected branches. Silver leaf, as the name suggests, causes the leaves of the affected tree (notably cherries and apples) to take on a silvery appearance, die and fall off as the fungus progressively kills off twigs and branches.

Action: There is no effective, affordable treatment for Dutch elm disease. There are some disease-resistant elm trees now on the market, which could be planted instead of the most susceptible

Right: Knopper gall on oak.

Below: Artichoke gall on oak.

Cherry gall (*Cynips quercusfolii*) on the underside of an autumn oak tree leaf.

Common spangle gall on an oak leaf caused by asexual generation of gall wasp *Neuroterus quercusbaccarum*.

Dutch Elm disease.

elm species. Trees infected with verticillium wilt may recover, and heavy watering and the application of ammonium-based fertiliser may assist in this. Reliable diagnosis, however, is likely to require specialist input, as symptoms may be confused with other issues (for example, drought or de-icing salt damage). Silver leaf can be potentially avoided by pruning trees after flowering (in the summer); sometimes removing the affected parts helps in preventing the spread. Removing and burning cut material is also prudent.

Symptom: Bacteria causing dieback

Certain bacteria also cause the wilting and dieback of foliage, twigs and branches. Most notable of these is possibly fireblight. Other species are also affected by bacterial cankers which kill off twigs and branches. Fireblight causes a widespread tip dieback and sometimes progressive death of larger branches in certain species in the Rosaceae family (whitebeam and hawthorn especially). Shoots may have a distinctive 'hooked' appearance. However, trees often spontaneously recover. Flowering cherry trees are prone to a bacterial canker related to that which causes bleeding canker of horse chestnut. Small twigs and sometimes larger branches may be girdled and die off. Gummy, sticky liquid exudes from the bark in places. Very rarely, stressed trees may die. Bacterial canker of poplar causes the death of poplar twigs and branches and also large cankers on stems and branches.

Action: It may be possible to prune out fireblight, removing branches 15cm (6in) below the infected part with sterilised tools. Burn the infected material immediately. Prevention is the best control for bacterial canker of cherries and poplars, pruning only in summer (cherries), maintaining good tree health with watering and mulching of young trees and perhaps sourcing resistant cultivars or species when planting out. Differentiating between the causes of various diseases of the foliage can be very tricky, and it is easy to confuse the signs of fungi, bacteria and environmental factors. Often, an experienced arboricultural specialist will be required to determine the precise cause of an ailment affecting your tree(s).

Bacterial canker of cherry on *Prunus × yedoensis*.

Cherry blackfly on a cherry.

Symptom: Insects disfiguring foliage

Other than the leaf miners and gall insects, a variety of creatures are known to feed on or cause the dieback of leaves and shoots as part of their lifecycle. These are documented on both broadleaved and coniferous species, causing distortion and death of shoots (for example as caused by cherry blackfly on cherry trees or balsam woolly aphid on fir trees and the pine shoot moth on pine trees). The damage can vary in its severity and is often more serious in young trees, being more of an aesthetic issue in older specimens.

Action: Rarely necessary. Maintaining good soil conditions, especially in young trees with watering and mulching when necessary, will improve growth rates and improve resistance to pests and diseases.

Symptom: Insects eating foliage

A number of insects defoliate trees, particularly broadleaf, deciduous species. It is generally the larval stage (caterpillars, grubs) that feeds on the leaves, growing and maturing as it does so. Trees are partially or sometimes wholly defoliated in heavy infestations. Their presence will sometimes be conspicuous, with numerous caterpillars feeding throughout the tree. Certain species create nests on the stem or larger branches (for example the oak processionary moth caterpillar). Others spin leaves together with fine threads, causing the leaf to roll up (for example the green oak tortrix).

Action: It may be possible to pick and destroy leaves where there are small infestations of harmless defoliating caterpillars. Beyond this, it can become impracticable and dangerous to do so. Beware, however, as the oak processionary moth caterpillar (which affects predominantly oaks in the London area at the time of writing, although it is spreading) should not be approached. Oak processionary moth caterpillars produce thousands of tiny, irritant hairs which can cause skin rashes and potentially breathing and eye problems. This can be especially problematic for pets and children. A contractor with appropriate expertise will be required to remove them.

Oak processionary moth.

Tree part: branches

The branch network of a tree generally covers the largest area and includes numerous parts which have both structural and transport functions. A variety of structural and physiological issues can arise with the tree's branch network. Signs of pests and diseases may be subtle or glaringly obvious.

Symptom: Cankers

Cankers occur on stems and branches of a whole host of broadleaf and coniferous tree species. They are caused by fungi, bacteria, water moulds and sometimes even insects. Cankers appear either as bleeds, with gummy or resinous substances or sometimes watery and foul-smelling liquids emanating from them, or as bark disfigurations where the causal agent has created a distinctive eruption or depression or some other kind of abnormality. They occur on a variety of scales from a few drops of liquid to large areas of dead bark, oozing around the edge. Certain types of canker will kill off healthy bark to the extent that twigs or branches become girdled and die altogether.

Action: Identifying the cause may require specialist input. There are many canker-causing species: host interactions which are likely to require an experienced eye to help you come to a decision on what to do. It is unlikely that any form of pruning or application of off-the-shelf treatments will make much difference. In many cases, maintaining good tree health may help to halt the spread of disease.

Symptom: Bark inclusions

Recent research has shown that bark-included unions occur when there is a lack of movement at the point where branches meet (i.e. at their union). The result is an acutely angled fork where the bark of the two branches is in contact. Bark-included unions are usually weaker than normally formed cup- or U-shaped unions. Their failure is by no means guaranteed, however, and the individual circumstances of each will have to be considered in terms of its environment.

Action: Recent research recommends that 'natural braces' (i.e. crossing, rubbing branches) should probably be retained in older, semi-mature and mature trees, especially in trees which overhang valuable property or busy areas. Formative pruning to remove crossing branches should be encouraged in young and newly planted trees, in order that bark-included unions have time to eventually develop into normally formed unions.

Symptom: Splits and cracks

Axial cracking (i.e. along the grain) often occurs in large, lateral limbs, in particular where there is an acute bend in the limb and sometimes where a heavy, straight limb extends laterally and subsides. Variously known as hazard beam splits and cracked or split elbows, they are not definite signs of imminent failure. Cracking occurs along the grain of a limb, splitting the fibres, often along the central or neutral plane. Broken limbs often remain loosely attached.

Action: There is no real means of preventing cracks and splits from occurring in larger branches. It is one of the consequences of the trade-offs in tree design. Removing broken, hanging branches over high-value property or busy areas may be wise.

Bark inclusion on a young oak.

Split branch.

Rubbing branches.

Symptom: Crossing/rubbing branches

Crossing and rubbing branches have been discussed briefly under bark inclusions on the previous page. They occur in trees of all shapes and sizes in branches of any diameter. Branches have grown so as to be in contact at their union. Sometimes the zone of contact in larger limbs occupies a large area of bark and is relatively static. In smaller limbs, or where a small limb crosses a large one, there is considerable movement. Sometimes, eventually one of the limbs will be shaded out and die off.

Action: As already stated, removing one or both crossing limbs in larger trees may be unwise, potentially destabilising a union lower down the tree. Where a significant defect appears to be forming at the point at which the branches meet (for example kinking in a large, heavy limb), specialist arboricultural advice may be required on the best course of action. Formative pruning in young trees is the best way to remove crossing limbs, to prevent structural defects from forming. Refer to page 88 for information on how to undertake formative pruning.

Symptom: Old pruning wounds/ damage/cavities

Trees don't really 'need' to be pruned, they're quite happy doing what they do. Often, however, people need to prune trees, to alleviate a nuisance, improve a sight line or increase the amount of light in a garden. Trees may also be damaged by the action of a high-sided vehicle or farm machinery, by a lightning strike or a traffic accident perhaps. All pruning is wounding, and will leave its mark on the tree. No matter the cause, the bark is breached, and the underlying wood exposed not only to the air but the fungal spores that drift along on it. The tree is able to defend itself quite well (although there is considerable variation between species) from pruning and wounding but larger wounds will expose larger areas of sapwood and require greater resources from the tree to defend and repair itself. Often, wounds in the region of branch unions and root crowns (the most common sites for tree failure to occur) may have a greater effect on the stability of these zones, if decay establishes and eventually weakens the underlying wood.

Action: The days of painting wounds with all sorts of chemicals and treatments is long since gone, as these have little if any long-term effect on preventing the establishment of decay, or any other health benefits on the tree. Where there is a collection of large wounds in close proximity on a stem, a large, older wound at the union of larger branches or extensive wounding around the base of the tree, further investigation to map the extent of decay may be required. You may want to engage the advice of an arboriculturist, especially if the tree overhangs valuable property or a busy area.

Basal damage caused by vehicle impact.

Historic squirrel damage high in the crown of a beech tree, which has developed into extensive decay.

Above and below: A storm-damaged oak tree in a park where a large limb has failed.

Symptom: Grey squirrel damage

Young, aggressive male grey squirrels often strip the bark from thin-barked trees (especially beech and sycamore). Patches of bark are stripped off, sometimes quite large and girdling entire stems or branches, causing the death of the affected part(s). It is often quite easy to spot damage in young trees; not always so obvious in the crowns of large trees, high above the ground. Squirrels target primarily broadleaf species and are one of the primary causes of tree failure when trying to establish new native woodland in the UK. Squirrel damage may act as an entry point for secondary pathogens and cause structural weakness in a tree in the years following.

Action: Grey squirrels cause extensive damage and financial loss in UK parks and woodlands. It is widely accepted that it would be physically impossible to eradicate the grey squirrel from the UK although there are projects underway to remove them from some areas. Subject to current legislation and restrictions, it is currently legal to trap and humanely kill grey squirrels.

Symptom: Storm/snow damage

Wind, ice and snow are responsible for the failure of limbs of any diameter from the structure of every tree species one could possibly name. Trees suffer damage and fall over in storms without there being any prior defect or damage, although the presence of a significant defect at a branch union or at the root crown is likely to increase the chances of failure. Failed trees and limbs will be obvious. Parts may be left broken and hanging; failed trees will be lying on the ground or resting in the crowns of adjacent trees.

Action: Quite often it will not be possible to prevent storm or weather-related failures. The prevention of waterlogging (if possible) and the unnecessary exposure of trees (by removal of adjacent trees) may help to limit the number of storm-related failures. Ensuring that tree roots are protected should there be any development pressure (e.g. a new garage or pathway through the garden) will also assist in this.

Tree part: main stem and root crown

The main stem and root crown are the most accessible and easily investigated parts of the tree. A wide array of potential issues can be observed in this region, some of which will be obvious, others more subtle, which may require a bit of additional exploration where soil meets tree.

Symptom: Bark diseases/complexes

Sometimes, a combination of factors or pathogens come together to create a disease or symptoms of decline in a tree. Damage or drought (amongst other things) can often act as a facilitator to secondary 'invaders'. Beech bark disease is a well-known issue, with either drought or the felted beech scale insect as a facilitator to fungal decay. In the case of beech bark disease, felted beech scale leaves a distinctive white fluffy material on the bark of trees. Prolonged infestation can create entry points for decay fungi. Subsequently, fungal fruiting bodies (sometimes minuscule) appear on the bark, as well as bleeding stem lesions (cankers), indicating that the bark is being killed off. Acute oak decline (AOD) has appeared as a disease in parts of England and can lead to the death of the affected tree. Various new species of bacteria, associated with native bark beetles have been isolated from extensive bark lesions (cankers). Crown symptoms follow, with trees dying in as little as 18 months from the onset of symptoms. Stem bleeds (lesions) in themselves are not necessarily symptoms of AOD, however. In many species, drought, insect infestation or pruning, for example, can weaken the tree and allow secondary invaders to take advantage, further stressing the tree and increasing the likelihood of significant decline or possibly even tree mortality.

Acute oak decline on a mature oak.

Action: Younger beech trees appear to succumb more readily than older, more established specimens. It is possible to apply a mild detergent scrub to wash off felted beech scale where heavy infestations occur and help limit the number of entry points for secondary invaders. Again, maintaining good tree health is key to limiting the impact of pests and improving the repair and defence mechanisms a tree naturally has. There is no known treatment for acute oak decline at present and research is ongoing into the disease.

Symptom: Cracks

As stated elsewhere, cracks in the structure of the tree can be bad news on a number of levels. Any part of a tree can develop a crack, with the location of the crack being crucial to the outcome for the tree. Cracks through the base in the timber of the tree, cracks along the grain in a large diameter branch, cracks originating below the union of stems or branches, expansion cracks in the bark as the tree grows… the list goes on! Cracks in the base of the tree may be quite subtle, definitely more so in a thick, rough-barked tree but may be a sign of imminent tree failure. Expansion cracks in bark of young trees may be quite obvious and look a bit alarming, but are actually of no real consequence to the healthy tree.

Action: Having a good look and poke around when inspecting trees will help you to spot any potential issues. As pointed out elsewhere, cracks in the wood below a bark-included union (as shown in the photo below) and shear cracks in the base of trees are of particular concern as potential signs of imminent failure. If the crack is present in the structure of a large tree which is within falling distance of valuable property or an area of high access, prompt action is required to remove or reduce the affected part.

A bark-included union in an ash tree, at the base of which a crack has formed.

Symptom: Cankers

Cankers occur in trees for a variety of reasons and are quite common in the bark of trees of all species. Variously known as stem lesions, stem bleeds and target cankers among other names, the host tree species, the cause of the canker and therefore the significance will vary. Whatever the cause, cankers are generally indicative

Inonotus hispidus fruiting bodies on ash.

of localised bark death or dysfunction. Black or resinous, watery or gummy liquids seeping from the bark, either in single or multiple locations, sometimes coalescing in larger patches, can be caused by drought, fungi, bacteria or various species of the water mould *Phytophthora*; bark eruptions and abnormalities also occur, with or without liquids or gummy residues, and again are caused by fungi or bacteria; sunken bark strip cankers are sometimes caused by wood decay fungi, as a result of localised destruction of wood.

Action: The cause of the canker will require close consideration. In some cases, the terminal decline of the tree may shortly ensue after the cankers become apparent and there may be nothing that can be done about it. An example may be cankers caused by the action of honey fungus as it kills off the cambium. More than

likely it will be a case of monitoring the tree to assess its ongoing health. Trees do sometimes display spontaneous improvements when infected by certain bacteria with some years apparently worse for the infection than others (for example, horse chestnut bleeding canker).

Symptom:

Cankers brought on by drought on the stem of a common alder.

The stem of an oak damaged by a lightning strike many years previously.

Lightning damage

Lightning damage can, at the extreme end of the scale, cause significant damage to a tree, effectively blowing it apart. Normally, however, lightning causes the removal or destruction of a strip of wood, sometimes extending the whole length of a tree. A strip of bark may be removed from the tree, often extending for some length up the stem and into the crown, exposing the sapwood beneath.

Action: As with other types of wounding, in addition to the direct damage caused, which, if sufficiently extensive may cause structural instability, wounds caused by lightning create an entry point for secondary invaders, such as fungal spores and the introduction of air, which may allow the development of a pathogen which is latent within the tree. Ongoing monitoring will help in the process of assessing the development of decay or any secondary problems which might arise, including dead or dying branches, which may need to be removed.

Symptom: Fire damage

Sometimes trees are damaged by wild fires, building fires or even when set fire to on purpose. Patches of foliage, branches or stems are blackened, charred and withered (in the case of foliage). Sometimes whole trees or groups of trees may be killed. The ground around the tree may be scorched and there may be other signs (for example a burnt-out vehicle).

The base of a giant redwood in a forest with old fire damage which has recovered.

Action: Broadly speaking, the action required will be the same as for other types of damage. If the damage is extensive and it is not possible to retain the tree as some sort of habitat, it may be necessary to remove it where it poses an unacceptable future hazard. In regions where wild fires are more common, new plantings could comprise species that have some resistance (for example the exceptionally thick-barked giant redwood (*Sequoiadendron giganteum*)).

Symptom: Graft incompatibility

Failure sometimes occurs in grafted trees where the rootstock is not properly compatible with the scion (the rest of the tree,

Unusual graft union on a *Fraxinus angustifolia*.

which forms the stem and crown). It can be difficult to spot external signs of graft incompatibility in trees. It is easy enough to spot a grafted tree as there is normally a line just above ground level encompassing the whole stem, which indicates the graft point. Sometimes, there is different foliage to the rest of the crown on any suckers which have been produced from the base of the tree. Where the rootstock and the scion are not compatible, there may be uneven or distorted growth above and below the graft line, although this is by no means a sign of structural instability. If a crack is forming at the graft, then this could well be a sign of incipient failure.

Action: It can be difficult to assess graft unions for compatibility and, even to the experienced eye, the extent of any dysfunction at the union may not be clear. Quite often, grafted trees are small, ornamental varieties which may pose less of a hazard.

Symptom: Girdling roots

Whilst girdling roots have been mentioned elsewhere in this book, they are worthy of a mention here as they appear to be slowly becoming more of an influence on tree failure. A root is described as girdling where it passes over and constricts another major root, generally quite close to the base of the tree. Girdling roots can have implications for stability in mature trees, as they restrict the radial spread of roots.

Action: It is difficult to ascertain to what extent a girdling root may restrict the radial spread of roots and thus the implications for stability. In high-value target zones, some excavation may be required to assess what is going on below ground. Trees with girdling roots may require crown reduction or removal if signs of immediate instability are discovered.

Girdling roots.

Symptom: Tree guards and grilles left in place too long

Trees that have been planted to provide a landscape effect in the grounds of a large estate or as part of a town-centre beautification scheme are often installed with ornate metal guards around the stem and maybe also grilles around the base. As the tree grows incrementally, it steadily encroaches on the guard and grille. As there is no give in the guard or grille, the tree distorts and is often damaged. The extent of the damage depends on how long the tree has been growing in contact with the ironwork around it. Where trees have been left for a number of years, damage may be so extensive that structural stability is compromised. If the tree has been extensively girdled, especially at the base (root crown), this may introduce a potential hazard point/hinge point which may increase the likelihood of failure. Sometimes a tree will assimilate all or part of a guard into its structure, forming new bark around the metal.

Action: Where damage is extensive, it may be necessary to remove the tree as the only viable course of action. It may be that the act of trying to remove a guard or grille may also cause extensive

damage, although if the tree is not in a busy area, it can be allowed some time to see if it can repair itself and continue to thrive. The precise impact on structural stability may require specialist arboricultural input. Of course, prevention is the best course of action so a system of inspection and proactive measures to remove or adjust guards as trees grow is best.

Tree guard.

Around the tree

The root network of a tree will, where there is room, spread a considerable distance from the trunk, exploiting the soil environment of its location. A number of factors can have an impact on root distribution and condition and it is worth considering the impact of change when building or altering the ground around trees. Knowing the history of a site may also give you some clues as to why a tree is in poor health.

Symptom: Trenching/damage

As has been mentioned elsewhere, tree roots can easily be damaged by construction activity on any scale. Even repeated passage of foot traffic over areas can affect the soil structure enough to cause root mortality, or restrict or prevent root development. Direct damage including the severance of large-diameter roots can be caused by hand-held tools or larger machinery. Evidence of damaged roots may be very obvious or very subtle, including open or recently closed trenches in close proximity to trees, the installation of a new track or road or a pedestrian 'desire line' across the grass adjacent to a tree. These, and many others, are all likely signs of root damage, although the scale and significance may differ greatly.

Action: It takes quite a lot of root damage to affect tree stability in the immediate short term and it may require prompt specialist inspection to assess the risk posed by a tree if root severance or damage is extensive. Moderate to minor damage can perhaps best be countered by maintaining healthy trees with a watering and mulching regime. Soil compaction can be alleviated by the use of a garden fork to turn the soil over if necessary, although proprietary machines are in production which use compressed air to improve soil structure (see page 100) and sometimes also inject fertiliser by various means. Where you're not sure of the best course of action,

A deep trench cut in close proximity to the base of a mature English oak tree has severed a number of large-diameter roots.

it may be wise to consult with your arboricultural professional to design a programme for you.

Symptom: Waterlogging

Excess water may be just as much of an issue as a lack of the wet stuff. Whilst some trees may be able to more easily withstand waterlogged conditions, prolonged standing water in the rooting zone of trees, particularly whilst the tree is actively growing, is likely to adversely affect them. The presence of excess water is often obvious and doesn't require much investigation. During

A mature English oak in winter which has become accustomed to seasonal waterlogging.

the winter in many areas, this is entirely normal and may present no real issue. However, excess water at other times of year may present more of a problem, as plant tissues may be more likely to be asphyxiated during warmer temperatures as the absence of oxygen for the roots to respire may more quickly become an issue. Following root death, crown decline symptoms may ensue, although trees may recover over the course of a season. Secondary infections may take hold, taking advantage of temporarily weakened trees. Notable amongst these are the *Phytophthora* water moulds, which are often associated with damp conditions and quite often bring about the tree's demise.

Action: It may be possible to drain small areas which become unexpectedly waterlogged around trees, although one must take care not to damage roots! Improving the drainage of larger areas may be possible through measures such as de-compaction and aeration or more industrial means to 'rip' the soil where an impenetrable layer is present (for example a plough pan in a frequently cultivated field).

Symptom: Drought

Odd as it may seem to suggest it, the effects of drought on the tree are similar in many ways to those caused by prolonged waterlogging. Root death may not be as extensive in the drought-affected tree but a lack of available water in both instances can lead to the death of leaves, twigs and branches. Prolonged shortage of rainfall, in particular during the spring and summer months in temperate climates, can be an issue. Keep an eye out also for the amenity tree that does not possess good drought tolerance which has been planted out in a drier area than it is accustomed to in its native ranges. Wilting, yellowing/browning of foliage and progressive dieback, as well as stem bleeds associated with cracked, dying bark can be indicative of the drought-affected tree. Secondary invaders, in particular wood decay fungi such as honey fungus, can take advantage quite quickly of the weakened tree.

Action: Avoiding drought-related problems is probably best achieved by good planning. For smaller trees, watering effectively to establish them properly in their formative years as well as planting them in a site with good soil conditions will help to

provide some additional resilience to water shortages. It is as much about managing the site prior to planting as managing the individual tree. Choosing species that display good drought tolerance when specifying species for dry climates or challenging urban sites is also a good way of minimising losses.

Trees and buildings

Subsidence and heave

Trees can cause damage to structures in a variety of ways. Direct damage can occur when roots lift or distort light structures and block drains, when trees or branches fall on or strike buildings and when leaves block gutters, potentially causing water damage.

Properties can also be damaged by volumetric changes in the soil that surrounds them. The most susceptible properties are those with shallow foundations, as they are more likely to move as the soil around them changes according to the amount of moisture in it. Subsidence and heave are more problematic where 'shrinkable soils' are in evidence. Shrinkable soils are those that have a high, fine-grained clay content. Building damage caused by soil subsidence is caused when shrinkable soil becomes excessively dry, thus causing it to shrink. Soil heave occurs when the shrinkable soil re-wets, normally in the autumn and winter months, causing it to swell. Normal seasonal fluctuations and vegetation growth account for much of the volumetric change but this doesn't usually lead to subsidence damage. However, conditions can be accentuated by tree planting, severe pruning or removal, changes to local drainage (for example leaky pipes or new, paved surfaces) and longer-term changes to local hydrology. In dry periods, the presence of trees and vegetation in proximity to buildings on shrinkable soils can cause excessive soil subsidence and increase the likelihood of building damage occurring.

Assessing the precise causes and potential remedies for building damage is normally the subject of rare specialist knowledge. Where trees are suspected to be causing or contributing to subsidence-related damage, you will need to engage an experienced professional as soon as you can. One has to be careful, as trees are sometimes unfairly blamed when other causes are overlooked, and unnecessary pruning or felling may lead to building damage occurring as soil water content increases after the tree work has been completed. It might be necessary to undertake some tree pruning in an attempt to manage the water demand.

Protecting trees during construction

Are you planning to build or remodel your home or garage? Are you going to expand or pave your driveway? Are your city's streets, kerbs, pavements, and buried utilities about to be widened, modernised, or replaced? Before construction begins, consider the impact on your trees.

Careful tree protection will help you avoid the expense and heartache of later repairing or removing trees that were located too close to construction activities. Depending on the type of construction and proximity to trees, you may be able to protect the trees yourself, or it may be best to consult with an arborist to design, implement, and enforce a tree protection plan.

Start planning early. To minimise the costs and increase the likelihood of successful tree preservation, start tree protection planning as soon as possible. Protecting trees during construction is important because many of the activities of building construction can easily damage trees. Of primary concern is to make sure that the soil around the tree is not compacted through the building process. One of the main ways of achieving this is to use a root protection area or zone.

ROOT PROTECTION AREAS (UK)

In the UK, development in proximity to trees is normally guided by the British Standard BS5837: 2012 'Trees in relation to design, demolition and construction Recommendations'. BS5837 sets out methodologies for assessing trees on a site prior to development and categorising them according to their amenity value (arboricultural, landscape and cultural values). BS5837 goes on to set out tree-related constraints that should be identified prior to site design and the potential for future conflict (which can be avoided with good design). The document also details how to construct the reports and plans that should be used by other professions to inform how they go about building whatever it is that is planned. During construction, the use of barriers and ground protection should be in place in order that both above and below ground parts of the tree are looked after. The extent of the protected area is most significantly influenced by the stem diameter of the tree, as larger trees would normally have a larger root spread and larger canopy. Other measures, including preventing ground-level changes and the storage of materials within root protection areas, are also recommended.

Root protection areas (RPA) UK

- For single-stemmed trees, the stem diameter at 1.5m (5ft) above ground level is multiplied by 12.
- For multi-stemmed trees with two to five stems: first, square the stem diameter measurements (i.e. multiply them by themselves). Then, combine the products of your calculations from step 1. Then, find the square root of your result from step 2. This gives you the RPA for that tree.
- For multi-stemmed trees with six or more stems: find the average stem diameter, and square it. Then, find the square root of your answer from step 1. The result is your RPA for that tree.
- The product of your calculations above gives the radius of the circle which, when plotted with the stem at its centre, gives the notional RPA. If the roots have developed asymmetrically according to site constraints, then it is necessary to modify the area protected.

Root protection zones (US)

- Measure the diameter (width) of the trunk at chest height, to the nearest inch. To do this, either wrap a tape measure around the trunk and divide that number by three or hold a yardstick up to the trunk and approximate the distance.
- Multiply that number by 1.5 for mature or stressed trees or by 1.0 for young, healthy trees. Express the result in feet.
- Measure that distance from the trunk of the tree. The area within this radius is the Protected Root Zone (PRZ).
- PRZ radius (ft) = 1.0 or 1.5 × trunk diameter (in).

If you are planning on undertaking some development near trees or you have concerns about some building works going on near you, then ensuring that a suitably qualified and experienced arboricultural professional has been engaged to advise on tree retention and protection throughout the course of development is very important.

Common wood decay fungi

Armillaria species, Honey fungus

Host species: A number of different species of honey fungus occur. Honey fungus has a broad tree and shrub host range although a small number of tree species appear to be more resistant to honey fungus than others.

Identification: Often appearing as clumps of toadstools around the base of a tree or stump. Cap honey-brown, underside with gills; distinct ring on stem below cap; quickly rots away.

Significance: Honey fungus operates on a number of levels, and is capable of operating as a 'butt rot', degrading the wood of living trees and causing a brown, cubical rot or as a cambium killer, quite quickly stopping the tree from functioning normally. Once again, promoting good tree health may prevent honey fungus from taking hold. If planting on a former woodland site or very close to a woodland edge, consider planting resistant species. Honey fungus is apparently much less pathogenic in woodlands, probably due to the presence of numerous 'mutualistic' fungi interacting with the roots, which prevent honey fungus from taking hold in living trees.

The base of an English oak with a clump of honey fungus fruiting on a hedge bank; note the stem 'bleed', caused by the pathogenic action of honey fungus killing the cambium.

Fistulina hepatica fruiting body at the base of a tree.

Fistulina hepatica, Beefsteak fungus

Host species: Almost always on oak species. Infrequently on sweet chestnut. Rarely on ash, beech, elm, hornbeam, lime, London plane and walnut. In Australia *F. hepatica* sometimes occurs on eucalyptus species.

Identification: Annual, soft-fleshed fruiting bodies August to November, decaying quickly after maturity; sometimes with a short stalk; 5–30cm (2–12in) across; first red, later brown; fine yellow tubes create pores on the under-surface; almost always appearing at the base of trees.

Significance: A brown rot causing fungus, *F. hepatica* degrades the heartwood of the host tree only very slowly and causes a brownish discolouration (highly sought after among wood workers). After many years, decay may contribute to failure at the root crown of the host.

Fomes fomentarius, Tinder fungus

Host species: *F. fomentarius* occurs on a range of host trees, apparently influenced by the climatic zone it is found in. Most commonly on common beech throughout Europe (in the northern half of the UK often on birch trees). Also found on oak, lime, maples and poplars. Very rarely on other hosts.

Identification: The fruit bodies of *F. fomentarius* are persistent and slightly variable in shape, ranging from a hoof shape to a flatter, bracket shape; top ranges from grey to black with concentric zone lines; underside changes from white to rusty brown from spring onwards.

Significance: *F. fomentarius* degrades all of the main components of the wood of the host tree, operating preferentially in the main stem. Wood becomes susceptible to a brittle fracture, which will occur much sooner in trees with a smaller stem.

Ganoderma adspersum (also *G. australe/ applanatum*), Artist's fungus

Host species: *G. adspersum* and *G. applanatum* have a broad host range of broadleaved trees but are most often found on common beech. Very rarely they will occur on conifers.

Identification: The fruiting bodies of *G. adspersum* and *G. applanatum* are often confused and can be hard to differentiate due to their similarities. The perennial, matt, hard fruiting bodies, reddish-brown with concentric zone lines, are found most commonly at the stem base and can extend to 50cm (20in) across; both species produce a whitish underside (*G. applanatum* in particular); *G. applanatum* fruit bodies have often been described as being more plate-like, flatter and with an upper, crust-like surface which can be easily indented.

Significance: *Ganoderma* species generally prefer to munch on the lignin component of the host tree's wood at the base of the stem and in the root crown. In colder climates, the decay is limited and generally much slower to progress, with trees able to live with *Ganoderma* for many years as they produce compensatory growth to account for strength loss in affected timber. Extensive decay may bring about whole tree failure at the root crown.

Fomes fomentarius fruiting body at the base of a tree.

Fruiting bodies of *Ganoderma applanatum* on the base of a dead tree.

Fruiting bodies of *Ganoderma resinaceum* at the base of a mature oak tree.

Ganoderma resinaceum

Host species: *G. resinaceum* occurs almost exclusively on oaks.
Identification: *G. resinaceum* also produces a resinous top surface but this is softer and more easily depressed compared with *G. pfeifferi*. Like the other *Ganoderma* species described here, *G. resinaceum* produces a stark white pore surface in the spring, which soon changes to a lightish brown.
Significance: There is little known about the decay potential of *G. resinaceum* but the decay is documented for all *Ganoderma* species as essentially being a degrader of lignin. Extensive decay may bring about whole tree failure at the root crown.

Grifola frondosa, Hen of the woods

Host species: *G. frondosa* is only known on oak.
Identification: Nearly always occurring at the base of the tree, the fruiting bodies occur in clumps of beige-grey fan-like fronds up to 250cm (8ft) across. The underside of the fronds is white and the fruiting bodies soon degrade after appearing in the autumn. *G. frondosa* seems to associate with *F. hepatica* quite often on oak.
Significance: *G. frondosa* degrades wood at the stem base/root crown. Initially thought to only degrade lignin, it appears that *G. frondosa* also degrades both cellulose and lignin in certain elements of wood. *G. frondosa* is rarely implicated in cases of tree failure as decay progresses very slowly in the healthy tree, although the seat of decay is inaccessible and very difficult to accurately inspect.

Grifola frondosa fruiting body at the base of a mature oak tree.

Fruiting body of *Heterobasidion annosum*.

Heterobasidion annosum, Fomes

Host species: *H. annosum* has a broad host range but is probably most often associated with conifers in commercial plantations, particularly pines and spruces.
Identification: Perennial fruiting bodies are produced at the base of the host tree. They are tough and consist of a reddish to dark brown, lumpy top surface and a stark, white underside (pore surface).
Significance: *H. annosum* is thought to spread by root contact in plantations, the freshly cut stumps of felled trees providing the entry site for the fungal spores. Decay progresses again in the stem base and root crown, with *H. annosum* preferentially degrading the lignin in wood, moving onto the cellulose much later, thus destroying wood entirely. *H. annosum* is more problematic in plantation settings and its decay pattern varies according to the host tree, with pines much less susceptible to stem decay.

Inonotus dryadeus, Oak bracket

Host species: *I. dryadeus* is again almost confined to oaks. Very rarely on horse chestnut, sweet chestnut, beech, London plane and elm. Oaks native to the UK are common hosts.
Identification: *I. dryadeus* forms an annual fruiting body, which takes the form of an irregular bracket at the base of the host tree, up to around 30cm (12in) across and often in tiers. Fruiting bodies are thick and lumpy and, when young, produce drops of liquid at

Distinctive *Inonotus dryadeus* fruiting bodies at the base of a mature holm oak.

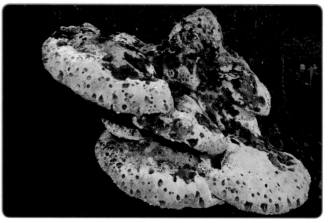

the margin. Fresh fruiting bodies are yellowish, progressing to a brittle, brown state as they age and decay.

Significance: *I. dryadeus* is very slow to degrade the wood of the host tree. Again, it prefers the lignin at the early stages of decay, operating in the roots and stem base. Eventually, all wood is destroyed but this takes a long time. This fungus has been nicknamed the Eiffel Tower fungus as at very advanced stages of decay, standing host trees have sometimes been left with functional columns of wood as if on stilts.

Inonotus hispidus, Shaggy bracket

Host species: *I. hispidus* has a relatively broad host range, preferring oaks native to North America when found there and when in Europe tending to occur mainly on common ash (*F. excelsior*), London plane, apple trees and walnut, rarely on other broadleaved tree species as well.

Inonotus hispidus on the stem of a common ash.

Identification: *I. hispidus* also forms an annual, bracket-like fruiting body, which can normally be found at height on both stems and larger diameter branches of the host tree. Fruiting bodies are red-yellow and felt-like when fresh with a white underside, often with droplets of liquid, degrading to a dark brown and eventually black, brittle state which persists.

Significance: *I. hispidus*, as with most decay fungi, varies in terms of its significance dependent on the species and how healthy the host tree is. Often, *I. hispidus* degrades both lignin and cellulose at a similar rate, thus locally destroying entire volumes of wood. This leads to sunken cankers on stems and branches and potentially brittle fracture of the affected part. *I. hispidus* is usually more significant on common ash and walnut than on London plane, which has generally greater resistance to decay.

Kretzschmaria deusta, Brittle cinder

Host species: *K. deusta* is found on a broad range of broadleaved host trees. Preferring common beech, lime, horse chestnut and maples, it may also be found less frequently on many other species.

Identification: *K. deusta* produces persistent, perennial, small, lumpy, black, crust-like fruiting bodies, which can easily be overlooked. Whilst normally found on roots or stem base, fruiting bodies may also be found encompassing large areas of stem at later stages of decay. Initially grey with a pale margin when

The asexual stage alongside the mature fruiting body of *Kretzschmaria deusta*.

immature, *K. deusta* matures to its black, crust-like state quite quickly.

Significance: *K. deusta* is dangerous due to its often inconspicuous nature, often buried beneath moss or leaf-litter. The decay establishes in roots, stem base and lower stem and seems to be most common in roadside trees, with damage to the roots and base of the main stem. *K. deusta* prefers the cellulose to begin with and advances to a more complete decay later on. However, trees have been known to fail after this degradation of the cellulose as it embrittles the wood quite significantly.

Laetiporus sulphureus, Chicken of the woods

Host species: *L. sulphureus* has a very broad host range amongst both broadleaved and coniferous trees across many different climate zones.

Identification: *L. sulphureus* forms annual fruiting bodies which take the form of bright yellow fronds with wavy margins, often in layered, overlapping clumps appearing out of pruning wounds and the sites of damage on stems and larger branches. The fruiting bodies degrade to a whitish, bleached state which may persist for several months.

Significance: *L. sulphureus* only very slowly degrades the wood of the infected host. However, the heartwood is primarily affected at first as *L. sulphureus* likes to have a go at cellulose first, making the infected wood very brittle. At advanced stages, the affected part (which includes the base of the stem) may become decayed enough to snap.

Young fruiting bodies of *Laetiporus sulphureus* on the stem of a tree.

Large fruiting body of *Meripilus giganteus* on the base of a mature beech tree.

Meripilus giganteus, **Giant polypore**

Host species: *M. giganteus* has a relatively narrow range of host tree species. It occurs almost exclusively on common beech (*F. sylvatica*), very rarely on oaks, London plane (*Platanus*) and monkey puzzle (*Araucaria araucana*).

Identification: *M. giganteus* forms a very distinctive fruiting body, although it is sometimes confused with *G. frondosa*. Large clumps of light brown, overlapping fronds, sometimes 50cm (20in) or more across can be found at the base of infected trees and also sometimes at distance from the tree above decayed roots. Multiple fruiting bodies often occur around one tree or stump. The fruiting bodies are annual and degrade to a blackened state, often when affected by frost.

Significance: *M. giganteus* is probably the most feared wood decay fungus amongst arborists. Operating in the roots and at the stem base, *M. giganteus* consumes both cellulose and pectin, which is like the glue that holds cells together. Once crown symptoms set in, a high chance of total failure exists.

Phaeolus schweinitzii, **Dyer's polypore**

Host species: *P. schweinitzii* is confined to coniferous host species but is most common on pines, Douglas fir, spruce, larch and cedar.

Identification: The fruiting body is an annual bracket which may or may not have a stem, appears from roots or at the stem base, very rarely on the stem. The fruiting body is dark brown with an orangey margin when young, bearing a soft, felty top surface and degrades to a blackened, crusty state which persists.

Significance: *P. schweinitzii* is one of a relatively small number of wood decay fungi which prefer to initially consume the cellulose within wood. This normally leaves degraded wood with a brown, cubical appearance. Advanced decay, where there may also be decline evident in the crown, can lead to brittle fracture at the stem base/root crown.

A large fruiting body of *Phaeolus schweinitzii* appearing from the roots of an infected tree.

Piptoporus betulinus, **Razor strop fungus**

Host species: *P. betulinus* is confined to members of the birch family.

Identification: The fruiting bodies of *P. betulinus* are persistent but not annual and form soft brackets on the stem of the host tree, almost always singly. The upper surface starts a silvery grey

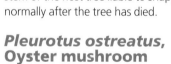

A fruiting body of *Piptoporus betulinus* on the stem of a silver birch tree .

and matures to a grey-brown with a silvery sheen. The top side curves downwards in mature fruiting bodies. The pore surface is whitish, darkening slightly in maturity.

Significance: *P. betulinus* is responsible for a brown rot. Practically this means that the cellulose in the wood is degraded first. Often, this fungus appears to have an effect where the tree is already in a state of decline, whether due to drought stress or some other factor and can render the stem of the host tree liable to snapping, normally after the tree has died.

Pleurotus ostreatus, **Oyster mushroom**

Host species: *P. ostreatus* is very common on a broad range of broadleaved trees.

Identification: Fruiting bodies of *P. ostreatus* form a soft, fleshy fan-shaped bracket which may or may not bear a short stem. They are annual, grey-brown when young, maturing to a brownish-buff colour. The underside consists of white gills.

Significance: *P. ostreatus* degrades both the lignin and cellulose of the host tree at a similar rate, which may lead to a localised cavity forming in the vicinity of pruning wounds. Decay can progress quite rapidly in trees which are already in a state of serious decline.

The fruiting bodies of *Pleurotus ostreatus* on the stem of a mature beech tree.

A fruiting body of *Polyporous squamosus* on the trunk of a common ash.

Polyporus squamosus, Dryad's saddle

Host species: *P. squamosus* occurs on a broad range of broadleaved trees, including maples (especially sycamore), beech, elm and ash.

Identification: Fruiting bodies of *P. squamosus* are soft, annual brackets on a short, stout stem and can be up to 40cm (16in) across. The top surface is distinctive and bears brown scales. The underside (pore surface) is white or creamy coloured.

Significance: The decay caused by *P. squamosus* is of low significance in the healthy tree and appears to be confined to dysfunction, which may have been caused by pruning or topping. Decay, where lignin is consumed first, can progress to cavity formation in the affected wood.

Rigidoporus ulmarius

Host species: *R. ulmarius* used to be much more common, occurring mostly on elms. With Dutch elm disease accounting for the majority of large, mature elms, this fungus has become quite rare in parts of Europe. It can still be found at times, however, on maples, oaks, poplars and horse chestnut.

Identification: *R. ulmarius* forms thick, woody, irregular perennial brackets at the base of trees. These can be over 30cm (12in) across. The top surface, normally a creamy honey colour in older specimens, is often discoloured by the presence of an algae to green. *R. ulmarius* is easily confused with *Perenniporia fraxinea* as they are

Fruiting body of *Rigidoporus ulmarius* growing at the base of a poplar.

quite similar. To distinguish them reliably, one has to cut the fruiting body open and examine the flesh. In *R. ulmarius*, the flesh and the tubes contrast, as they are pale and cinnamon coloured respectively. In *Perenniporia fraxinea*, no such contrast exists.

Significance: *R. ulmarius* causes a brown rot, preferentially degrading cellulose at the very base of the host tree. At advanced stages of decay, the stability of the host tree may be compromised. Detecting the extent of decay caused by this fungus (as with all trees operating in this zone) is very difficult to achieve.

Sparassis crispa, Cauliflower fungus

Host species: *S. crispa* is thought to be confined to coniferous species of tree. Most common on pines although also on firs, spruces and larch.

Identification: *S. crispa* forms a unique fruiting body, essentially formed from masses of curly fronds which are white, maturing to a honey-coloured state. The fruiting bodies form fairly round, lobed forms which can be over 30cm (12in) across. They degrade and disappear quickly.

Significance: *S. crispa* also causes a brown rot, preferring to munch on the cellulose at the stem base and in the root system of the tree. It can extend a few metres further up the stem in exceptional cases. Ultimately, the advanced stages of decay may bring about failure at the root crown.

A fruiting body of *Sparassis crispa*, growing from a root on the forest floor.

What to do if you cannot identify the fungus

As with other sections of this book it is not possible to list all of the fungi that you may encounter. You may need to obtain specialist advice to help identify potential pests and diseases. Contacting a local arboriculturist may be your first option as often a site visit and visual check of your tree(s) may be all that is required to correctly identify the problem and come up with a course of action. Sometimes, further investigation will be required and it may be necessary for the arboriculturist or the tree owner to send off samples. In the UK, services are provided by the Forestry Commission and their Tree Health Diagnostic and Advisory Service. At the time of writing, enquiries can be submitted via their Tree Alert Tree Pest and Disease sighting reporter on their website (https://treealert.forestry.gov.uk/index.php/thdas). This is a chargeable service.

Tree Manual

8 APPENDICES

Tree species
Planting site checklist
Maintenance schedule
Tree inspection
Service record
Resources and references
Glossary

Tree species

Key

Size	
1	Dwarf Tree = Mature Height up to 3m
2	Small Tree = Mature Height 3–8m
3	Medium Tree = Mature Height 12–17m
4	Large Tree = over 20m

Habit	
5	Columner
6	Pyramidal
7	Umbrella
8	Spreading
9	Weeping
10	Oval
11	Multi Stern

Good for	
12	Bees
13	Flowers
14	Leaves and autumn colours
15	Interesting bark
16	Smaller gardens
17	Parkland trees
18	Urban sites

BROADLEAVES

Genus *Acer* — The larger maples

Almost entirely originating from the northern hemisphere, the maples form a varied and fascinating genus of trees. Most are deciduous and often provide a good if not outstanding display of autumn colour when the weather allows. With most species having a number of cultivars available, there is almost certain to be a maple to suit any size garden and soil type.

Acer pseudoplatanus Sycamore maple

		4		8		14		18

Known as the sycamore maple to many, *A. pseudoplatanus* is a very large tree, and fast-growing for the first 20 years. It is also one of the toughest of all trees, tolerating air pollution and poor soil well.

Acer platanoides Norway maple

		4		8		14		18

A. platanoides (Norway maple) is a resilient tree, performing well in urban environments on any soil, tolerating both pollution and drought well. Norway maple is a large, fast-growing tree and tolerates pruning well.

Acer saccharinum Silver maple

		4		8				18

A. saccharinum (silver maple) is also a large, fast-growing tree. It copes well with the urban realm but can form brittle branches so should be afforded plenty of room. Silver maples cope well with wet sites.

Genus *Acer* — The medium-sized maples

The three maple species described here are all medium-sized trees at maturity. They are likely to be better suited to locations where space is more limited although they are no less striking than their larger relatives listed on the previous page.

Acer campestre Field maple

	3						10			14			18

Native to England, field maple is fairly tolerant of challenging urban sites. It can be pruned heavily and often and can form striking (if brief) autumn colour. Many cultivars (including Elsrijk and Louisa Red Shine) give more regular form and reliable autumn colour.

Acer cappadocicum Cappadocian maple

	3				8				14			

A. cappadocicum is prone to verticillium wilt. Care is required during establishment but the rewards are great as bark and foliage are very attractive. *A. cappadocicum* provides fantastic autumn colour, 'Aureum' provides yellow foliage throughout.

Acer x freemanii

	3				8				14			18

A cross between Canadian and silver maples, *A. x freemanii* is more tolerant of tough sites. This tree forms some gloriously colourful cultivars (some with more compact form) although branches can be a bit snappy like the parent silver maple.

Genus *Acer* — The small maples

These smaller maples are a sample of what is available for the more constrained garden or site. Very popular and often to be found in gardens all over the world, smaller maples are more delicate and pretty but no less pleasing on the eye than their larger cousins in the genus Acer.

Acer griseum Paperbark maple

	2				8		11		14		16		

A somewhat delicate tree, the paperbark maple requires shelter, shade and moist soil, not in urban sites. It does not tolerate drought. Fascinating, peeling bark and good autumn colour from an early age make this a great little tree.

Acer negundo Box Elder

	2				8				14		16		

The Box Elder is amazingly tolerant of all sorts of hardships and shows good resistance to Honey fungus. The leaves are compound and very different to most maples. The normal type is larger but smaller cultivars are available which are at their best when pruned hard, including the variegated 'Flamingo' and 'Variegata'. Tolerates heavy pruning.

Acer palmatum Japanese maple

	2				8				14			

Known as Japanese maple, but native to other parts of East Asia, this is a popular garden and park tree. Many cultivars are produced for various attributes although the autumn colour is always good. Moist, well-drained soil is necessary. These can often grow larger than anticipated.

Genus *Aesculus* Horse chestnuts

The horse chestnuts have always been a popular choice, in particular in parks and large gardens where these large trees have a chance to flourish and show off their attractive flowers and autumn fruits although autumn colour is not normally notable. The common horse chestnut in particular is found all over the world, despite being native only to a small area of south-eastern Europe.

Aesculus hippocastanum Common horse chestnut

	4		8		13		17	

A. hippocastanum is very attractive in late spring with its white, tinged yellow then pink, candle-like flowers. Subject to a number of pests including bleeding canker, leaf blotch and leaf miner, which make this tree a less attractive proposition than was once the case.

Aesculus x carnea Red horse chestnut

	4		8		13		17	

Red horse chestnut thrives in all soils and tolerates air pollution but it is best in spring and early summer when the pink/red flowers emerge. 'Plantierensis' is the best cultivar, being resistant to many of the afflictions that blight common horse chestnut.

Aesculus indica Indian horse chestnut

	4		8		13		17	

Indian horse chestnut is the prettiest of the horse chestnuts and appears to have good resistance to bleeding canker. It bears pink flowers and bronze foliage in spring and sometimes orange-yellow autumn colour. A particularly tall and majestic specimen.

Genus *Alnus* Alders

Alders are often unfairly overlooked when deciding on a tree species for a particular site. A variety of cultivars are available and they are generally tolerant of a wide variety of soils and moisture regimes as well as urban pollution. Alders make ideal screen plantings along the edge of gardens and under the right conditions can grow very quickly indeed.

Alnus glutinosa Common alder

	3		6			11	12	

A native of northern Europe (including the UK), where it is found fringing rivers and lakes, the roots of common alder can survive prolonged waterlogging. In youth *A. glutinosa* maintains a conical habit, when up to 2m of growth in a season is possible.

Alnus cordata Italian alder

	3		6			12		

Italian alder is a common urban tree and is very hardy indeed. A fast-growing, medium tree with a conical habit, its shiny, green, pear-like leaves last well into winter, particularly under street lights. *A. cordata* tolerates a wide range of soils.

Alnus incana Grey alder

	3		6			12		

Again, a very hardy, medium-sized tree, grey alder is tolerant of urban pollution and wet soils. A European native, it also does well in exposed sites. The cultivars 'Aurea' and 'Laciniata' are smaller and very attractive.

Genus *Amelanchier* Serviceberry

Amelanchiers are native to temperate regions of the northern hemisphere and include small shrubs to medium-sized trees. Differentiation between species is sometimes difficult. Most species are native to North America.

Amelanchier arborea

	2					8			12	13					

The cultivar 'Robin Hill' is considered to be the best serviceberry on the market by far. Requiring little maintenance, this tree forms a dense, oval habit and produces masses of spring flowers that open pink and turn white. Young spring leaves emerge coppery red, turning to green by late spring and then a vivid red in autumn.

Genus *Arbutus* Strawberry trees

Four species of Arbutus are native to Europe and North Africa and eight to North America (mostly western areas including Mexico). All species are small, shrubby trees with flaky red bark and edible red berries.

Arbutus unedo Killarney strawberry tree

	2					11				16			

Native to western Ireland and the Mediterranean region, the Killarney strawberry tree is a small evergreen with brown, shedding bark. Flowers and fruits are produced together in the autumn. This small shrubby tree tolerates coastal locations well.

Genus *Betula* Birches

Native to temperate and boreal climates of the northern hemisphere, birches are mostly relatively short-lived, pioneer species which do best where light levels are good. There are a large number of species and cultivars available, many of which are noted for their interestingly coloured, peeling bark, which provides interest throughout the year.

Betula pendula Silver birch

		3												15				

A native of northern Europe, the medium-sized silver birch is also known as the 'Lady of the Woods' – so called because of its slender and graceful appearance. Several cultivars exist including two weeping forms, 'Youngii' with a dense twiggy pendulous top and 'Tristis' which has an erect trunk with weeping branches.

Betula nigra River birch

	3					8			11			14	15	16		

This beautiful, tough tree is native to central and eastern USA and makes a medium sized tree to 15 metres high with a wide spreading crown. It has striking pinky-brown peeling bark and always colours up well with yellow leaves in the autumn. It like a moist but well-drained soil of any type. The best cultivar is 'Heritage'.

Betula utilis Himalayan birch

	3			6				11			15			

The Himalayan birch has very attractive white bark which peels away in layers. It makes a medium tree with ascending branches and the oval, dark green leaves turn yellow in autumn. By far the most prevalent variety is 'Jacquemontii'. Multi-stem specimens are particularly striking.

Genus *Carpinus* Hornbeams

Around 40 species of hornbeam are distributed across the northern hemisphere, concentrated in East Asia. Renowned for producing very hard timber which has been utilised in numerous ways including in simple machines and for flooring.

Carpinus betulus European hornbeam

			4				8					14	15			

The European hornbeam is a very hardy, versatile tree. Ideal for pleaching and producing a fine hedge which can be repeatedly pruned hard, the hornbeam is a large tree with a characteristic grey fluted trunk and oval, ribbed and serrated leaves which turn yellow in autumn. It grows well on most soils, including clay and chalk. Fastigiate cultivars ('Frans Fontaine' retains its form best) are available.

Genus *Castanea* Chestnuts

Chestnuts are generally sub-divided into American, European, Chinese and Japanese chestnuts. Generally trees of warm temperate and Mediterranean climate zones, chestnuts generally produce edible nuts in spiky cases with 1–7 individual fruits inside.

Castanea sativa European sweet chestnut

			4				8					14	15			

C. sativa is a versatile and beautiful, fast-growing tree, which is at its best in early summer when laden with its male and female catkins. Foliage in autumn turns yellowy orange. The deeply furrowed bark spirals around the trunk at maturity. This tree is native to southern Europe and north Africa but has long been naturalised in the UK. Temperatures throughout most of the UK are generally not high enough to produce significant fruit.

Genus *Catalpa*

Catalpas are normally medium to large deciduous trees from sub-tropical regions. Most have large, fleshy, heart-shaped leaves and showy white or yellow flowers in large panicles.

Catalpa bignonioides Indian bean tree

		3					8				13			

C. bignonioides hails from the South-Eastern United States and is a magnificent medium to large tree with a broad, spreading crown. It tolerates urban conditions very well but should not be planted in windy, exposed sites or paved areas. It produces white, orchid-like flowers in midsummer and subsequently the dangling seed pods in autumn.

Genus *Cercidiphyllum* Katsura

There are just two trees in the genus *Cercidiphyllum*. The 'species type' is detailed below and is a large tree in its native range of the genus in China and Japan. The other member of the genus is a much smaller tree, thriving at higher altitudes.

Cercidiphyllum japonicum Katsura tree

		3					8					14			

This tree requires deep, moist, fertile soil and does not tolerate drought well. New foliage can tend to be sensitive to frost. It is sensational both in spring with emerging coppery green leaves and autumn when the foliage turns yellow or pink whilst exuding a fragrant scent reminiscent of burnt sugar.

Genus *Cercis*   Redbuds

There are approximately ten species in this genus of small trees, most of which are native to Asia. Four species are native to North America. They are characterised by round to heart shaped leaves and flowers borne in spring on bare shoots.

Cercis siliquastrum Judas tree

	2					8					13				

A stunning sight in May when clusters of rosy-lilac, pea-like flowers wreathe the wood, sometimes springing direct from mature branches and even from the trunk. This tree takes a while to root, so additional support is recommended. Planting this tree in a sunny, warm position will help to get the best from it.

Genus *Corylus*   Hazels

Common to Asia, Europe and North America, the hazels form small trees and multi-stem shrubs. The nuts of all hazels are edible, but the main commercially important nut products come from the European hazel. A number of varieties have been selected and produced as ornamentals with contorted stems, weeping branches or coloured foliage.

Corylus avellana European hazel

	2						11				16			

Native to Europe and west Asia, this is a small tree with a rounded habit. It looks particularly striking in the early spring when it is adorned with its long yellow 'lamb's tail' catkins. The nuts in autumn are an important food source for many animals. A very good choice for gardens, parks and woodlands. Red and corkscrew are the most common varieties.

Genus *Cornus*   Dogwoods

This genus comprises mostly deciduous small trees and shrubs, the majority of which are commonly referred to as dogwoods. There are a number which are commercially available, and the show of flowers and autumn colours is often stunning. Care is required on choosing the right one for your local climate to get the best out of them.

Cornus kousa

	2					8					13	14			

There are a number of kousa varieties available, and they are probably the most reliable flowering types of dogwood. Flowers are borne in abundance in early spring and the foliage turns vivid colours by autumn. Cornus kousa do not tolerate alkaline soils.

Cornus controversa Japanese dogwood

	3					8				12	13	14			

This is a medium-sized architectural, deciduous tree to 15 metres high with the branches growing in tiered layers. It bears clusters of white star-shaped flowers in late spring, and is a good tree for pollinating insects, followed by the blue-black berries that follow which are sought after by feeding birds. The autumn colour is also a valuable attribute of this tree. The variegated cultivar with white margined leaves, known as the wedding cake tree is a good choice for the smaller garden.

Genus *Crataegus*   Hawthorns

Hawthorns are shrubs and small trees, nearly always thorny and producing a fruit which is correctly known as a 'pome'. This is a small, round fruit which resembles a berry and which is an important winter food, in particular for bird life. *C. monogyna*, *C. crus-galli* and *C. x laevigata* are probably the most common ornamental species.

Crataegus monogyna Common hawthorn

	2				8			12	13		

Native to Europe, the common hawthorn produces small, white, fragrant flowers which appear in May and June and are followed by small red fruits in abundance during autumn. A good choice for urban and coastal planting, it is also tolerant of air pollution. It does well in most soils, including very dry and wet soils. Tolerant of repeated, heavy pruning, this also makes a fantastic hedge plant.

Genus *Eucalyptus*   Gum trees

Trees belonging to the genus Eucalyptus are nearly all native to Australia, with just a handful of the 700 species in the genus naturally found outside the country. The genus includes the tallest flowering plant on earth (*Eucalyptus regnans*). As you would expect, many are cold sensitive and don't do well in temperate areas with low winter temperatures.

Eucalyptus gunnii Cider gum

		4				8								17	

A very well known Eucalyptus – and a very hardy one – this large, broadly pyramidal tree has smooth grey-pink to red-brown bark. The young leaves are a blue-green and provide a great contrast to gardens and municipal landscapes. This tree is native to south-east mainland Australia and Tasmania and copes with low temperatures well.

Genus *Fagus*   Beech trees

Trees belonging to the Fagus genus are normally referred to as beeches. Trees of temperate regions, they are found exclusively in the northern hemisphere. Most commonly cultivated, the attractive European beech (detailed further below) forms many fine cultivars.

Fagus sylvatica European beech

	4		8			14		17

European beech is difficult to establish when faced with extreme heat and drought. It has a wide range of uses as an ornamental tree – in woodland, parkland and in broad verge plantings – and it provides a fantastic rich copper autumn colour. European beech thrives just about anywhere other than exposed and coastal locations. Cultivars of fastigiate, weeping and dark purple forms are popular.

Genus *Fraxinus*   Ash trees

Again common across Europe, Asia and North America, trees in the genus Fraxinus are normally medium to large specimens of tree and are commonplace in amenity planting schemes everywhere. In Europe, the prevalence of ash dieback, which is now established across much of the continent, has led to import bans and in many areas a complete stop to the planting of trees of this genus.

Fraxinus excelsior European ash

		4			10				17	

Particularly susceptible to Chalara dieback of ash, the almost complete removal of this species from the landscape will have a dramatic effect. A large tree which casts a dappled shade from its crown, this tree is particularly important for native wildlife.

Genus *Ginkgo*

There is just one tree in this genus which dates back only about 200 million years or so. The survivor of a cataclysmic event which led to a mass extinction, this species is making a comeback as an urban tree due to its no-nonsense toughness.

Ginkgo biloba Maidenhair tree

		4		6					14			

A potentially large tree, the conical form is only maintained if the central leader is left untouched. It is a good choice for parks and avenues, tolerating paved areas well. It has a deep root system, and curious, fan-shaped leaves. A number of cultivars have been developed for their compact habit and smaller size. Autumn colour can be very good indeed.

Genus *Gleditsia*　　Locust

Native to North America and Asia, there are around 12 listed species in this genus. Often thorny and adaptable to a variety of conditions, these deciduous trees can be invasive.

Gleditsia triacanthos Honey locust

	3			8				14			18

A number of attractive cultivars are produced of this species with the species type hailing from moist soils in river valleys of central North America. It copes well with a variety of urban environments and produces profuse, long spiny thorns. Spineless forms are available with 'Sunburst' possibly the best as it also has yellow foliage.

Genus *Ilex*　　Holly

There are around 500 species in this genus spread throughout the temperate and subtropical regions of the world. Trees, shrubs and climbers are included in the genus, which are evergreen and bear berries (technically 'drupes') of various hues and sizes.

Ilex aquifolium Common holly

	2			6						16		

The 'type species' for the genus, the common holly is beautiful in its simplicity and brings cheer at the darkest time of year. Native to Europe, this is a small, conical, evergreen tree which provides year-round interest, but is particularly attractive in autumn and winter with its dark foliage and red berries. A number of attractive cultivars are available, chosen for their less spiny or variegated foliage.

Genus *Juglans*　　Walnuts

All species of Juglans are deciduous and form trees which are between 10 and 40 metres tall. Native to North and South America as well as Europe and Asia, all species in this genus produce walnut fruit and many species are also harvested for their prized timber.

Juglans nigra Black walnut

		4		6								17	

A number of *Juglans* species are described as black walnuts. This is perhaps the best known and makes a large tree with a broadly pyramidal crown. It is a very good choice for parkland settings. *J. nigra* produces an abundance of nuts over a long period but extracting them from their hard shells is difficult.

Juglans regia Common walnut

	3				8						17	

By far the most commercially important species in the genus, *J. regia* is native to south-eastern Europe and makes a splendid and stately subject for parkland and avenue plantings. A slow-growing tree, common walnut develops a broad crown at maturity and does best in the full sun. Fruit production is best in warmer, drier climates.

Genus *Liquidambar* Sweet gums

Trees of warm temperate and sub-tropical climates, this is a small genus of deciduous trees most prevalent in eastern Asia and North America. They are most renowned for their coloured foliage.

Liquidambar styraciflua Sweet gum

		3		6							14				

With a number of cultivars to its name, this tree is one of the very best for autumn colour, producing stunning crimsons and golds. Often mistaken for a maple, this makes a large tree with a broad, pyramidal crown if its central leader is retained although smaller and more uniform cultivars are available. This tree does not like chalky soil.

Genus *Liriodendron* Tulip trees

This genus contains just two species of deciduous trees. Given the name tulip tree on account of the flowers which superficially resemble tulips. Both species are relatively similar, and hybridise freely although they are geographically isolated with one species native to China, the other to North America.

Liriodendron tulipifera Tulip tree

		4		6						13					

L. tulipifera and *L. chinense* are very similar, originating from a common parent a few million years ago. They both form potentially very large trees, *L. chinense* bearing smaller flowers and more deeply lobed leaves. Autumn colour is good but these trees need a lot of room and fertile soils. Only mature trees will give a summertime floral display.

Genus *Magnolia*

Very large and ancient genus of trees, members of the genus are found across North and South America and Asia, generally preferring warmer tropical and sub-tropical regions. Many are evergreen although some species are tolerant of cold and are deciduous. Magnolias are renowned for their floral displays and many species and cultivars are available.

Magnolia grandiflora Southern magnolia

		3								10			13		

Native to sub-tropical southern states of the USA, the evergreen Southern magnolia can establish in colder regions given adequate shelter and a south-facing position. Capable of becoming a medium to large tree under the right growing conditions, it is a magnificent, round-headed specimen. The large, cream flowers, which are delicately scented, are borne through summer and into autumn and look stunning against the shiny, dark green leaves. It does best in rich, fertile soil and, given this, will tolerate lime.

Magnolia x soulangeana Saucer magnolia

	2					8				13			16		

This small tree is a hybrid with over a hundred named cultivars making it one of the most commonly planted magnolias in the British Isles. It is deciduous with large flowers in early spring in various shades and colours from white, pink and purple.

Genus *Parrotia*	Ironwoods

A genus of just two species of deciduous tree, native to the Caucasus (*P. persica*) and Eastern China (*P. subaequalis*). Both species produce attractive autumn colour and attractive, flaking bark when mature.

Parrotia persica Persian Ironwood

	2					10		14	15			

As the name suggests, this species hails from the Caucasus and northern Iran. Growing larger in its native range, this is normally marketed as a small tree in cultivation. One of the finest trees for autumn colour, this tree does well on most soil types and, typical for the genus, forms attractive flaking bark when mature.

Genus *Platanus*	Plane trees

A small genus with around ten members, plane trees are mostly found in wetter, riparian habitats in their native ranges in Central America (the majority of species are found here) and Asia. All but one of the members of this genus are deciduous, forming potentially very large specimen trees.

Platanus x hispanica (syn. x acerifolia) London plane

			4			8					15		17	18

Probably the most commonly cultivated member of this genus, it is a hybrid between *P. occidentalis* and *P. orientalis*. London plane produces very interesting, patchwork bark. Renowned for being a particularly tough and resilient urban tree, able to thrive in challenging environments, nevertheless in recent years Massaria disease and canker stain have taken their toll on this much-loved species.

Genus *Populus* Poplars/Cottonwoods/Aspens

Around 30 tree species make up this genus, which is relatively diverse. Poplars are found from tropical to sub-arctic regions, mostly in the northern hemisphere. Many poplars are important in riparian and sub-arctic ecosystems.

Populus alba White poplar

			4						10			14					

This large, fast-growing tree is ideal for exposed and coastal plantings. The vivid white undersides of its foliage give it its name and it can be very striking in the right situation. Space is needed to accommodate the expansive root system. This tree does well on chalky soils.

Populus nigra Black poplar

			4						10								

True black poplars, native to Europe and western Asia, are hard to find. *P. nigra* forms a large, fast-growing tree, with heavy branches and often burred stem. This tree also does well on exposed, wet sites and is often confused with imported lookalikes.

Genus *Prunus* Cherries

This large and diverse genus contains hundreds of recognised species, which are mostly found in northern temperate regions. Home to many commercial fruits, including cherries, peaches, plums and almonds, there are also many flowering ornamentals of various sizes which are often prized for their floral displays. Cherries also often produce very interesting bark with pronounced lenticels.

Prunus avium Wild cherry

			3							10			13	14			

Native to northern Europe, this tree is the parent of many cultivated cherry tree species. A medium to large tree with a rounded form, white flowers in spring are followed in autumn by good autumn colours of reds, pinks and golds. Well drained soil is required to get the best out of this tree. Often shallow rooted, the cultivar 'Plena' is a better bet for paved surfaces.

Prunus sargentii Sargent's cherry

		2								10			13	14			

One of the Japanese flowering cherries (in fact, this is probably the best), this forms a small, rounded tree. Profuse pink flowers in early spring are followed by oranges and reds quite early on in autumn. Dark brown bark contrasts nicely with the autumn colour.

Genus *Quercus* The oaks

Native to the northern hemisphere, the two main centres of oak diversity are North America (with approximately 200 species) and China (with over 100). The 600 or so species are divided into sections including the white oaks (for example English oak, *Q. robur*) and red oaks (for example northern red oak, *Q. rubra*). Common to all oaks is the acorn, the fruit which is produced with or without a stalk and borne in a cupule.

Quercus ilex Holm oak

		4		8						18

Native to Mediterranean regions of Europe, the Holm oak is ubiquitous throughout the region, particularly in coastal regions of the UK and Ireland where it could almost be said to be naturalised. A versatile and hardy tree which tolerates urban pollution well, it forms a good hedge, screen or a fine, large, individual evergreen tree when left to its own devices.

Quercus palustris Pin oak

	4		6					14		

An American oak, and perhaps one of the most graceful of the genus, this tree, which has stunning autumn colour, forms a large specimen with a pyramidal crown. It does best in freely draining, slightly acidic soil.

Quercus robur 'Fastigiata' Cypress oak

	4	5					14	16	18

This is a popular narrow compact form of the common English oak that can grow to 20 metres high, making it a very useful avenue tree. It has lobed, glossy leaves turning golden brown in autumn.

Quercus robur English oak

	4		8					17	

The range of the English oak significantly overlaps that of the Sessile oak and they are generally quite similar trees. Preferring deeper, more fertile soils than *Q. petraea*, the English oak is a majestic tree in maturity, with gnarly, deeply furrowed bark.

Genus *Robinia* — Locusts

Native to North America, the small number of trees and shrubs of the *Robinia* genus are deciduous. Many *Robinia* species are thorny and produce long racemes of flowers.

Robinia pseudoacacia False acacia

		4		8		13				

A large irregular crowned tree with soft, green, pinnate leaves that emerge in early May. Racemes of sweetly scented white flowers in June are replaced by purple tinged seed pods in autumn. It thrives on any soil, and tolerates urban pollution, but is not good in windy, exposed locations due to its rather brittle branches. Many cultivars exist, with 'Frisia' particularly notable for its yellow foliage.

Genus *Salix* — Willow

Mainly native to cold and temperate regions of the northern hemisphere, *Salix* includes willows, sallows and osiers. There are around 400 species including shrubs and large trees and everything in between. Nearly all species in this genus will take root readily from cuttings. Numerous naturally occurring and cultivated hybrids occur.

Salix alba White willow

		4		8						

Native to Europe, there are a large number of cultivars and hybrids which derive from this large, fast-growing tree. The species type is found on riverbanks in its native habitat but it does well on most soils and is tolerant of wet sites. Subjected to regular, heavy pruning, this tree recovers well.

Genus *Sorbus*

The exact number of species which belong in this genus is disputed, with recent work further dividing the genus into various sub-genera. Variously known as whitebeams, rowans and service trees and distributed across the northern hemisphere including north Africa, sorbus are normally small to medium-sized specimens.

Sorbus aria Common whitebeam

	3				10	12	13	14		

A popular and widely distributed tree, the various whitebeam cultivars form small to medium-sized trees noted for the stunning white underside of the foliage, white flowers in spring and red berries later in the autumn. There is interest throughout nearly every season.

Sorbus aucuparia Rowan

2					10	12	13	14		

Again a European native, the Rowan is a very pretty small tree, with white spring flowers and red autumn berries which are great for birdlife. The species type prefers cooler temperate and upland habitats in acidic soil. There are a large number of cultivars available which can be chosen for greater uniformity of habit (e.g. Rossica Major), yellow berries (e.g. Golden Wonder) and various other traits.

Genus *Tilia* — Lime (linden, basswood)

There are around 30 species of lime across North America, Europe and Asia (which has the highest species diversity). In the wild and in cultivation, limes hybridise freely and are almost all large, deciduous trees. Most limes readily tolerate heavy pruning and cyclical coppicing.

Tilia tomentosa 'Petiolaris' Weeping silver lime

		4			9			13	14			17	

This is one of the most graceful of the large weeping trees to 20 metres high, with large leaves, which are silver on the underside, giving a beautiful display of shimmering foliage on a warm breezy day. It also produces sweetly scented white flowers in early summer. The silver leaves make it aphid free, so it doesn't produce honey dew drip, which is a major bonus for this tree.

Tilia cordata Small-leaved lime

		4			8			12				18

Native to Europe, *T. cordata* forms a large tree with a broadly oval crown. More regular cultivars (e.g. 'Greenspire') are in production. The small, heart-shaped leaves are dark green on top and pale green beneath. Creamy white flowers are produced in July. *T. cordata* grows at moderate pace and is often used for avenues and parks. This tree also bears air pollution very well. *T. cordata* is one of the parents of *T. x europaea*, which forms a more vigorous, large-leaved tree but which often has issues with honeydew and sooty moulds on cars and hard surfaces beneath its canopy.

CONIFERS

Genus *Cedrus* — Cedars

Cedars make magnificent trees. However, cedars are also large trees meaning that their huge size will make them unsuitable for most homeowners. A quick rule of thumb to recognise the different cedars is that Atlantica has ascending branches, Deodars go down and the Cedar of Lebanons are level. These trees are best in a well-drained site that receives full sun.

Cedrus atlantica Atlas cedar

		4			8						17	

Atlas cedars make the most imposing and stately subjects, perfect for large gardens and estates. It is a native of the Atlas mountains of Algeria and Morocco. The glaucous cultivar of this tree has beautiful blue green foliage and of the cedars is probably the most tolerant to urban pollution.

Cedrus deodara Deodar cedar

		4		6								17	

Different from all other cedars due to its drooping leader and broadly conical shape, this large conifer has a gently pendulous habit and soft, blue-green foliage. It thrives on most soils but, like all cedars, does not do as well in wet ground. Grown for timber in southern Europe and as an ornamental elsewhere.

Cedrus libani Cedar of Lebanon

		4			8						17	

There is little to choose between *C. libani* and *C. atlantica* in the imposing grandeur stakes with *C. libani* forming a majestic, tiered mature form. Widely planted in parks and large gardens although slower-growing than *C. Atlantica*, again this tree does not appreciate wet soils.

Genus *Chamaecyparis*   False cypresses

The coniferous trees of this genus are native to eastern Asia and the western and eastern fringes of North America. Generally forming large, evergreen trees in their native ranges with several species of high commercial importance as ornamentals.

Chamaecyparis lawsoniana Lawson cypress

1			4		6										16	17	

There are dozens of Lawson cypress cultivars available on the market, which have been selected for all sorts of different traits including dwarf, blue, yellow and columnar varieties so there is likely to be one to suit your needs. The species type forms a large specimen tree and is often utilised in hedges as an alternative to the more vigorous Leyland cypress. It dislikes water logged ground and thrives on well-drained sunny sites.

Genus *Cupressus/Cuprocyparis*   Cypresses

Cupressus is not the only genus of tree which is commonly referred to as belonging to the cypresses. It is, however, probably the main genus within the group. Mostly native to warm temperate zones in the northern hemisphere, extensive cultivation has produced many ornamental trees which are widely planted and often highly valued, with options for any size garden and budget.

Cuprocyparis leylandii Leyland cypress

			4		6											17	

Not a 'true' cypress, perhaps, but this is included here as it is a hybrid between Nootka cypress and Monterey cypress. Fast-growing and making an excellent screen or close-clipped hedge, this hardy tree is ubiquitous in the UK and Ireland. It needs room, however, although the excellent 'Castlewellan' is slower-growing and makes the best hedge.

Genus *Metasequoia*

There is just one living species in this genus, which are also one of the few referred to as redwoods. Before the 1940s, only fossilised forms were known, when the species described below was discovered in China.

Metasequoia glyptostroboides Dawn redwood

		4		6						14	15		17	

Since its discovery this attractive, deciduous conifer has become a firm favourite. Called by many a 'living fossil', *M. glyptostroboides* is often confused with *Taxodium*. It is, however, notably different if they are seen together. A large tree with pyramidal form, it makes a grand park or specimen tree.

Genus *Picea* 'The Spruces'

Found mostly throughout the northern temperate and boreal regions of the world, there are approximately 35 trees in this genus, which are mostly large, always coniferous specimens. Common to all trees in this genus is the fact that the needles occur on little pegs (known as pulvini).

Picea abies Norway spruce

		4		6															

This well known spruce is common over most of northern and central Europe. Known by many as the Christmas tree of choice although its propensity to lose too many needles has seen it replaced by conifers less likely to shed. This species is quick to grow and does well on most moist, free-draining soils.

Genus *Pinus* 'The Pines'

There are just under 130 species accepted in this genus. The majority are medium to large trees, with a number of species, however, growing much larger. Some are dwarf species, growing just a few feet tall. Characteristic of the species are the needles of various length which are borne in different numbers and which can be used as a means of identification.

Pinus nigra Austrian pine

		4		6												

A great choice for coastal areas and exposed sites, this two-needled pine is a tough tree. Displaying a dense habit, *P. nigra* also has a broadly pyramidal form. When younger, the ability of the crown of this tree to diffuse the wind is fantastic.

Pinus radiata Monterey pine

		4														17

A large tree with a deeply fissured bark, Monterey pines bear their (often up to 15cm long) needles in threes. This pine is also very tolerant of windy coastal locations. This pine also produces a dense crown and the cones persist for years on the branch.

Pinus sylvestris Scots pine

		4		6									15			

The only pine native to the UK, Scots pine is a tree of variable form often seen growing as a low, windswept tree in exposed locations. This tree does best when not waterlogged but tolerates most soil types and can form a large, impressive tree with distinctive bark which is orangey when young.

Genus *Sequoia/Sequoiadendron* 'The Redwoods'

Whilst not genetically that similar, these two genus are placed together as they are both referred to as redwoods. There is also just one species in both the *Sequoiadendron* and *Sequoia* genera (see below). Native to North America, trees from these two genera form the largest living things on Earth!

Sequoiadendron giganteum Giant redwood

		4		6									15		17

Notable for being THE largest living thing on the whole planet, the giant redwood is native to California, doing best on the western slopes of the Sierra Nevada. Needless to say, *S. giganteum* forms a very large, fast-growing conical tree which must be given plenty of room! The bark is very interesting, being a rich red-brown and forming a very thick, dense fibrous barrier.

Sequoia sempervirens Coast redwood

		4		6									15		17

If the giant redwood is the biggest, the coast redwood is probably the tallest. Native to the coastal region of California and Oregon, the few remaining trees in the wild are a truly impressive sight. A large, conical evergreen, it also has a thick, fibrous, red-brown outer bark, which is soft and spongy to the touch. This tree also needs lots of room and plenty of water when young to establish it.

Genus *Taxodium*

A genus in the cypress family, containing just a few species, *Taxodium* is native to North America. Notable for their extreme tolerance to water logging, species are either evergreen or deciduous, depending on the climate where they are found.

Taxodium distichum Swamp cypress

			4		6									14	15		17	

Often confused with *Metasequoia, Taxodium distichum* is also a large, deciduous conifer of broadly pyramidal form. It is also a good choice for parks and has interesting red-brown bark. Preferring wet soils, it requires plenty of water to establish it properly.

Genus *Taxus*   Yew

Trees in the genus *Taxus* are found distributed across most of the globe. However, there are only nine or so species (depending upon which authority you consult). Coniferous trees, yews are slow-growing and produce some of the oldest living things on the planet. A yew in Wales, UK has been dated at over 5,000 years old. With the exception of the fleshy aril which surrounds the seed, all parts of the yew can be toxic to humans.

Taxus baccata Common yew

		3					8									18

A medium tree of conical appearance, its hard wood can support this evergreen to a great age. Often used for hedging, it also makes a fine specimen tree. Very good for parks and gardens and can thrive on very alkaline or very acidic soils. The springy, durable wood of this tree was once used for bow making and the species has high cultural significance in parts of Europe.

Genus *Thuja*   The aborvitaes

A group of evergreen conifers in the cypress family represented by five species from North America and eastern Asia of varying sizes from small to very tall. The foliage is in flattened sprays and aromatic when crushed. There are several cultivars of Thuja occidentalis regularly grown in our gardens.

Thuja plicata Western red cedar

			4	5									16	17	

This is a large to very large tree from western north America, ranging up to 65 to 70 m (213 to 230ft) tall. It has a reddish-brown stringy bark and shiny green sprays of foliage that smells of pineapple when crushed. It retains its branches to the ground and makes a good hedging plant.

Planting site checklist

Use this form to help guide your decision on what tree species to plant.

Sketch plan

Sketch out the planting site and any nearby buildings, walls or features. Estimate distance and consider the ultimate mature size of the tree in relation to the static features.

Checklist			Notes
Climate			
Exposure	Is the site exposed to high winds?	Consider staking, wind scorch and tree shelters	
	Which direction is the prevailing wind?		
Sunlight	Full Sun	Also consider shade and reflected heat and light from the sides of large buildings	
	Partial Sun		
	Shade		
Frost	Is the site in a frost hollow?	Even in small sloping gardens frost can become trapped against walls	
Soil			
pH	What is the pH level?		
Texture	Is the soil Clayey, Loamy or Sandy?		
Compaction	Is the soil un-compacted, severely compacted or somewhere inbetween?	Also consider soil depth and volume. Is there enough for the mature size of tree being considered?	
Drainage	Is the soil… Poorly drained	<10cm (4") per hour	
	Moderately drained	10-20cm (4-8") per hour	
	Well drained	>20cm (8") per hour	
Other	Consider indications of soil disturbance from construction works, are there any signs of soil erosion or soil contamination from road salts etc		
Structures			
Buildings	What is the distance and orientation to the envisaged planting space?		
Utilities	Are there any overhead utilites? Estimate the distances from the planting site and include in the sketch plan		
	Are there potentially any underground utilities? Grilles and covers may indicate their presence.		

Maintenance schedule

Item	At planting	Years 2–3				Years 4–10				After 10 years				Notes
		Spring	Summer	Autumn	Winter	Spring	Summer	Autumn	Winter	Spring	Summer	Autumn	Winter	
Watering	✔	✔	✔	✔		✔	✔				✔			Once established water if needed during drought periods in the summer.
Mulching	✔	✔		✔		✔		✔		✔		✔		If planted on hungry soil, the mulch may require topping up more often, but ensure the mulch has almost disappeared before topping up. Do not mulch on top of mulch.
General tree protection	✔													Build a basket around the tree for protection from mammals immediately after planting and remove when considered safe to do so.
Trunk protection	✔	✔												Inspect annually to make sure it is not cutting into the tree, that weeds are not growing up inside it or that it has not become a mouse nest!
Staking	✔	✔												Remove the stake and tie after the first or second year following planting, depending on the stability of the newly planted tree.
Tree ties	✔	✔	✔	✔	✔									Check and adjust the tree tie regularly through the first one or two years that the tree is staked, especially following strong winds.
General health	✔		✔	✔			✔	✔		✔	✔			Regular checks for general health and appearance.
General safety										✔	✔			After ten years it may be necessary to start regular inspections for safety reasons.
Pruning	✔									✔				Carry out formative pruning before and after planting. Carry out pruning as required, but sooner rather than later if removing major branches to prevent large pruning wounds.
Feeding		✔				✔				✔				Check young trees in the first spring following planting and feed if needed. Most trees will never need feeding, especially if organic mulching is maintained.

Tree inspection

Use this form to keep a record of your tree inspection. It can also assist in discussing your tree with a tree care professional. Work through the checklist and tick off any issues that apply.

Tree ID and/or Species		Survey Date and Time			
Weather Conditions		Age/class of tree (Circle)	Young Mature	Semi-Mature Over-Mature	
Approximate Height		Overall Health or Vigour (Circle)	Good	Ok	Poor

Checklist		Y/N ?	Notes
Whole Tree	Is the tree leaning?		Try to comment on the extent of any item found, for example the severity of any lean or the % of any dieback in relation to the rest of the crown or trunk area.
	Is the crown of the tree complete?		
	Is there an unstable root plate around the tree?		
	Has there been recent construction work around the tree?		
Crown	Is there any dieback or poor foliage in the crown?		
	Are there signs of the tree being poorly pruned in the past?		
	Has the tree been pollarded in the past?		
	Are there any gaps in the crown?		
	Are there any dead, snapped or hanging branches in the crown?		
Branches	Are there long, heavy limbs present?		
	Are there branches overhanging any structures?		
	Are there any narrow forks?		
	Are there any dead branches?		
Trunk	Are there any bleeds or exudates from the trunk of the tree?		
	Are there any fungi or cankers present?		
	Are there any hollows present?		
	Is there flaking or dead bark present?		
	Has the trunk grown around old walls/fences, etc?		
Trunk to Root	Are there any fungi present?		
Roots	Is there damage to any roots? How extensive is it? Does the root damage correspond to dieback in the crown of the tree?		
	Are there any girdling roots?		
	Are there any fungi present?		

Service record

Use this form to keep a record of the work completed on your trees.

Tree ID or species	Date	Description of maintenance	Works undertaken by:	Date of next inspection

Resources and references

Resources

Biosecurity
www.planthealthportal.defra.gov.uk

Endangered trees
Global Trees Campaign – www.globaltreescampaign.org

Felling licences
Forestry Commission – www.forestry.gov.uk

High hedges
Settling differences without involving the local authority (UK)
www.gov.uk/government/publications/over-the-garden-hedge

Hiring an Arborist or Arboriculturist
The Arboricultural Association (UK) –
    www.trees.org.uk
International Society of Arboriculture – (RoW) –
    www.isa-arbor.com

Pruning Tools
Silky Fox Saws: silkysaws.com
Felco Pruning tools: felco.com
Bellota Pruning tools: agricareUK.com
Niwaki tripod ladders: niwaki.com

Tree Measurement Tools and Educational Equipment
Invicta: www.invictaeducationshop.com

Tree benefits
Green Cities Good Health: www.depts.washington.edu/hhwb/

Tree Identification Guides
Collins Tree Guide by Owen Johnson, published by Harper Collins

Tree planting materials
Tree ties: Big cushion tree ties: bigcushion.com
Mulch mats: Landscape Supplies: www.landscapesuppliesni.co.uk
Gardening tools: Spear and Jackson: spear-and-jackson.com
Treegator® Slow Release Watering Bags: treegator.com

Other Useful Tree Organisations for Information
Arbor Day Foundation: www.arborday.org
The Tree Council: www.treecouncil.org.uk
Woodland Trust: www.woodlandtrust.org.uk

UK Tree Nurseries
Barcham Trees, Ely, Cambridgeshire: barcham.co.uk
Bluebell Nursery, Ashby de la Zouch, Leicestershire: bluebellnursery.com
Burncoose Nurseries: burncoose.co.uk
Credale Maple Nursery, Leominster, Herefordshire: credale.co.uk
Deepdale Trees Ltd, Sandy, Bedfordshire: Deepdale-trees.co.uk
Hillier Trees, Romsey, Hampshire: hillier.co.uk
Landford Trees, Landford, Wiltshire: landfordtrees.co.uk
Majestic Trees, St Albans, Hertfordshire: majestictrees.co.uk
Frank P. Matthews Trees for Life, Tenbury Wells, Worcester:
    frankpmatthews.com
Oakover Nurseries, Ashford, Kent: oakovernurseries.co.uk
Place for Plants, East Bergholt Place, Suffolk: Placeforplants.co.uk
Tendercare mature and formal hardy plants, Uxbridge, Middlesex:
    tendercare.co.uk
Wyevale Nurseries, Hereford, Herefordshire: wyevalenurseries.co.uk

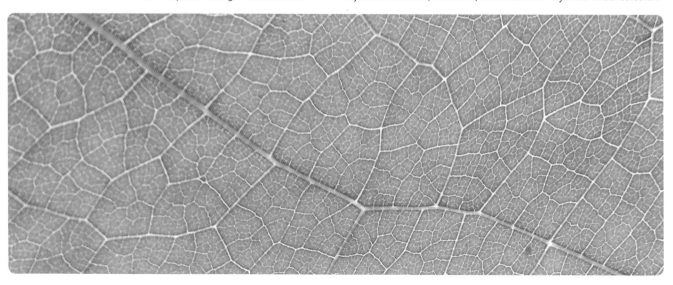

References

American National Standards Institute. (2008). *"Pruning" Part 1 of Tree Care Operations* A300. ANSI.

Bean, W. J. (1970). *Trees and Shrubs Hardy in the British Isles*, 8th edition, 4 volumes. John Murray.
(Online) International Dendrology Society. beantreesandshrubs.org

Bird, R. (2006). *How to Prune Fruiting Plants*. Southwater.

Bradley, S. (2009). *The Pruner's Bible: A Step-by-Step Guide to Pruning Every Plant in Your Garden*. Reader's Digest. UK.

Brickell, C. & Joyce, D. (2017). *RHS Pruning and Training*. Revised new edition, Dorling Kindersley, UK

British Standards Institute (1992) *Nursery Stock Specification for Trees and Shrubs* BS 3936-1, BSI.
British Standards Institute (2010) *Tree Work Recommendations* BS 3998:2010, BSI.
British Standards Institute (2014) *Trees from Nursery to Independence* BS 8545:2014, BSI.
British Standards Institute (2012) *Trees in Relation to Design, Demolition, and Construction: Recommendations* BS 5837:2012, BSI.

Brown & Kirkham, T. (2004) *The Pruning of Trees, Shrubs and Conifers*, Revised & enlarged by T Kirkham. Published January, Timber Press, Portland, Oregon, USA.

Brown & Kirkham, T. (2017) *Essential Pruning Techniques*, Timber Press, Portland, Oregon, USA.

Glover, M. (2016) *Time for Trees: A Guide to Tree Selection for the UK*, Barcham Trees, Edition 3.

Goodwin, G. (2017) *The Urban Tree*, Routledge Press, UK.

Porter Felt, E. (2011) *The Photographic Guide to Pruning Fruit Trees*, Husband Press.

Flanagan, M & Kirkham, T. (1995) *Tree planting at the Royal Botanic Gardens Kew and Wakehurst Place. RHS The New Plantsman* Vol 2 Part 3 Pp. 142–151.

Gilman, E. F. (2001) *An Illustrated Guide to Pruning*, 3rd edition. Delmar Cengage Learning.

Hirons, A & Thomas, P. A. (2018) *Applied Tree Biology*, Wiley, Blackwell, Oxford, UK.

Harris, R. (1991) *Arboriculture: Integrated Management of Landscape Trees, Shrubs and Vines*. 2nd Edition, Prentice Hall.

International Society of Arboriculture. (2008) *Best management Practices: Tree Pruning*, 2nd edition. ISA. USA.

Lancaster, R. (2014) *The Hillier Manual of Trees and Shrubs*, RHS. UK.

Li, Qing. (2017) *The Art and Science of Forest Bathing*, Penquin Random House.

Lonsdale, D. (2013) *Ancient and Other Veteran Trees: Further Guidance on Management*, Tree Council.

Lonsdale, D. (1999) *Principles of Tree Hazard Assessment and Management (Research for Amenity Trees)* DETR/ Forestry Commission. UK.

Mattheck, C. (2007) *The Body Language of Trees (Encyclopedia of Visual Tree Assessment)* Karlsruhe Institute of Technology, Germany.

National Tree Safety Group (2011) *Common Sense Risk Management of Trees*, Forestry Commission, UK.

Read, H. (2000) *Veteran Trees: A Guide to Good Management*, English Nature

Smiley, T. & Gilbert, E. A. (2004) *Picus Sonic tomography for the quantification of decay in white oak (Quercus alba) and Hickory (Carya spp.)*, Journal of Arboriculture, ISA. USA.

Shigo, A. (1991) *Modern Arboriculture*. Shigo and Tree Associates. USA.

Strouts, (2002) R.G. & Winter, T.G. *Diagnosis of Ill Health in Trees*. D.O.E. Forestry Commission. UK.

Van Den Berk, (2015) *Van Den Berk on Trees,* Second Edition. Van Den Berk, Holland.

Watson, B. (2007) *Trees: Their Use, Management, Cultivation and Biology*. The Crowood Press Ltd.

Watson, G. & Himelick, E. B. (2013) *The Practical Science of Planting Trees*, International Society of Arboriculture. USA.

Watson, G. (2011) *Fungi on Trees – An Arborists' Guide*. Arboricultural Association. UK.

Watson, G. (2013) *Tree Pests and Diseases – An Arborists' Guide*. Arboricultural Association. UK.

Wilson, P. (2018) *The A to Z of Tree Terms: A Companion to British Arboriculture*, Orange Pippin. UK.

Glossary

AA Arboricultural Association, the largest professional and trade body for arboriculture in the UK, established in 1964 and now with about 2,000 members. The AA exists 'to advance the science of arboriculture for the public benefit'. It is concerned with maintaining and promoting high standards in the profession through education and training, research, certification schemes, publication of the *Arboricultural Journal*, technical guidance and a quarterly magazine, the organisation of an annual conference, consultation exercises and public relations.

Abiotic factors Factors due to non-living things, therefore physical or chemical in nature. Many adverse conditions affecting trees are due to abiotic (as opposed to biotic) factors, such as frost, exposure, nutrient deficiency and pollution.

Airpots & Spring rings A form of pot for container-grown plants whose sides and base are partly open to the air, encouraging roots to stop extension growth (called 'air pruning').

Adventitious shoots Shoots that develop other than from apical, axillary or dormant buds; see also 'epicormic'.

Aeration Provision of air to the soil to alleviate soil compaction and improve its structure.

Aesthetic Pleasing to the senses, visually or otherwise. Artistic.

Air cultivation tools Equipment providing a jet of compressed air to a hand-held device which helps to excavate roots almost non-destructively.

Alkaline Having a pH greater than 7.0. Contrast with acid.

Angiosperms Those seed plants, including broadleaf trees, distinguished from the gymnosperms by having flowers, and seeds enclosed in an ovary.

Annual rings A kind of growth ring in which a cylinder of wood is laid down in one year to increase the diameter of a woody stem, generally easily distinguished.

ANSI Acronym for American National Standards Institute. .

AOD Acute Oak Decline A syndrome leading to the decline of native oaks which can lead to death within four to five years. AOD is thought to have arisen in the 1920s but appears to have become more prevalent in the last few decades. Most reports are from the midlands and south-east of England.

Apical growth The ability of a shoot apex to continue growing while inhibiting the axillary buds.

Arboriculture The selection, production, planting, maintenance and removal of all woody plants for amenity purposes.

Arborist An individual engaged in the profession of arboriculture who through experience, education and training possesses the competence to provide for or supervise the management of trees and other woody plants.

Arboriculturist A person skilled or knowledgeable in the field of arboriculture.

Arisings The green waste material produced from a pruning operation.

Axial cracking Cracking along the grain of large lateral branches and scaffolds.

Bacteria/bacterium One of the five kingdoms of living things.

Some cause disease, many are decomposers and some are beneficial (such as nitrifying bacteria and those in the gut of animals).

Bare root system A tree removed from the ground for re-planting without any soil around the roots.

Bark A term usually applied to all the tissues of a woody plant lying outside the vascular cambium, thus including the phloem, cortex and periderm; occasionally applied only to the periderm or the phellem.

Batter The slope on the front and back face of a hedge (wider at the bottom and narrow at the top).

Biodiversity A measure of biological variation, whether represented by genes, species, habitats or ecosystems (gene pool, species diversity, habitat diversity or ecosystem diversity). Human environmental impact has reduced habitat and ecosystem diversity, for instance by clearing forests and draining wetland, increasing the rate of species extinction above the natural rate and causing population loss in many other species.

Biosecurity A set of precautions to reduce the risk of accidentally introducing (or otherwise spreading) alien invasive species (AISs), including potential pests and pathogens. The frequency with which alien invasive species are being introduced into Britain and elsewhere is increasing in proportion to international trade and other transport. The Forestry Commission's 'Contingency plan for serious pest outbreaks in British trees', written in 2011, lists pest-specific contingency plans for 21 potential alien invasive species not yet arrived in Britain.

Branch attachment point The point at which a branch is attached to a parent branch or trunk.

Branch bark ridge The raised arc of bark tissues that forms within the acute angle between a branch and its parent stem.

Branch collar Area where a branch joins another branch or the trunk. This is created by the respective overlapping of xylem cells.

Brown rot Fungal wood rot characterised by the breakdown of cellulose. Contrast with soft rot and white rot.

BSI Acronym for British Standards Institution.

Bud Small lateral or terminal protuberance on the stem of a plant that may develop into a flower or shoot. Undeveloped flower or shoot containing a meristematic growing point.

Burlapped Tree dug up and removed from the ground in a root-ball for re-planting, with the roots and soil wrapped in hessian fabric and wire mesh. .

BVOCs Biogenic Volatile Organic Compounds.

Callus tissue Protective, undifferentiated growth of cells at the edges of wounded areas on trees.

Cambium vascular The unspecialised tissue one cell thick separating the xylem from the phloem, either within discrete vascular bundles or in the form of a continuous cylinder following secondary thickening. The cambium divides indefinitely to give new xylem and phloem.

Cambium bark Layers of meristematic cells on the outer side of the phloem that give rise to the bark.

Canker A persistent lesion formed by the death of bark and cambium due to colonisation by fungi or bacteria.

Canopies Collective branches and foliage of a tree or group of trees.

CAT Cable Avoiding Tool used for the detection of underground services such as electricity and other cables.

Cavity A hole in the trunk or scaffold branches of a tree caused by the loss of a limb or some other form of structural damage and usually associated with decay.

Codominant stems or twin leaders Usually two forked branches of the same diameter originating from the same growing point on the trunk.

Container grown Of plants grown in pots of whatever size and design.

Conservation Area (CA) A protection order that allows a local planning authority six weeks to place a Tree Preservation Order (TPO) on a tree.

Crotch The inner surfaces of a fork in a tree which is sometimes cupped, allowing water or organic matter to accumulate.

Crown/Canopy The head of the tree that is made up of the main scaffolds and branches bearing the foliage; these terms are interchangeable.

Crown lifting Removal of limbs and small branches to a specified height above ground level.

Crown thinning The removal of a proportion of secondary branch growth throughout the crown to produce an even density of foliage around a well-balanced branch structure.

Crown reduction/shaping A specified reduction in crown size whilst preserving, as far as possible, the natural tree shape.

Deadwood Branch or stem wood bearing no live tissues, serving no further purpose for the tree.

Decay The progressive decomposition of wood caused by specialised fungi, which consume it as a food source. The main modes of decay are white rot, brown rot, simultaneous rot and soft rot outdoors, and wet rot and dry rot in wood in service.

Defect In relation to tree hazards, any feature of a tree which detracts from the uniform distribution of mechanical stress, or which makes the tree mechanically unsuited to its environment.

Disease A malfunction in or destruction of tissues within a living organism, usually excluding mechanical damage; in trees, usually caused by pathogenic micro-organisms.

Dormant bud An axial bud which does not develop into a shoot until after the formation of two or more annual wood increments; many such buds persist through the life of a tree and develop only if stimulated to do so.

Dripline The outer edge of a tree's canopy.

Ecological tree planting Planting the smaller, bare-root trees from seedlings or transplants to whips that don't require an engineered planting pit or a means of support.

Ecosystem A unit of ecology consisting of a more or less discrete community of species, interacting with each other and with their physical environment, with emphasis on the interactions comprising the system. .

Ecosystem services The ways in which humanity relies on ecosystems for the continued provision of clean air and drinking water, an equable climate, the productivity of agriculture, forestry and the oceans, the control of flooding, soil erosion and coastal erosion, carbon sequestration, decomposition of wastes, etc.

Engineered tree planting Planting the larger nursery stock trees which have a large, well-grown root system needing a planting pit and possibly staking to support the tree until it can support itself.

Epicormic shoot or growth A shoot system growing on a mature portion of the main stem, trunk or branch. Often these shoots are in clusters in the region of wounds or burrs, having originated from adventitious shoots or dormant buds.

Exotic A species that is not native, more commonly applied to plants than to animals. Most exotic plants in Britain were introduced in the first instance for cultivation in gardens including botanic gardens.

Extension growth The shoots of a tree which have grown either in the current growing season (if observed in summer) or in the previous season (if observed in winter), typically giving the outermost shoots of the crown which are up to one year old.

Fastigiate A variety or form with erect and often clustered growths.

Feathered tree A young tree with a central leader and the lateral branches retained on the trunk from the ground .

Flush cutting The complete removal of a limb to a parent branch or trunk, cutting as close to the origin as possible and removing the branch collar and branch bark ridge.

Frass The powdery waste left by wood-eating beetles and other plant-feeding insects.

Fungal fruiting body The reproductive (spore-bearing) part of a fungus, taking various forms depending on species: mushroom-like with gills or pores on the underside of the cap, bracket-like excrescences whether woody or soft, etc.

Fungal pathogens A fungal parasite that causes disease.

Galls Any abnormal plant growth caused by a parasitic bacterium, fungus, nematode, mite or insect.

Genotype The part of the *genetic* makeup of a *cell*, and therefore of any individual, which determines one of its characteristics.

Girdling root A root which circles and constricts the stem or roots possibly causing death of phloem and/or cambial tissue.

Girth measurement The measurement around the circumference of something of more or less circular cross-section such as a stem. Girth is commonly used as a descriptor for planting stock.

Glyphosate A non-selective ('broad spectrum') systemic herbicide which is absorbed through leaves and freshly cut stems.

Graft or budded Various techniques of vegetative propagation in which complementary cuts are made, generally in a rootstock and scion, which are then bound together so that the two vascular cambia are in as much contact with each other as possible. The two parts fuse together and, after some growth, function as one.

Girdled/girdling Woody roots may strangle each other if they cross each other or are tangled at transplanting, when they remain fixed in this configuration.

Gymnosperm Seed-bearing plants whose seeds are not enclosed in an ovary. There are four groups, ginkgo, cycads (plants superficially like palms but more primitive), conifers and gnetophytes.

Habit The overall growth characteristics, shape of the tree and branch structure.

Halophytic Trees which grow in saline conditions.

Hazard beam An upwardly curved part of a tree in which strong internal stresses may occur without being reduced by adaptive growth; prone to longitudinal splitting.

Heading cuts The point where a branch is cut anywhere along the length of the branch back to an outward facing bud to encourage vigorous regrowth below the cut.

Heartwood In a branch, main stem or root of sufficient diameter, the non-living inner wood, in contrast to the sapwood in which the xylem parenchyma cells are alive.

Heave Upward movement of ground and affected structures. Heave occurs when a building is built on shrinkable soil. Following building the soil hydrates and swells for some reason, pushing the structure upward.

Hedge A line of closely planted woody plants, generally marking a boundary, enclosing farm animals, creating a screen and/or providing shelter, and generally trimmed at the sides and on top from time to time so that the hedge stays dense and foliated to near ground level.

Hedgerow A line of a hedge, often with trees, commonly seen separating agricultural fields. The hedgerow still marks a boundary but does not necessarily fulfil any of the other purposes of a hedge.

Heeling in To store dormant bare-rooted trees outdoors in winter, after lifting but prior to planting out, by digging a shallow trench, laying the trees cross-wise with their roots in the trench, then loosely back-filling.

Honey dew A sticky deposit, largely of phloem sap, found on trees and objects in their vicinity, excreted by sap-sucking insects such as aphids or scale insects feeding in the crown.

Included bark & Inclusions Bark that is pushed inside a developing crotch, causing a weakened structure.

ISA International Society of Arboriculture, an international body promoting professional practice in arboriculture through research, technology and education.

Leader A dominant shoot whether at the uppermost tip of a whole tree (centre leader) or at the tip of a branch (leading shoot).

Lions tailing A term applied to a branch of a tree that has few if any side-branches except at its end, and is thus liable to snap due to end-loading.

Maiden tree A young top fruit tree for transplanting or further growth in the nursery, 1–2m tall depending on the influence on vigour of the rootstock and variety. A maiden consists of a main stem and centre leader with little or no side branching.

Microclimate The climate of a site as modified by local site factors. The relevant scale depends on the context. Trees affect the microclimate in numerous ways, for instance by providing shelter and shade.

Mulch Material laid down over the rooting area of a tree or other plant to help conserve moisture; a mulch may consist of organic matter or a sheet of plastic or other artificial material.

Multi-stem A tree with several main stems arising from the ground or on a short stem.

Mycorrhizae Highly specialised root inhabiting fungi which form beneficial relationships with the roots of trees.

National tree safety group (NTSG) A partnership of many organisations seeking to develop nationally recognised guidelines on tree safety management. The overall approach is that a balance should be struck between the risks and benefits of trees.

Native Present in a defined region for a certain amount of time without having been brought by humans (cf. exotic), for instance in Britain since the English Channel was flooded in the early part of the present interglacial about 6,000 years ago.

Necrosis The premature death of specific areas of living tissue owing to some adverse factor.

Oblique staking A means of supporting a root balled tree with a tree stake positioned at 45 degrees to the tree

Occlusion The process whereby a wound is progressively closed by the formation of new wood and bark around it.

Pathogen A micro-organism which causes disease in another organism.

Phoenix regeneration The renewal of the aerial part of a tree, after decline or collapse, by growth from relatively near ground level of epicormic shoots, remnants of the crown, layering or suckering.

Photosynthesis The process whereby plants use light energy to split hydrogen from water molecules, and combine it with carbon dioxide to form the molecular building blocks for synthesising carbohydrates and other biochemical products.

Pneumatophores or knees An above-ground structure arising from the root system of some wetland species such as swamp cypress (*Taxodium distichum*), said to be knee-like in this species, assisting the roots to exchange gases with the air when the soil is waterlogged or flooded.

Pollarding The removal of the tree canopy, back to the stem or primary branches. Pollarding may involve the removal of the entire canopy in one operation, or may be phased over several years. The period of safe retention of trees having been pollarded varies with species and individuals. It is usually necessary to re-pollard on a regular basis, annually in the case of some species .

Pot-bound Potted plants, kept in a pot for too long so that the roots have become lignified, in a more or less unnatural (usually encircling) form.

Pruning The removal or cutting back of twigs or branches, sometimes applied to twigs or small branches only, but often used to describe most activities involving the cutting of trees or shrubs.

Reaction zone Area of wood that reacts and actively resists the growth and spread of micro-organisms.

Removal of dead wood Unless otherwise specified, this refers to the removal of all accessible dead, dying and diseased branch-wood and broken snags.

Rigid plastic containers The traditional plant pot.

Root balled The root volume of a tree contained in a bag or basket of soil to minimise root damage during transport (i.e. after being dug up in the nursery and before transplanting).

Root collar or Root crown The transitional area between the stem/s and roots.

Root plate That part of the root system (excluding the small outermost roots) needed to keep a tree wind-firm.

Root protection area (RPA) An area of ground surrounding a tree that contains sufficient rooting volume to ensure the tree's survival. Calculated with reference to BS5837 (2012).

Rootstock In grafted trees, the part below the graft union that gives rise to the lower main stem and root system.

Root wrapped The protection for bare-root trees to prevent the roots from desiccating in wind and sun.

Root zone Area of soils containing absorptive roots of the tree/s described. The primary root zone is that which we consider of primary importance to the physiological well-being of the tree.

Saprophytic fungi Fungi that are dependent on dead or dying wood as part of their lifecycle.

Sapwood The outer wood (xylem) of a secondarily thickened branch or main stem which is typically pale (in contrast to the often coloured inner heartwood). Sapwood contains living cells (xylem parenchyma) and has numerous functions, including the transport of water and nutrients.

Scaffold branches The major framework branches growing from the trunk on a tree.

Scion In grafted or budded trees, that part above the graft union that gives rise to most of the aerial part of the tree, typically desired for fruit or ornament.

Shinrin-Yoku Forest bathing – the Japanese practice of walking mindfully through a woodland.

Soft tagging Temporarily marking up a tree in the nursery and awaiting a quote before confirming a sale.

Spiral tree guard A spiral strip of plastic forming a narrow tube around the stem of a newly planted tree, protecting against small mammals and strimmer injury. The spiral yields as the tree trunk flexes or grows radially.

Spur A slow-growing and usually dwarf shoot system with a rosette of leaves, usually associated with flowering and fruiting trees.

Stag headed The appearance of a tree where the tree is failing in health and dieback has generated dead branches protruding through the living canopy resembling the antlers of a stag, hence the term.

Stomata Microscopic pores on a leaf (on the underside in broadleaf trees) which allow gas exchange when open.

Stog or Snag In woody plants, a portion of a cut or broken stem, branch or root which extends beyond any growing point or dormant bud; a snag usually tends to die back to the nearest growing point.

Strimmers and brushcutters A power tool worn on a shoulder harness consisting of a boom with a rotary head from which two short lengths of nylon line or fixed blades protrude. As the lines/blades fly round they sever grass and other light vegetation close to ground level.

Subsidence In relation to soil or structures resting in or on soil, a sinking due to shrinkage when certain types of clay soil dry out, sometimes due to extraction of moisture by tree roots.

Succession In ecology, the change in the species composition of the plants and animals living in an area of whatever size, as occurs naturally over time.

Target pruning The final pruning position to the outside of the branch collar and the branch bark ridge. The opposite of flush cutting, and the correct form of pruning.

Topping The indiscriminate cutting back of the major scaffolds to stubs or lateral branches that are not large enough to take on the terminal role.

Transpiration The evaporation of moisture from the surface of a plant, especially via the stomata of leaves; it exerts a suction which draws water up from the roots and through the intervening xylem cells.

Transplants The smallest specification of bare-rooted nursery stock, minimum height about 25cm, and so-called because it is transplanted in the tree nursery. Transplants may also be transplanted.

Transplanting The lifting and replanting of young trees.

Tree A woody perennial plant, typically having a single stem or trunk growing to a considerable height and bearing lateral branches at some distance from the ground.

Tree officer The officer of a local authority responsible for the council's trees, administering the guidance and legislation to do with trees and hedges, evaluating tree reports, etc.

Tree preservation order (TPO) An order made by a local planning authority to protect amenity trees and woodland.

Tree shelters A plastic tube open at both ends largely enclosing a newly planted tree and fixed in a vertical position with a small stake. The tube is intended to provide support and a sheltered greenhouse-like environment, and protects the tree from small mammals.

Tree tie A specially made tie used to secure a newly planted tree to a tree stake. .

Tree watering bags A bag that is positioned around newly planted trees, filled with water that is slowly released over the top of the root ball.

Tripod ladders Tripod ladders are essential for large topiary and hedges. Depending on the slope, you can either work face-on, with the third leg poked into the hedge, or sideways, with the ladder parallel to the hedge. The three legs and wide base are very adaptable and give extra stability.

Trunk or Bole The lower part of the main stem of a tree, visually well-defined and generally lacking side branches.

Targets In tree risk assessment (with slight misuse of normal meaning) persons or property or other things of value which might be harmed by mechanical failure of the tree or by objects falling from it.

Tree shelters A plastic tube open at both ends largely enclosing a newly planted tree and fixed in a vertical position with a small stake. The tube is intended to provide support and a sheltered greenhouse-like environment, and protects the tree from small mammals.

Undercutting The drawing of a horizontal blade through the soil at a certain depth below a bed of young bare-rooted trees in a tree nursery to sever the deeper roots, encouraging a more fibrous root system to develop and improving the quality of the trees when transplanted.

Urban forest Trees and other woody vegetation in the built environment considered collectively over an extensive area (e.g. the jurisdiction of a local authority).

UHI Urban Heat Island effect.

Veteran tree A loosely defined term for an old specimen that is of interest biologically, culturally or aesthetically because of its age, size or condition and which has usually lived longer than the typical upper age range for the species concerned.

Volcano mulching A large build-up of mulch around the base of young trees, that resembles a volcano, hence the term.

Waterlogged Saturation, implying a lack of oxygen, for instance in wood or soil. Roots in waterlogged soil are asphyxiated and killed in a time that varies with species and their degree of metabolic activity.

Watering loop A loop installed adjacent to a newly planted tree which protrudes above the soil surface at one end and extends at least to the depth of the roots at the other. The tree is watered via the tube as appropriate, minimising weed growth and evaporation losses and encouraging the tree to develop a relatively deep root system.

Wildlife corridors An area of habitat, such as a hedgerow, meadow or beetle bank, connecting otherwise fragmented wildlife populations. A discontinuous corridor is said to consist of 'stepping stones'.

Windbreak Any artificial obstacle to the wind intended to reduce its force, such as a fence.

Whip Young tree for transplanting consisting of a centre leader with few or no side branches.

Wind-firm Having no elevated risk of wind-throw.

Wound sealants A protective paint applied to pruning wounds.

Woven geotextile fabrics A kind of geosynthetic consisting of fibres of a synthetic material woven into a fabric and therefore porous to liquids and gases.

Xylem The tissue in vascular plants that transports mainly water and nutrients from the roots through the aerial part of the plant to the leaves and buds. Xylem occurs in localised vascular bundles in herbs and some species with ligneous stems.